Anita,
a taste of
Texas for your
kitchen — Martha
April, 2006

M000106574

The Dining Car

Collections
&
Recollections
of
Denison's First 125 years

MISSOURI - KANSAS - TEXAS

DAVID CROCKETT

THE DINING CAR

For information on purchasing additional copies please write or call:

The Denison Service League, Inc.
P.O. Box 4
Denison, Texas 75021-0004
903-463-8400

E-mail Address:
serviceleague@texoma.net

ISBN# 0-9657672-0-5

Copyright © 1999
Denison Service League, Inc.
Denison, Texas

First Printing 5,000 copies 1999

Printed in the USA by

WIMMER
The Wimmer Companies
Memphis
1-800-548-2537

The Dining Car

WELCOME! *The Dining Car* awaits your pleasure! Climb aboard the Katy, the Missouri-Kansas-Texas Railroad, as we take you on a journey through time. Ride the rails from General Dwight D. Eisenhower's Birthplace, past native persimmon groves, pecan trees, and wild grapevines, to the shores of Lake Texoma. On the way, hear tales of the unique culinary heritage of Denison, founded in 1872 as the MKT prepared to head south into Texas.

In *The Club Car,* start with beverages to wet your whistle and tidbits to whet your appetite. Sipping Champagne Punch, toast the importance of viticulture in our region. Town father T.V. Munson saved the French wine industry from the dreaded phylloxera, going on to become in 1888 the second American to receive the French Legion of Honor.

Wake up to the conductor's *First Call,* bread and brunch recipes to help you work up a full head of steam. *Clickety Clack* moves you down the line with a first course of soups and salads galore. Just in time for *Dinner on Board* are main dishes that will have you ringing the buzzer for seconds. You might get *Side Tracked* with our delicious accompaniments, but be sure to leave room for a stop at *Sugar Bottom.* How it got its name is still a sweet mystery.

Rounding Preston Bend, you'll find *The Texas Special* waiting to tantalize your taste buds with special recipes from the Lone Star State. Finally, hop on the caboose for *Half Fare,* a selection of fun recipes to try with the kids.

From delicious quick-fixing meals for a busy family to an elaborate candlelit dinner for two, *The Dining Car* is on the right track for exceptional dining. *ALL ABOARD!*

About The Artist

Talented artist Penny Webb Hyman, a Denison native, has created our cover and graphic pages. After graduating from Denison High School, she attended Texas A & M at Commerce where she received a Bachelor of Science Degree for Advertising Art with an emphasis on Illustration.

Trained in a variety of media from the traditional - pen & ink, pencils, oils, watercolors and pastels - to the digital of photo imaging, vector drawing and desktop publishing, Penny is currently an Internet Graphic Designer. She resides in Denison with her husband and young son.

Volunteers give of their time and resources for many reasons, but perhaps most of all, they give because they care. The countless determined hours given to the creation of *The Dining Car* were buoyed by the realization its benefits would reach beyond immediate enjoyment and pleasure, even far into the future. Proceeds from the sale of *The Dining Car* will be returned to the community through Denison Service League supported educational, cultural, social and civic endeavors.

Table of Contents

 **THE DINING CAR**

The Dining Car *Committee is deeply grateful to those who submitted their favorite recipes and to the testers who contributed their time, their palates and their critiques to assure the high quality of the recipes offered here. Recipes in this book have been collected from Service League members, family and friends. The Service League of Denison believes the recipe ingredients and directions will be successful!*

Some recipes have a symbol by the title to quickly identify useful information:

 Make Ahead

 Freezes Well

 Overnight

 Quick & Easy

 Low Fat

The
Club Car

Denison
Arts & Wine
Renaissance

March 22, 1997
"Charter Year"

*P*olly Erzinger's entry, "Choices", won the competition for the Denison Arts & Wine Renaissance poster and wine label for the first year. It was done with goose quill pen, India ink and watercolor on paper.

Denison's superbly diverse colony of artists and artisans, coupled with the amazing Munson grape heritage, have propelled the success of this celebration.

Appetizers & Beverages

Almond Bacon Cheese Crostini (Little Crusts)

1	French baguette (long loaf)	⅓	cup mayonnaise or salad dressing
3-4	slices bacon, cooked and crumbled	¼	cup sliced almonds, toasted
1	cup shredded Monterey Jack cheese	1	tablespoon chopped green onions
		¼	teaspoon salt
			Toasted sliced almonds, garnish

Preheat oven to 400 degrees. Slice baguette into 36 (¼ to ½ inch) slices; place on a baking sheet lined with aluminum foil. Bake for 5 minutes or until lightly browned. Combine bacon and next 5 ingredients; spread on bread slices. Bake for 5 minutes more or until cheese melts. Garnish with almonds, if desired, and serve immediately. Yield: 3 dozen.

🕐 Spicy Artichoke Dip

1	(16 ounce) can artichoke hearts (not marinated) cut up	1	cup Parmesan cheese
1	cup mayonnaise		Dash garlic powder
			Paprika, to sprinkle on top

Mix all ingredients until smooth. Spread evenly in an 8-inch square greased baking pan and bake at 350 degrees for 30 minutes.

Optional: 2 to 3 dashes hot pepper sauce and/or pinch cayenne pepper; or spicy: 1 (4½ ounce) can green chiles; 1 cup shredded Cheddar cheese in place of Parmesan cheese.

Crab Dip Supreme

1	(6 to 7 ounce) can crab meat, drained	1	tablespoon sherry
1	cup mayonnaise	1	teaspoon lemon juice
½	cup sour cream	1	teaspoon chopped parsley
			Salt and pepper to taste

Remove any shell fragments from crab. Combine all ingredients. Chill at least 2 hours before serving. Yield: 2 cups.

Cheese Puffs

2   cups grated Cheddar cheese
½   cup softened butter
1¼ cups flour

½   teaspoon salt
½   teaspoon paprika
48 small stuffed green olives

Blend grated cheese with softened butter. Stir in mixture of flour, salt and paprika; mix well. Wrap 1 teaspoon of dough around each olive. Arrange on a flat pan; freeze. After dough freezes, place in a plastic bag; store in freezer. When ready to use, remove from bag and arrange on cookie sheet. Bake at 400 degrees for 15 minutes.

Broccoli Dip

1 (10 ounce) box frozen chopped broccoli
1 (10 ounce) can diced tomatoes and green chiles, drained

1 (10¾ ounce) can cream of celery soup
1 cup shredded Cheddar cheese

Preheat oven to 350 degrees. Cook broccoli as directed on package; drain well. Put in bottom of baking dish that can be used for serving. Drain diced tomatoes and green chiles. Sprinkle over broccoli in an even layer. Spread celery soup evenly over other ingredients. Sprinkle cheese over top. Bake until bubbly, about 20 to 30 minutes. Serve hot with your favorite dipper. Corn chips are especially good.

Broccoli-Cheese Dip

½ cup chopped green onion
½ cup chopped celery or green bell peppers
2 tablespoons margarine
1 (10¾ ounce) can cream of mushroom soup

1 (16 ounce) package mild Mexican processed cheese loaf
1 (10 ounce) package frozen chopped broccoli, cooked and drained

Sauté green onion and celery in melted margarine until tender. Melt cheese with soup in double boiler; add onion, celery and broccoli. Serve warm with chips.

Can substitute broccoli with 1 pound of hot or mild sausage, cooked, crumbled and drained.

Elegant Seafood Dip

16 ounces cream cheese, softened
1   tablespoon lemon juice
    Hot pepper sauce to taste
    Garlic salt to taste
1   teaspoon Worcestershire sauce
1   medium size can shrimp, drained

1   can crab meat, drained and
    checked for shell pieces
1   can chopped clams, drain,
    RESERVE juice
1   tablespoon fresh parsley, chopped
1   loaf Italian bread rounds or
    Shepherd's bread

In a medium bowl, cream the cheese. When soft, add lemon juice, hot pepper sauce, garlic salt, Worcestershire sauce, and reserved clam juice. After thoroughly mixed, add the seafood and parsley. Prepare bread rounds by cutting top off. Scoop out inside of loaf; fill with mixture. Replace lid on loaf and double wrap with aluminum foil. Bake at 300 degrees for 2 hours. Serve with fresh vegetables or bread slices for dipping. Can be reheated. Yield: 10 servings.

Hot Broccoli Dip

1   (1½ pound) round loaf sourdough
    bread
½   cup finely chopped celery
½   cup chopped red bell pepper
¼   cup finely chopped onion
2   tablespoons margarine

1   (16 ounce) package processed
    cheese loaf, cubed
1   (10 ounce) package frozen
    chopped broccoli, cooked and
    drained
¼   teaspoon dried rosemary leaves,
    crushed

Preheat oven to 350 degrees. Cut slice from top of bread loaf, remove center leaving a 1 inch shell. Cut removed bread into bite-size pieces. Cover shell with top, place on cookie sheet with bread pieces, bake 15 minutes. Sauté celery, peppers and onions in margarine; add processed cheese and stir over low heat until melted. Stir in remaining ingredients; heat thoroughly, stirring constantly. Spoon into bread loaf. Serve hot with toasted bread pieces and vegetable dippers. Yield: 6 to 8 servings.

Crab Imperial

1 stick margarine, softened	½ teaspoon seasoned salt
1 jar sharp, processed cheese spread, softened	7 ounces crab meat, drained and checked for shell pieces
1½ teaspoons mayonnaise	6 English muffins
½ teaspoon garlic salt	

Mix margarine and cheese spread together with mayonnaise, garlic and seasoned salts; add crab meat. Spread mixture on English muffins. Freeze for 10 minutes for ease in cutting. Cut into eighths; broil or bake until bubbly and crisp.

Harriet, 16, patted the yeast bread dough into the pans and lifted them to the mantle so fireplace heat would hasten rising....

So began this day in 1843 on the Bradley farm on Iron Ore Creek. Mama had died. Pa left a week ago to sell farm produce downriver. At home were her brothers Thomas, Joe and Wesley, little sister Sarah and hired hand Anse. Little did they know what was in store for them.

Renegade Indians were discovered creeping closer and closer. Wesley rode for help. Thomas and Anse hid in the barn. Harriet, Sarah and Joe huddled in the cellar under the house, watching out the gun ports all night and into the next day.

Suddenly they heard splintering wood overhead. Indians were in the cabin! Paralyzed with fear, Joe managed to point his rifle upward just as the trap door was flung open!

Sagging with relief, they saw Pa's face. Pa, two neighbors and Wesley had arrived. The Indians had fled.

The four loaves of dough on the mantle had risen well above the pans, more than ready to be popped into the fireplace oven.

Sarah Elizabeth Dye rocks in front of the fireplace where Harriet's yeast bread was baked. Her family tree includes Thomas Bradley who in 1847 built the house, now at Denison's Frontier Village. She is the author of the book "The Cabin by the Spring" from which this story was taken.

THE CLUB CAR

With the panorama of the countryside flashing past wide windows and elegant table service inside, passengers enjoyed the Katy's famous table d'hote meals. Katy menus were advertised as offering a wide choice of tempting, delicious well cooked foods appetizingly served at moderate prices. In the 1930's, the lure of the "air-cooled diners" alone would be an irresistible new experience for most travelers.

Finger Pizza

½ cup chopped bell pepper
½ cup chopped onion
1-2 tablespoons cooking oil
½ pound sausage
½ pound ground beef
1 (10 ounce) can diced tomatoes and green chiles
1 (8 ounce) can tomato sauce
½ cup chopped mushrooms

1 pound American cheese, grated
1 pound sharp Cheddar cheese, grated
1 cup chopped olives, green or black
100 pepperoni slices (1 per roll), optional
5 packages small party rolls (20 rolls per package)

Sauté pepper and onion in oil; reserve. In the same pan, brown sausage and ground meat; drain. Combine the next 6 ingredients. Scoop out center of rolls with a spoon, making a well in top. Preheat oven to 350 degrees. Fill rolls with pizza mix and bake for 10 minutes. Pepperoni slices may be put on top if desired. Mixture may be made ahead and frozen or refrigerated for several days. Serve piping hot. Yield: 100.

Save scooped-out center of rolls to make luscious bread crumbs.

Party Rye Hors d'oeuvre

1 pound hot sausage
1 pound ground lean meat

1 pound processed cheese loaf
2 loaves party rye bread

Brown both meats and crumble; drain and remove from heat. Melt cheese and mix with meats. Spread about 1 teaspoon of mixture on each slice of bread. Freeze on cookie sheet; put into plastic bags. Use as needed, keeping the remaining slices frozen. Bake on a cookie sheet at 450 degrees for 12 to 15 minutes. Yield: 50 slices.

Sausage Balls in Cranberry Sauce

1	pound bulk pork sausage	1	(16 ounce) can jellied cranberry sauce
2	eggs		
1	cup fresh bread crumbs	1	tablespoon prepared mustard
1	teaspoon salt	½	cup water
½	teaspoon poultry seasoning		

Mix sausage, eggs, bread crumbs, salt and poultry seasoning in a large bowl. Shape into 24 small balls. In a large skillet over medium heat, brown meatballs well. Drain on paper towel. Pour all grease from skillet; wipe skillet clean. In same skillet over low heat, melt cranberry sauce, stirring occasionally. Stir in mustard, meatballs and water. Cover; simmer 20 minutes or until meatballs are tender. Yield: 24 meatballs.

⧖ Almond Ham Roll-Ups

1	(8 ounce) package softened cream cheese	¼	teaspoon paprika
		⅛	teaspoon black pepper
2	tablespoons mayonnaise	⅛	teaspoon hot pepper sauce
1	teaspoon minced onion	1	tablespoon finely chopped almonds, toasted
1	teaspoon Worcestershire sauce		
¼	teaspoon dry mustard	1	(12 ounce) package thinly sliced boiled ham

Combine all ingredients except ham. Spread 1 tablespoon of mixture on each ham slice. Roll and chill at least 12 hours. Use a sharp knife and cut in ¼ inch slices. May be frozen for 1 month. Thaw at room temperature 1 hour before serving. Yield: 5 dozen.

🕐 Cheese Dip

1	(16 ounce) package processed jalapeño cheese loaf	1	cup chopped Spanish olives
		1	cup real mayonnaise
1	(5½ ounce) can evaporated milk	1	cup chopped onions
1	cup chopped pecans		

Melt cheese and milk together. Mix in other ingredients; chill. Serve with corn chips or other chips.

Asparagus Roll-Ups

18 slices white bread (approximately) remove crusts	1 (15 ounce) can small green asparagus spears, drained
½ cup mayonnaise seasoned with drops of hot pepper sauce or seasoning of your choice	⅛ teaspoon salt
	⅛ teaspoon freshly ground pepper
½ teaspoon anchovy paste, mixed into mayonnaise	2 tablespoons French dressing
	1 stick butter or margarine, melted (for hot sandwiches only)

Roll out bread; spread each slice with mayonnaise and anchovy mixture. Place one asparagus spear on bread; sprinkle each with salt, pepper and a few drops of French dressing. Roll up the bread from a corner or jelly roll style. Secure with a toothpick (when ready to serve, remove toothpick). To serve as a hot appetizer, brush each roll-up with melted butter and broil until lightly browned.

Why was Ashburn's Peach Ice Cream better than the rest? Bill Ashburn says it was special attention to details. In the latter part of the season, with peaches at their flavorful best, a man from Colbert, Oklahoma, took his pickup to Arkansas to get them. While neighborhood women peeled and pitted the peaches, Ashburn's furnished them ice cream. In five gallon metal cans, the sugared peaches were stored in the cold vault for mixing into ice cream the next year. When you bit into the ice cream, you knew those good peaches were there.

Ashburn's on Main Street.

Sauerkraut Dip

16 ounces Mexican processed cheese loaf, softened	3 tablespoons chopped onion
	1 (2 ounce) jar diced pimento
8 ounces cream cheese, softened	1 (15 ounce) can chopped sauerkraut, drained
3 tablespoons chopped green pepper	

Mix processed cheese (can partially melt in microwave) and cream cheese well. Add other ingredients. Serve with crackers.

Shrimp Dip

1   (8 ounce) package cream cheese, softened
½   cup sour cream
Juice from one lemon
2   green onions, finely chopped

1   package dry Italian salad dressing mix
Salt and pepper to taste
2   pounds cooked and peeled shrimp, diced

Mix all ingredients together; chill 6 hours. May be used as a dip or salad.

Spinach Balls

2   (10 ounce) packages frozen chopped spinach
2   cups herb seasoned stuffing mix
2   medium onions, finely chopped
½   cup Parmesan cheese, grated

2   teaspoons garlic salt
1   teaspoon ground black pepper
1½ teaspoons thyme
¾   cup margarine or butter, melted
5   large eggs, beaten

Cook spinach according to package directions, omitting salt. Drain thoroughly, patting moisture out with paper towels. Add stuffing mix, onions, cheese, garlic salt, pepper and thyme to spinach. Stir thoroughly. Add melted margarine and then eggs; mix well. Form into walnut size balls (chill for easier handling). On a greased cookie sheet bake at 350 degrees for 18 to 20 minutes. Yield: 7 dozen.

Curried Chicken Balls

2   (3 ounce) packages cream cheese, softened
2   tablespoons orange marmalade
2   teaspoons curry powder
¾   teaspoon salt
¼   teaspoon white pepper

3   cups finely chopped cooked chicken
3   tablespoons minced green onions
3   tablespoons minced celery
1   cup finely chopped macadamia nuts or almonds, toasted

Combine first 5 ingredients in a mixing bowl; beat at medium speed with mixer until smooth. Stir in chicken, green onions and celery. Shape into 1 inch balls and roll in nuts. Chill up to 2 days, or freeze up to 1 month. Yield: 3½ dozen.

Fish in streams, creeks and the Red River were an important source of food for our ancestors. But the fishing itself was one of the simple pleasures shared with family and friends as described in this excerpt from Nancy Bradley's letter to her husband, Wesley, during the Civil War. It is dated May 20, 1864.

"Dear Wesley,

...I was glad to hear that you was well and to hear that the feds had got another whitten...I ben afishing today, and had a fine time, tho it was not mutch ajonament (enjoyment) to me if you had been along, I could have injoied the trip fine. there was about 15 along. ole Mr. and Mrs. Chils came by and I went with them. We only caut enough for us to eat at the creak...."

Cocktail Puffs

1 cup water	1 cup mayonnaise
½ cup butter or margarine	½ cup finely chopped celery
1 cup all-purpose flour	1½ teaspoons minced onion
¼ teaspoon salt	1 tablespoon Worcestershire sauce
4 eggs	1 teaspoon hot pepper sauce
1½ cups fresh lump crabmeat	Fresh parsley sprigs, garnish
2 cups (8 ounces) shredded sharp Cheddar cheese	

Combine water and butter in a medium saucepan; bring to a boil. Add flour and salt all at once, stirring vigorously with a wooden spoon until mixture leaves sides of pan and forms a smooth ball. Remove from heat; cool 5 minutes. Add eggs, one at a time, beating with a wooden spoon after each addition; beat until batter is smooth. Drop batter by teaspoons 2 inches apart onto lightly greased baking sheets. Bake at 400 degrees for 20 minutes. Turn oven off; remove puffs. Make a horizontal slit about one-third of the way down in top of puffs (do NOT cut completely through). Return puffs to oven for 10 minutes to dry out. Remove from oven; cool on wire racks. Complete slit to slice top from each puff. Combine crabmeat and remaining ingredients; stir well. Spoon about 2 teaspoons crab mixture into each puff; replace tops. Cover and chill until ready to serve. Garnish, if desired. Yield: 4½ dozen.

One pound fresh medium shrimp, boiled and peeled, can be substituted for crabmeat.

Crab-Stuffed Cherry Tomatoes

1 (6 ounce) can all-white crabmeat, drained	⅛ teaspoon red pepper
1 cup (6 ounces) chopped imitation crabmeat	1 tablespoon lemon juice
	¼ cup mayonnaise
2 green onions, chopped	30 large cherry tomatoes
	Parsley sprigs, garnish

Using knife blade in food processor, combine the first 6 ingredients in bowl of processor. Process 30 seconds or until smooth. Cut an X on the bottom of each tomato, cutting to within ½ inch of stem end. Carefully spread out sections of each tomato to form a cup. Spoon crab mixture into each tomato; top with parsley sprig. Yield: 2½ dozen.

☾ Herbed Cheese Spread

2 sticks butter, softened	¼ teaspoon dill weed
2 (8 ounce) packages cream cheese, softened	¼ teaspoon marjoram
	¼ teaspoon black pepper
2 cloves of garlic, pressed	¼ teaspoon thyme
½ teaspoon oregano	Coarse ground pepper, garnish
¼ teaspoon basil	

Mix all ingredients thoroughly in a mixer. Refrigerate overnight. Spread cheese on crackers and sprinkle with coarse ground pepper. Serve at room temperature.

❄ Four Cheese Ball

1 cup small curd cottage cheese	1 medium onion, finely grated
1 (16 ounce) package cream cheese, softened	2 tablespoons Worcestershire sauce
	Dash of seasoned salt
½ cup finely shredded sharp Cheddar cheese	½ cup pecans, divided (¼ in cheese and ¼ to roll balls in)
2 ounces crumbled blue cheese	½ cup parsley

Combine first 7 ingredients. Shape into 2 balls. Roll in nuts and parsley mixed; chill.

Cheese Ball

1   bunch green onions
1   (8 ounce) package cream cheese, softened

1   tablespoon Worcestershire sauce
1   (2½ ounce) package smoked chopped beef

Chop onions finely; separate the white part of onions from the green. Mix white part with cream cheese and Worcestershire sauce. Cut chopped beef into tiny pieces; mix well with cream cheese mixture. Roll into a ball, then coat the outside of the ball with the chopped green portion of onions.

Cheese Roll

2   pounds processed cheese loaf, softened (do NOT use low fat)
3   ounces cream cheese, softened
2   bunches green onions, chopped

1   (2 ounce) jar pimentos, chopped and well-drained
1   (8 ounce) can pickled peppers, well-drained

Take softened processed cheese and place between wax paper to roll and flatten. Spread cream cheese on top of flattened cheese, then layer with well drained vegetables. Roll between wax paper. Refrigerate; slice. Serve with crackers.

Smoked Salmon Pâté

6   ounces canned or fresh smoked salmon
2   tablespoons lemon juice
½   cup melted butter or margarine
½   cup sour cream

1   tablespoon snipped fresh dill OR ½ teaspoon dried dill weed
    Salt, pepper and lemon slices, if desired

Place salmon and lemon juice in blender; blend until smooth. Add butter in a slow steady stream, scraping sides of container occasionally. Place mixture in a bowl and stir in sour cream and dill. Taste and adjust seasonings. Cover and refrigerate up to 2 days.

Make your own smoked salmon by adding Liquid Smoke to canned salmon.

Crab Spread Superb

8 ounces softened cream cheese
½ cup mayonnaise
½ cup or 2 ounces shredded sharp Cheddar cheese
½ teaspoon garlic salt

¼ teaspoon Worcestershire sauce
¼ teaspoon black pepper
6 ounces frozen crab meat, thawed, drained and checked for shell pieces

Combine cream cheese and mayonnaise until creamy in a mixer or processor. Add remaining ingredients. Keep chilled. Serve with crackers or vegetables.

☽ Creamy Olive Spread

6 ounces cream cheese, softened
½ cup mayonnaise
1 cup chopped salad olives

½ cup chopped pecans
2 tablespoons olive liquid
   Dash of black pepper

Beat cream cheese well; stir in mayonnaise. Add remaining ingredients; stir well. Cover; chill 24 hours. Yield: 2 cups. Serve with crackers or chips.

Laura's Shrimp Dip

8 ounces cream cheese
3-4 teaspoons milk
1 can small shrimp, drained (may use ¾ cup fresh, cooked shrimp)
1 small can sliced black olives, drained

½ medium onion, chopped
1 (12 ounce) jar cocktail sauce or chili sauce
8 ounces grated Monterey Jack cheese

Mix cream cheese and milk. Spread mixture on bottom of dish. Layer remaining 5 ingredients in the order they appear.

Crab Meat Spread

12 ounces cream cheese, softened
¼ cup chopped onions
1 teaspoon Worcestershire sauce
1 teaspoon lemon juice
1 cup chili sauce

Lemon juice to taste
Horseradish to taste
1 can white crab meat, drained and checked for shell pieces
Chives or parsley, garnish

Mix together cream cheese, onions, Worcestershire sauce and lemon juice; mold on a plate. Mix together chili sauce, lemon juice and horseradish to taste and pour into molded cream cheese. Top cream cheese and chili sauce with crab meat. Garnish with chives or parsley. Serve with crackers.

Spinach Spread

1 (10 ounce) package frozen chopped spinach, thawed
1 cup mayonnaise
8 ounces sour cream

1 (1⅝ ounce) package dry vegetable soup mix
1 (8½ ounce) can water chestnuts, drained and finely chopped
1 small onion, finely chopped

Squeeze all water from spinach. Combine with other ingredients and refrigerate at least 2 hours, preferably a day ahead. Serve with rye bread. This spread works well as a dip in a hollowed-out bread round; as a dip using potato chips or crackers; and as a stuffing for raw mushroom caps.

Choice Tidbits

In the late 1800's, Denison boasted the tallest building in Texas. Dallas residents would make the trek north just to see it.

The Eternal Flame for President John F. Kennedy's gravesite was designed, practically overnight, by a Denisonian.

The fall of 1890 saw the founding of the XXI Club, a visionary ladies cultural club still going strong. By 1896 they had the first Women's Club building in Texas and were a charter member of the Texas Federation of Women's Clubs.

A Strawberry Festival enlivened the summer of 1873 when Denison was about three months old. Two unnamed women were looking for a way to establish themselves as social doyens. After finally agreeing a strawberry festival would be much classier than a peanut or corn festival, they realized there were no clubs or lodges in the fledgling city to serve as sponsors. So the wannabe socialites latched on to the Presbyterian Church. After all, the church had been around for six months or more and had important members.

There were no strawberries produced in Texas at that time; the berries were first introduced four years later by Mr. Tone on one of his Denison farms and thence scattered all over the state. Undaunted by such an annoying detail, the women airily declared they would be ordered from Galveston.

The two women found citizens eager to "up-build" their new town. Donations were already rolling in when the Presbyterian minister and his congregation heard the news. The momentum, and perhaps other considerations, overcame their consternation. In due time, a $167 strawberry order was dispatched to Galveston.

The appointed time of the Festival arrived. Alas, the berries did not. As fate would have it, Galveston had no strawberries so the order was sent to New Orleans. Shipped out of New Orleans on a sailing vessel on a scorching day without any ice, the hapless strawberries were transferred to a slow train to Houston and then laid on a hot platform to await forwarding the next day to Denison. Glory be!

The Strawberry Festival sailed forward without the featured attraction. The chagrined Presbyterian ladies endured the event with rigid backs and poker faces, vowing thereafter to conduct their own affairs.

Apple Dip

¾ cup brown sugar	1 (8 ounce) package cream cheese
¼ cup white sugar	¼ teaspoon vanilla extract

Mix together with a mixer until well blended. Serve with sliced apples!

Vegetable Bars

12 ounces cream cheese, softened
½ cup sour cream
¾ cup mayonnaise-type salad
    dressing
1 package dry original ranch
    dressing mix

2 packages refrigerated crescent
    rolls
¾ cup each finely chopped
    cauliflower, broccoli and carrots

Combine first 4 ingredients; set aside. Roll out 2 packages of rolls on one long cookie sheet. Bake at 350 degrees for 8 to 10 minutes. Cool! Spread cheese mixture on cooled rolls. Sprinkle finely chopped vegetables on top of cheese. Refrigerate. Cut into 60 pieces. Keeps several days.

Crunchy Cinnamon Snack

3 cups apple-cinnamon-flavored
    cereal
2 cups pecan halves
1 cup whole almonds
1 cup chow mein noodles

  Nonstick cooking spray
2 egg whites
1 cup granulated sugar
2 tablespoons ground cinnamon
½ teaspoon salt

Preheat oven to 300 degrees. Combine first 4 ingredients; spread on a sprayed cookie sheet. Combine remaining ingredients in a small bowl. Pour over dry ingredients; stir to coat well. Bake 35 to 40 minutes; stir frequently to break apart. Pour onto waxed paper to cool. Yield: about 8½ cups.

Party Pretzels

6 cups pretzels (assorted shapes if
    desired)
½ cup margarine, melted

1 package original ranch party dip
    mix
1 tablespoon Worcestershire sauce
½ teaspoon seasoned salt

Preheat oven to 250 degrees. Place pretzels in a large shallow baking pan. Combine remaining ingredients in a small bowl. Pour mixture over pretzels; mix well. Bake 1 hour; stir every 15 minutes. Pour onto waxed paper to cool. Store in airtight container. Yield: 6 cups.

Rumaki

Oriental Sauce

¼ cup soy sauce
¼ cup salad oil
2 tablespoons ketchup

1 tablespoon vinegar
¼ teaspoon pepper
2 cloves garlic, crushed

Mix all ingredients. Yield: approximately 1 cup.

6 chicken livers, cut in half
1 (5 ounce) can water chestnuts, drained and cut into 12 slices, or use 12 slices fresh water chestnuts

6 slices bacon, cut in half
¼ cup brown sugar

Pour Oriental Sauce over chicken livers and water chestnuts in baking dish. Cover dish with plastic wrap; refrigerate 4 hours. Set oven control at broil and/or 550 degrees. Remove chicken livers and water chestnuts from marinade. Wrap one chicken liver and water chestnut slice in each piece of bacon; secure with wooden toothpick. Roll in brown sugar. Broil 3 inches from heat for 10 minutes; turn occasionally, until bacon is crisp. Yield: 12 appetizers.

Chafing Dish Meatballs

1 pound ground beef
½ cup fine dry breadcrumbs
⅓ cup minced onion
¼ cup milk
1 egg, beaten
1 tablespoon minced fresh parsley

1 teaspoon salt
½ teaspoon Worcestershire sauce
⅛ teaspoon pepper
¼ cup cooking oil
1 (12 ounce) bottle chili sauce
1 (10 ounce) jar grape jelly

Combine first 9 ingredients; mix well. Shape into 1 inch meatballs. Cook in hot oil over medium heat for 10 to 15 minutes or until browned. Drain on paper towels. Combine chili sauce and grape jelly in medium saucepan; stir well. Add meatballs, simmer 30 minutes; stir occasionally. Yield: 5 dozen.

Crazy Crunch

2	quarts popped corn	1	cup margarine
1⅓	cups pecans	½	cup white corn syrup
⅔	cup almonds	1	teaspoon vanilla extract
1⅓	cups sugar		

Mix popped corn and nuts on a cookie sheet. Combine sugar, margarine and syrup in a 1½-quart saucepan. Bring to a boil over medium heat; stir constantly 10 to 15 minutes or until mixture turns a light caramel color. Remove from heat; stir in vanilla. Pour over popped corn and nuts, mix to coat well. Spread to dry. Break apart and store in a tightly covered container.

▧ Bellinis

6	cups sliced fresh or frozen peaches	2	cups apricot nectar
		6⅔	cups champagne

Combine half each of peaches and apricot nectar in container of an electric blender; process until smooth. Repeat process with the remaining fruit and nectar; freeze.

Remove peach-apricot mixture from freezer 30 minutes before serving. To serve, spoon about ⅔ cup of mixture into each stemmed glass; add ⅔ cup champagne. Yield: 10 servings (about 13 cups).

♥ Lo-Cal Cocoa Mix

3	cups powdered milk	Powdered coffee creamer if
3	tablespoons cocoa	desired for rich flavor
1½	teaspoons sugar substitute	

Mix first 3 ingredients and store. Use ⅓ cup of mix and add 1 cup hot water; stir. Add coffee creamer for richer flavor.

Gluhwein

1	quart hot, strong black tea	1	orange, sliced
2	quarts dry red wine	1	lemon, sliced
½	cup brown sugar (increase according to taste)	½	teaspoon whole cloves
4	cinnamon sticks	½	cup rum

Brew the tea. Simmer wine; do NOT boil. Mix remaining ingredients in a pot, adding hot wine and tea. Simmer for about half an hour. Serve!

Holiday Punch

1	quart cranberry juice	2	3 inch cinnamon sticks
1	quart unsweetened apple juice	6	whole cloves
¼	cup water		Cinnamon sticks for garnish, optional
1	(6 ounce) can frozen orange juice, undiluted		

Combine all ingredients except optional cinnamon sticks. Bring to a boil, reduce heat and simmer for 10 minutes. Remove spices. Serve warm; garnish each cup with a cinnamon stick. Yield: 9 servings.

Amy's Punch

2	(46 ounce) cans pineapple juice	¾	cup of red hots candies
2	(46 ounce) bottles apple juice	½	cup fresh or bottled lemon juice
1	cup brown sugar		

Combine all ingredients; heat and serve. Yield: 32 servings.

"In The Pink" Champagne Punch

1	pint raspberry sherbet	2	cups orange juice
½	cup lemon juice	48	ounces cranberry juice
¾	cup sugar	2	(28 ounce) bottles champagne

Combine softened sherbet, lemon juice, sugar, and orange juice. Just before serving, add cranberry juice and champagne.

Hot Fruited Tea

5	cups boiling water	½	cup sugar
5	tea bags or 5 teaspoons loose tea	¼	cup lemon juice
10	whole cloves	⅓	cup orange juice
¼	teaspoon cinnamon	3	unpeeled orange slices, cut in half

Pour boiling water over tea, cloves and cinnamon. Cover and let steep 5 minutes. Strain tea, stir in sugar and fruit juices. Heat to just below boiling. Serve hot with orange slice in each cup. Yield: 6 servings.

Wassail

Wassailing is an ancient English custom, part of the feasts and revelry of New Year's Eve and New Year's Day. The master of the English household drank to the health of those present with a bowl of spiced ale, and each in turn after him passed the bowl along and repeated the Saxon phrase Wass hael, "be whole", or "be well".

1	cup sugar	2	cups orange juice
4	cinnamon sticks	6	cups claret
	Lemon slices	½	cup lemon juice
2	cups pineapple juice	1	cup dry sherry

Boil sugar, cinnamon sticks, and 3 lemon slices in ½ cup water for 5 minutes and strain. Heat but do not boil the remaining ingredients. Combine with syrup, garnish with lemon slices, and serve hot. Yield: 20 servings.

Excellent Cappuccino

1 pound coffee	4 cups whipping cream, whipped
2 cinnamon sticks	Shaved chocolate, garnish
1 teaspoon cinnamon	Crushed peppermint candy,
½ cup sugar	garnish

In a 30-cup percolator, filled with water, brew first 3 ingredients. When brewing is complete, add sugar. Serve whipped cream, shaved chocolate and crushed peppermint in bowls allowing guests to prepare as desired. Yield: 30 servings.

Champagne Punch

24 ounces frozen undiluted lemonade concentrate, thawed	6 cups water
	66 ounces ginger ale, chilled
24 ounces frozen undiluted pineapple juice concentrate, thawed	28 ounces tonic water, chilled
	1 bottle champagne, chilled
	Lemon rings, optional

Combine first 3 ingredients; chill well for several hours. When ready to serve, gently stir in remaining ingredients. Garnish with lemon rings, optional. Yield: 1½ gallons.

To keep punch cold while serving, freeze either cubes or a block of the lemonade/pineapple mixture and then gently stir in remaining mixture and ingredients.

Enjoying a once-a-year event and turning it into a social occasion, the young people of the community pose by the sorghum mill on the C. L. Holder Farm in 1895.

Lemon Almond Tea

3 tablespoons lemon flavored (pre-sweetened) decaffeinated instant tea	1 (12 ounce) can frozen lemonade
	1 tablespoon almond extract
	1 tablespoon vanilla extract
2 cups hot water	

Mix tea with hot water to dissolve the tea. Add remaining ingredients; mix well. To 1 cup of this mixture add 2 cups hot water. Pour over ice or serve hot. Good for brunch or afternoon tea.

Almond Tea Punch

½ cup fresh lemon juice	2 tablespoons almond extract
2 cups sugar	1 tablespoon vanilla extract
1 cup strong brewed tea	1 (2 liter) bottle chilled lemon lime carbonated soda or ginger ale
1 quart water	

Mix first 6 ingredients together; freeze. May use zip-top plastic freezer bags. Remove from freezer, thaw slightly, and add a 2 liter bottle of chilled soda of your choice. Yield: 20 to 25 servings.

"Punch" is the English rendering of the Hindustani "pauch", meaning five, for the five ingredients - spirits, water, sliced lemons or limes, sugar, and spice.

Coffee Punch

1 (2 ounce) jar instant coffee	1 quart ginger ale
2 quarts hot water	1 pint heavy cream, whipped
2 cups sugar	1 half gallon vanilla ice cream
2 quarts half & half	

Dissolve coffee into hot water; cool. Add sugar and half & half; mix well. Just before serving, add cold ginger ale, heavy cream and ice cream. Stir to mix. Pour half at a time into punch bowl. Keep other half refrigerated and use as needed.

Marty's Punch
Good For A Crowd!

1	pint cranberry juice cocktail	1	(46 ounce) can pineapple juice
1	(6 ounce) can frozen orange juice	2	quarts chilled ginger ale
2	(6 ounce) cans frozen limeade	1	pint chilled club soda
1	(6 ounce) can frozen lemonade	1	(fifth) bottle Vodka
4	cups water	1	ice ring

Mix all ingredients and pour over ice ring and serve.

Golden Punch

2	cups lemon juice, chilled	2	cups cold water
2	cups orange juice, chilled	4	quarts ginger ale, chilled
2	cups sugar		

Combine fruit juices, sugar and water in a large punch bowl. Stir until sugar dissolves. Just before serving, pour ginger ale down side of bowl; stir gently. Float Iced Fruit Garland (directions follow) in bowl, if desired. Garnish with mint leaves. Yield: approximately 40 servings, ½ cup size.

Iced Fruit Garland
In a ring mold, arrange alternating slices of lemons and oranges with washed unhulled strawberries. Add just enough water to partially cover fruit. Too much water will float the fruit. Freeze. When frozen, add water to fill mold ¾ full; freeze. Unmold and float fruit side up in punch bowl.

Fuzzy Navel Punch

9	cups orange juice	1	(750 ml) bottle champagne, chilled
3	cups peach schnapps		Crushed ice or frozen ice ring

Combine orange juice, peach schnapps, and champagne. Pour into punch bowl; add crushed ice or frozen ice ring. Yield: 1 gallon.

Lemonade Punch

1 (12 ounce) can lemonade, thawed
   and undiluted
1¾ cups orange juice, chilled
¾ cup fresh lemon juice, chilled

1 (2 liter) bottle lemon-lime
   carbonated beverage, chilled
1 quart club soda, chilled

Combine first 3 ingredients in punch bowl; stir well. Slowly add last 2 ingredients;
mix well. Serve over ice if desired.

Summer Cooler Punch

1 (46 ounce) bottle cranberry,
   raspberry, strawberry juice
   beverage from concentrate, chilled

1 (2 liter) bottle diet lemon-lime
   carbonated soda, chilled

Pour 1 bottle each into punch bowl; add ice cubes or an ice ring. This also makes an
excellent individual drink; measure equal quantities and pour over ice.

Shower Punch

1½ cups white grape juice
1 (2 liter) bottle cherry lemon-lime
   carbonated soda or raspberry
   ginger ale

Cranberry or cran-grape or cran-
raspberry juice

Combine first 2 ingredients. Add enough cranberry juice to color as desired; cran-
grape gives a mauve color; cran-raspberry gives a purple color.

Frothy Raspberry Drink

1 pint raspberry sherbet, softened
12 ounces club soda

Raspberries, garnish

Beat together the sherbet and club soda. Garnish with raspberries. Serve immediately.
Yield: 4 servings.

Creamy Orange Drink

6   ounces frozen orange juice
     concentrate
1½ cups water
½   cup milk

⅓   cup sugar
1   teaspoon vanilla extract
2   cups ice
1   cup vanilla ice cream

Place all ingredients in a blender. Mix for 30 seconds. Yield: 4 twelve ounce servings.

Amaretto Eggnog

½   gallon carton refrigerated eggnog
½-1 cup amaretto liqueur

1   quart vanilla ice cream, softened
     Nutmeg, garnish

Pour eggnog into punch bowl. Add amaretto; stir until blended. Gently fold in ice cream. Sprinkle with nutmeg.

The Cabernet Sauvignon from Homestead Vineyards and Winery, photographed by Gary Carter in front of the Katy Depot, was chosen the official wine of the Denison Arts and Wine Renaissance Festival.

Homestead owners, Gabe and Barbara Parker, came back to their old stomping grounds to launch their nearby vineyards. Their tasting outlet on historic Main Street caters to wine enthusiasts, whether novices or connoisseurs.

Sangría - Red Wine & Fruit Punch

½	lemon cut in ¼ inch slices	1	bottle dry red wine (about a fifth)
½	orange cut in ¼ inch slices	¼	cup brandy
½	large apple, cut in half, lengthwise, cored and cut in thin wedges		Club soda chilled, to taste
			Ice cubes, optional
¼	cup sugar, more if desired		Fresh orange and/or lemon slices, garnish

Combine lemon, orange, apple and ¼ cup of sugar in a large pitcher. Add wine and brandy; stir well. Taste and add sugar; up to ½ cup more. Refrigerate 1 hour. Pour in chilled club soda (up to 24 ounces); pour into ice filled glasses. Garnish with fresh orange or lemon slice. Yield: 4 to 6 servings.

She grew her own hops. That's what you had to do if you wanted to make yeast rising bread. Or make persimmon beer. Or a few other beverages.

Christina Wiest, with her husband Jacob, immigrated to Denison in 1886. Her baking skills were exceptional; her bread was in demand.

Jacob was drawn to Denison by the work available in the Katy railroad car shops. Industrious Christina did her part to help with the money needed to provide for their seven children. She planted cuttings from hop vines, harvested the cones, then

dried and boiled them to make her own yeast.

Much to her daughters' chagrin, Christina entrusted her extra yeast to them to sell all over town. On the packets were printed "Mrs. Wiest's Hops Yeast".

The Wiest Family

First Call

*S*crambling eggs on Main Street in 1947, Kenneth Mills does the stirring while Judd Sampson stands ready to do some hot lifting. Verne Murray seems very content with his plateful as he talks with a friend.

Down home Main Street cooking is still a crowd-pleaser several times a year in Denison. Instead of eggs, however, recent Fall Festival breakfasts featured pancakes and sausage.

Bread & Brunch

 **FIRST CALL**

A TOAST! As you open your next bottle of wine, fill your glass and raise a salute to the man who rescued the grape vines of Europe: Dr. Thomas Volney Munson of Denison.

An epidemic root disease, phylloxera, was devastating the vineyards of Europe in the 1880's. With their wine industry in peril, the French government asked for Munson's help. Using the hardy and disease resistant native grapes he had found prospering along the Red River, Munson organized shipment of Texas grapevine rootstocks to France for grafting to their plants, thereby literally saving them from extinction.

In gratitude, the French government sent its Minister of Agriculture to Denison in 1888 to confer upon Munson France's highest accolade, the Legion of Honor, with the title of "Chevalier du Merite Agricole".

At that time the only other American recipient of the French Legion of Honor was inventor Thomas Alva Edison. General Dwight David Eisenhower, born in Denison, has since been so honored for his leadership during World War II.

Cognac, France, is the sister city of Denison, Texas. Cognac can be made only in the Charentes region around Cognac using methods dating back to the 16th century. Their vineyards still produce fine grapes for cognac because of Munson's efforts over one hundred years ago.

The T. V. Munson home.

Angel Biscuits

1   package yeast
¼   cup warm water (101 degrees)
⅓   cup shortening in 1 cup water
¼   cup sugar

¼   teaspoon salt
2½   cups flour
Butter

Dissolve yeast in ¼ cup warm water. Soften shortening in the water. Add sugar, salt and yeast mixture. Stir and add flour. Cover; let rise until double (1½ to 2 hours). Roll out; cut into rolls and let rise 1 hour. Put butter on top of each roll and bake in a preheated oven of 400 degrees until golden brown, approximately 10 to 12 minutes. Yield: about 14 large biscuits.

☺ Muffin Biscuits

1   stick margarine, softened
1   cup sour cream

2   cups biscuit baking mix

Preheat oven to 350 degrees. Cream all ingredients. Fill greased mini muffin pans with batter. Bake for 12 to 15 minutes or until golden brown. Serve warm!

Southern Biscuits

2   cups sifted flour
3   teaspoons baking powder
1   teaspoon salt

6   tablespoons shortening
⅔   cup milk

Preheat oven to 450 degrees. Sift together dry ingredients; cut shortening in finely. Stir in milk to make soft dough. Round up on lightly floured cloth-covered board. Knead lightly about 30 seconds. Roll or pat out about ¼ inch thick; cut. Place on an ungreased baking sheet. Bake for 10 to 12 minutes until golden brown. Yield: about 20 biscuits. Serve piping hot with any of the following: butter, jelly, honey, syrup, etc.

Unusual Apricot Nut Bread

1	cup dried apricots	¼	cup shortening
2	cups sifted flour	1	egg
2	teaspoons baking powder	¼	cup water
1	teaspoon salt	½	cup orange juice
¼	teaspoon baking soda	½	cup chopped walnuts or pecans
1	cup sugar		

Cover dried apricots with warm water and let stand 15 minutes. Drain and cut or chop into pieces. Sift together flour, baking powder, salt and soda. Cream sugar and shortening; add egg and beat well. Add half of dry ingredients and mix well. Add water and orange juice, then remaining dry ingredients; blend. Stir in nuts and apricots. Turn into a greased and floured 9-inch loaf pan and let stand for 20 minutes. Preheat oven to 350 degrees. Bake for 60 minutes or until bread tests done. Cool thoroughly before slicing.

The General's Wife's Bread

⅔	cup mayonnaise	⅔	cup finely chopped small green
⅔	cup Parmesan cheese		onions
		1	loaf enriched French bread, sliced

Mix first 3 ingredients and stir thoroughly. Spread on 1 side of each slice of French bread. Wrap in aluminum foil and bake at 200 degrees for 2 hours.

When the water pump was invented, it didn't take Denison pioneers long to figure out they could dig a well, then build their house on top of it. Wow! Indoor plumbing!

The Nettie Bass home, built in 1858 and now located at Denison's Frontier Village, boasted the very latest construction features. Not only did it have a kitchen sink with water but also glass window panes.

Stella's Banana Nut Bread

This venerable banana bread recipe has been enjoyed by four generations of a pioneering Denison family. Stella Miller Jennings, daughter of Arrena and James Miller, was one of the first babies born in the new township. The log home where she was born, which now has a State of Texas historical marker, is pictured with the story about Arrena and the wounded Indian. Her recipe has been shared with successive daughters-in-law, first Eva Jennings and then Carol Jennings. It's Good!

1	cup sugar	¼	teaspoon salt
½	cup shortening	3	very ripe mashed bananas, any size
2	eggs		
2	cups flour	½	cup chopped nuts, optional
1	teaspoon baking soda		

Cream sugar, shortening and eggs. Add flour, baking soda and salt until smooth. Fold in bananas and nuts (DO NOT mix with mixer). Pour in a greased and floured loaf pan. Bake at 325 degrees for an estimated 60 minutes, or 2 small loaf pans for an estimated 45 minutes.

Bananas can be frozen. When you have ripe bananas on hand, mash them and put in an airtight container until you are ready to make the recipe.

🕐 Blueberry Banana Bread

1	cup shortening	3	cups flour
1	teaspoon butter flavoring	2	teaspoons baking soda
2	cups sugar	½	teaspoon salt
4	eggs	½-1	teaspoon cinnamon
2	cups mashed ripe bananas	1	cup black walnut pieces
1	cup quick oats	1½	cups fresh blueberries

Preheat oven to 350 degrees. Grease and flour two 9-inch loaf pans. Cream shortening and butter flavoring; gradually add sugar, beating until light and fluffy. Add eggs one at a time, beating well after each. Beat in bananas. Mix in oats, flour, baking soda, salt, cinnamon, and walnuts. Gently fold in blueberries. Bake 50 to 55 minutes. Let cool in pan 10 minutes.

Poppy Seed Bread

3	cups flour	1½	cups milk
1	teaspoon salt	1½	tablespoons poppy seeds
1½	teaspoons baking powder	1½	tablespoons vanilla extract
2¼	cups sugar	1½	tablespoons almond extract
1⅛	cups vegetable oil	1½	tablespoons butter flavoring
3	eggs		

Blend flour, salt and baking powder; set aside. Blend sugar and oil together. Add eggs and milk to sugar mixture; mix well. Add dry ingredients to sugar mixture, then add poppy seeds, vanilla, almond and butter flavorings; mix well. Bake at 350 degrees until tests done. TIME VARIES ACCORDING to the size of pan which you use. A Bundt pan takes about 45 minutes.

Glaze

¼	teaspoon almond extract	⅛	cup orange juice
¼	teaspoon butter flavoring	⅔	cup powdered sugar
½	teaspoon vanilla extract		

Blend all ingredients together and pour over hot bread.

Broccoli Cornbread

2	(6 ounce) packages cornbread mix	1	(10 ounce) container cottage cheese
4	eggs	1	onion, chopped
1	(10 ounce) package chopped frozen broccoli (microwave for 8 minutes)	1	stick melted margarine
		1	cup shredded Cheddar cheese

Mix above ingredients (except Cheddar cheese) and pour half of mixture into an 8 x 12-inch greased pan. Sprinkle with 1 cup shredded Cheddar cheese; then cover with remaining mixture. Bake at 375 degrees for 30 minutes. Let cool about 10 minutes before cutting.

Can substitute with 1% cottage cheese as well as lowfat sharp Cheddar cheese.

Cranberry Bread

2 cups flour	¼ cup shortening
1 cup sugar	¾ cup orange juice
1½ teaspoons baking powder	1 egg
½ teaspoon baking soda	½ cup pecans, optional
1 teaspoon salt	2 cups cranberries, cut in half

Sift dry ingredients together. To keep cranberries and nuts from going to bottom, save out a little flour and coat cranberries and nuts slightly. Cut in shortening. Combine orange juice and egg. Pour into dry ingredients; fold in pecans and cranberries. Do NOT Beat! Bake at 350 degrees for 1 hour. Cool in pan.

❄ Pumpkin Bread

⅔ cup shortening	2 teaspoons baking soda
2⅔ cups sugar	½ teaspoon baking powder
4 eggs	1½ teaspoons salt
2 cups pumpkin	1 teaspoon cinnamon
⅔ cup water	1 teaspoon ground cloves
3⅓ cups all-purpose flour	⅔ cup raisins

Cream shortening; gradually add sugar; beat well. Add eggs; mix well. Stir in pumpkin and water; combine with all dry ingredients. Fold in raisins. Pour into 2 greased and floured 9-inch loaf pans. Bake at 350 degrees for 1 hour or until tests done. Cool in pan.

🕐 Garlic Bread Sticks

2 packages hot dog buns, split in half	Garlic Spread Concentrate
3 sticks butter, softened	Parmesan cheese

Mix softened butter with garlic spread. Generously spread on divided buns; cut into strips. Place on cookie sheet and sprinkle with Parmesan cheese. Bake at 200 degrees until crisp and toasted; 20 to 30 minutes. Can be served at room temperature. They keep well tightly wrapped.

Pull Apart Seasoned Bread

1 cup chopped green pepper	½ cup Parmesan cheese
1 cup chopped green onion	½ pound bacon, cooked and
¼ cup chopped chives	crumbled
2 sticks margarine, melted	1 heaping tablespoon all-purpose
3 cans refrigerated biscuits	Greek seasoning

Sauté vegetables in melted margarine; cool. Cut each biscuit into 4 pieces; mix all ingredients together. Place in an ungreased Bundt pan; bake at 325 degrees for 45 minutes. Cool 5 to 10 minutes before cutting.

Zucchini Pineapple Bread

3 eggs	1½ teaspoons cinnamon
2 cups sugar	¾ teaspoon nutmeg
1 cup oil	1 teaspoon salt
2 teaspoons vanilla extract	2 teaspoons baking soda
2 cups raw, grated zucchini, unpeeled	½ teaspoon baking powder
	1 cup raisins or chopped dates
1 cup crushed pineapple, drained	1 cup chopped walnuts or pecans
3 cups sifted all-purpose flour	

Beat eggs; mix in next 5 ingredients. Sift flour; add remaining dry ingredients; mix thoroughly. Add raisins or dates and nuts. Mix and pour into 2 greased and floured 9-inch loaf tins. Bake at 350 degrees (do NOT preheat oven) for 45 minutes or until a toothpick comes out clean. Let cool in baking pans.

Goodbye, Soot in the Butter!
Farewell, Cinders on the Tablecloth!

Katy dining cars already lavishly catered to their patrons, but this new level of comfort was astonishing. The railroad trains were taking their own weather with them! "Manufactured Weather", later called air conditioning, was the most comfortable kind of land travel ever known and Katy was quick to install it on their heavy equipment diners.

❄ Zucchini Bread

3 eggs, slightly beaten	½ teaspoon baking powder
1 cup oil	1 teaspoon cinnamon
2 cups peeled and grated zucchini	3 cups flour
1 teaspoon vanilla extract	2 cups sugar
1 teaspoon baking soda	½ cup chopped nuts, optional
1 teaspoon salt	

Mix eggs and oil together; blend in zucchini and vanilla. Add soda, salt, powder and cinnamon; mix well. Gradually add flour, sugar and nuts. Preheat oven to 350 degrees. Pour into 2 lightly greased and floured 9-inch loaf pans. Bake for 50 to 55 minutes or until done. Let cool in pans. Makes great muffins!

❄ Chocolate Nut Zucchini Bread

3 squares unsweetened chocolate	4 eggs
3 cups flour	3 cups sugar
1½ teaspoons baking powder	1½ cups oil
1 teaspoon salt	3 cups grated zucchini
1 teaspoon baking soda	1 cup chopped nuts, optional

Melt chocolate; let cool. Sift flour, baking powder, baking soda and salt; set aside. Beat eggs on high speed until thick and light; add sugar ¼ cup at a time. Add oil and melted chocolate; mix well. Add flour mixture and beat until smooth. Add zucchini and nuts; mix with a spoon. Preheat oven to 350 degrees. Pour into 3 greased and floured 9-inch loaf pans; bake for 50 minutes or until done.

This makes a wonderful cake baked at 350 degrees in a greased and floured 10-inch tube pan for 1 hour and 10 minutes or until done.

Aunt Bessie's Doughnuts

Bessie was born in 1881, her mother was born in 1850. Bessie handed down the recipe with these words "From My Mother".

One cup sugar and one cup milk.

Two eggs beaten fine as silk.

Salt and nutmeg, lemon will do.

Baking powder, teaspoons two.

Lightly stir the flour in.

Roll on pie board, not too thin.

Cut in diamonds, twists or rings.

Handle with care the doughy things.

Drop into fat which briskly swells.

Evenly the spongy cells.

Fry them brown, just short of burning.

Watch with care the time for turning.

Roll in sugar, serve when cool.

Price 25 cents for this rule.

Tri-Berry Muffins

3	cups all-purpose flour	2	large eggs
1	tablespoon baking powder	1	cup unsalted butter, melted
½	teaspoon baking soda	1	cup fresh blueberries
½	teaspoon salt	½	cup diced fresh strawberries
1½	teaspoons cinnamon	½	cup fresh raspberries
1¼	cups milk	1½	cups sugar

Preheat oven to 375 degrees. Line or grease 20 muffin cups. Stir flour, baking powder, baking soda, salt and cinnamon together in a large bowl. Make a well in the center of the flour mixture. Add milk, eggs and butter to the well; stir quickly just to combine. Add berries and sugar; stir quickly again just to combine. Spoon batter into cups, almost to the top. Bake about 20 minutes.

"I HAD FOUND MY GRAPE PARADISE" wrote *Thomas Volney Munson of his arrival in Denison in April of 1876. Grape paradise? Denison? Texas? Yes!*

In 1909 he wrote "Foundations of American Grape Culture", still a basic text for the study of grape culture. Moreover, housed in the United States Department of Agriculture in Washington, D. C., is the most complete botanical display for the whole grape genus ever made. It is Munson's work.

His legacy lives through the acclaimed Viticulture and Enology program offered by Grayson County College in Denison, which is one of the few degreed grape growing and wine making studies in the country, and through the Memorial Vineyard and Museum.

Botanical plate from Munson's book.

New Year Fritters

1	package dry yeast	3	eggs, beaten
¼	cup warm water	3½	cups flour
1	cup milk, scalded	1	cup raisins
¼	cup margarine		Oil for frying
¼	cup sugar		Dash of vanilla extract, if desired
¾	teaspoon salt		for additional flavoring

Dissolve yeast in warm water. Melt margarine in scalded milk; add remaining ingredients to liquid. Mix and let stand until double in bulk. Batter will be spongy. Dip spoon in hot fat and spoon a small amount of batter into the fryer. Deep fat fry. Roll fritters in sugar after removing from fryer.

Scald: to bring a liquid such as milk to a temperature below the boiling point at which bubbles appear around the sides of the surface. Milk scorches easily and should be scalded over hot water rather than over direct heat.

English Scones

2 cups all-purpose flour	6 tablespoons very cold or frozen
⅓ cup granulated sugar	unsalted butter
1½ teaspoons baking powder	½ cup buttermilk
½ teaspoon baking soda	1 large egg
¼ teaspoon salt	1½ teaspoons vanilla extract
	⅔ cup currants or raisins, optional

Preheat oven to 400 degrees. In a large bowl, stir together all dry ingredients. Grate butter over flour mixture; stir with a fork. In a small bowl, stir together the buttermilk, egg and vanilla. Add the buttermilk mixture to the flour mixture and stir to combine. Stir in currants, if desired. With lightly floured hands, pat dough to ½ inch thickness and cut into triangles. Place triangles on an ungreased baking sheet. Bake for 10 to 15 minutes, or until the top is lightly browned and a cake tester or toothpick inserted into the center of a scone comes out clean. Let cool for 5 minutes. Serve warm. To serve cool, remove scones to wire rack to cool completely and store in an airtight container. Serve with Devon Cream. Yield: 15 scones.

Devon Cream

1 cup heavy cream	½ cup sour cream
1 cup granulated sugar	1 teaspoon vanilla extract

Whip cream with sugar until soft peaks form. Fold in the sour cream and vanilla. Serve with scones.

Blueberry Muffins

2 cups flour	½ cup milk
1 cup sugar	2 eggs
2 teaspoons baking powder	1 teaspoon vanilla extract
½ teaspoon salt	2½ cups blueberries
½ cup butter	

Preheat oven to 375 degrees. Grease and flour a 12 cup muffin pan. In a medium bowl, combine dry ingredients. With a pastry blender, cut in butter until it resembles coarse meal. In a bowl, combine milk, eggs and vanilla. Add to dry ingredients; stir until moistened. Crush ½ cup of blueberries; add to batter. Fold in remaining berries and spoon into muffin pan. Sprinkle with sugar. Bake for 30 minutes or until centers are cooked. Cool in pan 5 minutes.

Pecan Muffins

⅓ cup margarine or butter at room
     temperature
2   eggs
1   cup brown sugar

½   cup plus 2 tablespoons flour
1   teaspoon vanilla extract
1   cup pecans

Cream margarine or butter. Add well beaten eggs; add brown sugar, mix well. Mix flour in gradually. Add vanilla. Mix in pecans. Fill well-greased tiny muffin pans half full. Bake at 350 degrees for 25 minutes. Yield: 2½ dozen muffins. Cool and glaze.

Glaze:
1½ lemons, squeezed
1   teaspoon salad oil

Confectioners' sugar

Take the juice from 1½ lemons and the oil and bring to a boil. Slowly add enough confectioners' sugar to hot mixture until it makes a thin paste. Pour over muffins. Cool and remove from pans.

Mattie Howard's Original Hot Rolls

½   cup warm water
2   packages dry yeast
2   cups warm milk
½   cup sugar

½   cup soft margarine
2   teaspoons salt
2   eggs
6½ cups flour, divided

In a large warm bowl, soften yeast in ½ cup (105 degrees) water and a little sugar (let set to proof). Heat milk to 115 degrees, add milk to sugar, margarine, salt and eggs; beat well. Add 3 cups flour, mix well; stir in remaining flour until easy to handle. Place in a greased bowl, turn once to grease top, cover loosely with foil. Refrigerate at least 2 hours. When dough rises, punch down occasionally. Remove from refrigerator, cut off amount needed, return remaining dough to refrigerator. Will keep 3 to 4 days. May skip refrigeration and let set on cabinet top about 1 hour, then proceed. Grease pans lightly. Make into any shape roll you wish; parker, clover, fan, crescent, folded. Bake at 325 degrees for 23 minutes until golden brown.

Katy Kornettes

This original recipe is typical of the unique choices for those enjoying meals in the luxury of the MKT Dining Car.

1	pound white corn meal	1	teaspoon salt
½	cup butter	1	quart boiling sweet milk
1	tablespoon sugar		

Mix well all ingredients. Let stand about 5 minutes. Drop through pastry bag about the size of a silver dollar on baking pan which has been greased very lightly. Cool about 15 minutes at room temperature before baking. Bake in hot oven for about 20 minutes. Yield: serves 6.

Cinnamon Rolls

1	(10 count) can of refrigerated biscuits	½	stick margarine
1	(3 ounce) package cream cheese	½	teaspoon cinnamon
¼	cup brown sugar	¼	cup chopped pecans

Preheat oven to 425 degrees. Cut slits in biscuits. Cut cream cheese into 10 squares and insert 1 square into each cut biscuit. Place in baking pan. Heat margarine, brown sugar, cinnamon and nuts to boiling. Pour over biscuits; bake about 12 to 15 minutes or until done.

Almond Biscotti

1	stick butter	2	eggs
1	teaspoon vanilla extract	1	cup sugar
1	teaspoon almond extract	1	cup almond slices
1½	teaspoons baking powder	2	cups flour

Melt butter; stir in remaining ingredients. Spray a 9 x 13-inch baking dish with a nonstick cooking spray. Pat mixture into baking dish. Bake at 350 degrees for 30 minutes. Slice or use a pizza wheel to cut.

Spray a little nonstick cooking spray on top of dough and it will pat easier.

Breakfast Casserole

1   pound sausage
1   stick margarine
6   cups tater tots, thawed
2½ cups shredded sharp Cheddar
       cheese

10 eggs, beaten
     Chopped parsley
     Seasonings of choice

In a large skillet, brown sausage; drain. Remove sausage to a small bowl; set aside. Melt margarine in skillet, stir in tater tots until crumbly. Do NOT brown. Stir in sausage; sprinkle with cheese. Pour eggs over top; cover and cook over medium-low heat until eggs are set. Do not disturb lid as eggs must steam to cook. Garnish with parsley. Yield: 10 servings.

☽ Egg and Sausage Strata

6   slices bread, crusts removed, and
       one side buttered
1   pound bulk pork sausage, cooked,
       crumbled and drained
1½ cups sharp Cheddar cheese,
       grated

6   eggs, beaten
2   cups half and half
1   teaspoon salt
½   teaspoon dry mustard

In a greased 9 x 13-inch baking dish place bread slices with the buttered side up. Sprinkle sausage over bread slices; sprinkle cheese over top. In a medium bowl place eggs, half and half, salt and dry mustard; beat them together. Pour mixture over cheese. Cover dish with foil; refrigerate overnight. Remove dish from refrigerator 30 minutes before you are ready to bake. Preheat oven to 350 degrees. Bake covered for 35 minutes; remove foil. Bake for 10 minutes more, or until set. Remove strata from the oven; let sit for 10 minutes. Yield: 8 to 12 servings.

Cinnamon Sugar Butter

½   cup butter, softened
2   cups sugar

2   teaspoons ground cinnamon

Mix all ingredients and beat until thoroughly blended. Mixture will be crumbly. Store in a jar in the refrigerator. Sprinkle mixture on bread and broil for excellent cinnamon toast.

A Dining Car Menu for a

Tea for the Ladies
Chicken Fruit Sandwiches
English Scones with Devon Cream
Apricot Sticks
Neiman Marcus Bars
Bonbons
Lemon Almond Tea

Eggs Bel-Mar

¼ cup butter or margarine	½ pound fresh mushrooms, sliced
¼ cup all-purpose flour	3 tablespoons butter or margarine, melted
2 cups milk	1 tablespoon butter or margarine
1 teaspoon salt	18 eggs, slightly beaten
½ teaspoon pepper	1 cup soft breadcrumbs
1 (6 ounce) package Canadian bacon, chopped	2 tablespoons butter or margarine, melted
¼ cup chopped green pepper	
¼ cup sliced green onions	

Melt ¼ cup butter in a heavy saucepan over low heat; add flour, stirring until smooth. Cook 1 minute, stirring constantly. Gradually add milk; cook over medium heat, stirring constantly, until thickened and bubbly. Stir in salt and pepper; set aside.

Sauté Canadian bacon and next 3 ingredients in 3 tablespoons butter in a skillet until vegetables are crisp-tender; drain.

Melt 1 tablespoon butter in skillet, tilting to coat bottom; add eggs. Cook without stirring until mixture begins to set on bottom. Draw a spatula across bottom of pan to form large curds. Continue until eggs are thickened but still moist; do NOT stir constantly. Remove from heat. Gently stir in Canadian bacon mixture and white sauce. Spoon egg mixture into a greased 9 x 13-inch baking dish.

Combine breadcrumbs and 2 tablespoons melted butter, stirring well; sprinkle evenly over egg mixture. Bake, uncovered, at 350 degrees for 20 to 25 minutes or until thoroughly heated. Yield: 12 servings.

To make ahead: prepare casserole as directed, but do NOT bake. Cover and refrigerate up to 24 hours. Remove from refrigerator; let stand 30 minutes. Bake as directed.

Banana Nut Pancakes

1 cup flour	1 egg, slightly beaten
2 tablespoons sugar	2 tablespoons oil
2 teaspoons baking powder	1 medium banana, chopped
½ teaspoon salt	¼ cup chopped walnuts
1 cup milk	

Combine flour, sugar, baking powder, and salt; set aside. In a large bowl, stir milk, egg and oil until blended. Add flour mixture; blend well. Stir in banana and walnuts. Pour ¼ cupfuls onto hot, lightly greased griddle. Cook until golden brown, turning once.

Puffy Baked Pancake

3 tablespoons butter	1 teaspoon vanilla extract
½ cup flour	2 eggs
½ cup milk	

Preheat oven to 425 degrees. Melt butter in a 10 to 12-inch skillet. Lightly beat together ingredients. Batter will be lumpy. Pour batter into skillet with melted butter. Bake 15 to 20 minutes until puffy and golden.

Serve with fresh fruit, sprinkle confectioners' sugar and fresh lemon juice over pancake.

Richer Waffles or Pancakes

3 eggs	2 teaspoons baking powder
1½ cups buttermilk or sour milk	½ teaspoon salt
1 teaspoon baking soda	½ cup soft shortening
1¾ cups sifted flour	½ teaspoon vanilla extract

Heat waffle iron while mixing batter. Beat eggs well; mix in remaining ingredients. Beat until smooth. This is a thin batter. Bake in a hot waffle iron. Yield: 8 waffles.

Sausage Mushroom Breakfast Casserole

2¼ cups seasoned croutons	1 (4 ounce) can sliced mushrooms,
1½ pounds sausage	drained
4 eggs, beaten	¾ teaspoon dry mustard
2¼ cups milk	2 cups (8 ounces) shredded
1 (10¾ ounce) can cream of	Cheddar cheese
mushroom soup	

Spread croutons in a lightly greased 9 x 13-inch baking dish; set aside. Cook sausage until browned, stirring to crumble; drain well. Sprinkle sausage over croutons. Combine eggs, milk, soup, mushrooms, and mustard. Mix well and pour over sausage. Cover and refrigerate at least 8 hours or overnight. Remove from refrigerator; let stand 30 minutes. Bake uncovered at 325 degrees for 50 to 55 minutes. Sprinkle cheese over top. Bake an additional 5 minutes until cheese melts.

Apple Pancake Tier

6 eggs	6 cooking apples, cored and sliced
1 cup all-purpose flour	¼ cup butter or margarine
1 teaspoon salt	½ cup sugar
½ teaspoon ground nutmeg	2 teaspoons grated lemon peel
1 cup milk	Confectioners' sugar
¼ cup butter or margarine, melted	Warm syrup

Preheat oven to 400 degrees. Beat eggs thoroughly in a large mixing bowl. Beat in flour, salt and nutmeg at low speed until moistened. Stir in milk and ¼ cup melted butter. Pour 1 cup batter into each of 3 greased 9-inch pie pans. Bake until pancakes are light brown and puffy, 15 to 20 minutes. Prepare apples while pancakes bake. Cook and stir apples in ¼ cup butter for 5 minutes; stir in sugar. Cook until apples are tender, about 10 minutes. Place largest pancake first on serving plate and top with ⅓ of the apple mixture and lemon peel; repeat 2 times. Garnish with confectioners' sugar. Cut in 4 pieces to serve. Pass the syrup! Yield: 4 servings.

Easy Quiche

2 tablespoons butter
6 green onions, chopped
12 eggs, beaten
1⅓ cups milk
¾ teaspoon seasoned salt

1½ cups diced ham or bacon
3 cups shredded Swiss cheese, divided
1 cup mushrooms, optional

Melt butter in skillet over medium heat. Sauté onions (and mushrooms if used) until soft. In a large bowl, beat eggs. Add milk, salt, ham, onions and all but ½ cup of cheese. Pour egg mixture into a greased casserole. Bake, uncovered, at 350 degrees for 35 to 40 minutes or until mixture is set. Sprinkle with remaining cheese and continue baking until cheese melts. Yield: 8 servings.

✳ Sausage Sandwich

1 pound hot sausage
½ cup chopped onion
¾ cup chopped celery
1 loaf French bread
½ teaspoon sage

½ teaspoon pepper
2 eggs, beaten
¼ cup milk
1 cup grated cheese or 6 slices
   Butter for spreading on bread

Cook sausage with onion and celery until brown; drain grease. Slice loaf of bread lengthwise. Make a well in each side of bread by pulling out centers. Tear centers into small pieces. Mix sausage mixture with bread, spices, eggs, and milk. Place mixture into the bottom half of loaf. Cover mixture with cheese. Top with top half of loaf. Butter top of loaf lightly. Wrap in foil. Bake at 400 degrees for 20 minutes. Slice; serve warm. This can also be frozen.

The White Pig flourished in the 40's and 50's golden era of drive-in eateries and juke boxes. Carhops wore silk shirts, slacks and hats to serve orders on aluminum trays clamped to car windows.

An order of a "stretched wild shot" and "one all the way in a basket" was White Pig jargon for a large cherry coke and a hamburger with french fries.

Pate's Cheese and Grits Casserole

4½	cups water	1	roll sharp cheese, divided
1	cup grits	2	jalapeños, chopped
1	teaspoon salt	5	slices bacon, crisply cooked and
1	stick butter		crumbled
1	cup chopped onions	2	eggs
1	teaspoon garlic powder		Milk
1	roll garlic cheese		

Cook water, grits and salt until very thick. Sauté onions in melted butter. Add the next 5 ingredients and stir until melted. Add eggs (broken in measuring cup filled with milk to equal ½ cup); mix well. Pour into baking dish. Crumble remaining ½ roll sharp cheese over top. Bake at 300 degrees for 30 minutes. Yield: 12 servings.

In early times, Denison had a wild and rowdy reputation. Migrant railroad workers were partly to blame, but most of the credit can be laid to the cowboys who regularly drove herds in from the south and west. With the coming of the railroad, these huge herds no longer had to cross the Red River and be driven northward but could be delivered to holding pens until loaded into rail cars.

After hard riding rounding up the steers, the cowhands wrangled the cattle across the state, trying to push the herds no more than ten miles a day to maintain all the weight possible. During the weeks on the trail, they had been eating and sleeping outdoors with a cloud of dust hanging over them.

Most of the cattle were shipped out of Denison on Thursday to reach the Monday morning market in Chicago. After the last steer was loaded and the cattlecar door banged shut, the cowhands had done their job. Whooping and shouting, they felt they had earned the right to a long weekend in town. Perhaps Denison gained its rowdy reputation so the rest of the United States could enjoy steak.

Calla Lily Sandwiches

1 (2 ounce) package slivered
   almonds
2-3 drops of yellow food coloring
54 slices white sandwich bread

1 (8 ounce) package cream cheese,
   softened
2 tablespoons orange marmalade

Combine almonds and food coloring in a jar; cover with lid, and shake vigorously until almonds are evenly coated. Roll each slice of bread to ⅛ inch thickness with a rolling pin; cut with a 2½ inch biscuit cutter. Combine cream cheese and marmalade; spread about 1 teaspoon on each bread round. Pinch edges of one portion of the circle together to form a calla lily. Press a tinted slivered almond into the pinched portion to represent the flower's stamen. Yield: 4½ dozen.

Cucumber Rounds

1 large cucumber
1 (8 ounce) package cream cheese,
   softened
1½ teaspoons mayonnaise

⅛ teaspoon seasoned salt
1 loaf multi-grain bread
   Parsley sprigs

Cut cucumber in half horizontally. Peel, seed, and shred half of cucumber. Measure ⅓ cup shredded cucumber. Slice remaining cucumber for garnish. Cut cucumber slices in half, set aside. Combine cream cheese, mayonnaise, and seasoned salt; mix until blended. Stir in shredded cucumber. Cut two 2 inch rounds from each bread slice. Spread each round with 1 teaspoon cucumber mixture. Garnish each round with a thin half slice of cucumber and a sprig of parsley. Yield: 48 rounds.

Chicken-Fruit Sandwiches

1 cup finely chopped cooked
   chicken
1 (8¾ ounce) can crushed
   pineapple, drained

⅓ cup finely chopped pecans
½ cup mayonnaise
¼ teaspoon salt

Combine all ingredients; chill well. Spread on bread of your choice. Cut into triangles; serve.

Spinach-Ham Rolls

1   cup cottage cheese
¾   cup sour cream
1   (10 ounce) package frozen
    chopped spinach, thawed and
    drained
1½ cups herb-seasoned stuffing mix
1   egg, beaten
¼   cup minced onion

½   teaspoon dry mustard
12 (⅛ inch thick) slices ham (about
    1½ pounds)
    Cheese sauce, recipe follows
    Paprika
    Green onion tops, sliced
    Parsley sprigs

Combine cottage cheese and sour cream in container of a blender; process until smooth. Combine sour cream mixture, spinach and next 4 ingredients; mix well. Spoon ¼ cup of mixture on each slice of ham. Roll up and place rolls, seam side down, in a lightly greased 9 x 13-inch baking dish. Top with cheese sauce; sprinkle with paprika. Bake at 350 degrees for 20 to 25 minutes. Garnish with onion tops and parsley. Yield: 12 servings.

Cheese Sauce

1   tablespoon cornstarch
1   cup milk
2   tablespoons butter or margarine

¼   teaspoon salt
⅛   teaspoon black pepper
1   cup (4 ounces) shredded Cheddar
    cheese

Combine cornstarch and milk; stir until smooth. Cook over medium heat, stirring constantly, until mixture comes to a boil. Boil 1 minute. Add butter, salt, pepper and cheese; stir until smooth. Yield: 1¼ cups.

Broccoli Bacon Quiche

1   (9 inch) pie shell, baked slightly
3   eggs, beaten
1   (10 ounce) package chopped
    broccoli, cooked and drained
⅓   cup chopped onion

1   cup cream
½   cup bacon bits or 6 slices bacon
    crisply cooked and crumbled
½   cup grated Cheddar cheese
¼   teaspoon nutmeg

Preheat oven to 350 degrees. Combine all ingredients and pour into a partially cooked pie crust. Bake approximately 40 minutes or until center is firm.

Greek Spinach Quiche

1 (9 inch) pie shell	1/4 teaspoon salt
3 large eggs, slightly beaten	1/4 teaspoon pepper
1 cup milk	Dash of ground nutmeg
1/4 cup butter or margarine, melted	1 (10 ounce) package frozen
2 tablespoons all-purpose flour	chopped spinach, thawed and
3 tablespoons grated Romano	well drained
cheese	1 cup crumbled Feta cheese

Preheat oven to 400 degrees. Put pastry into a 9-inch quiche dish; trim excess pastry around edges. Prick bottom and sides with a fork. Bake for 8 minutes. Remove from oven; reduce temperature to 350 degrees. Whisk eggs; mix with next 7 ingredients until blended. Stir in spinach and cheese. Pour into baked pastry shell. Bake for 35 minutes or until set. Let stand for 10 minutes before slicing.

Maple Cream Coffee Treat

1 cup firmly packed brown sugar	1 (8 ounce) package cream cheese,
1/2 cup chopped nuts	softened
1/3 cup maple flavored syrup or dark	1/4 cup powdered sugar
corn syrup	2 tablespoons margarine, softened
1/4 cup margarine, melted	1 (10 ounce) can refrigerated flaky
	biscuits

Preheat oven to 350 degrees. In an ungreased 9 x 13-inch baking pan, combine brown sugar, nuts, syrup and 1/4 cup margarine. Blend cream cheese, powdered sugar and remaining 2 tablespoons margarine until smooth. Separate dough into 20 biscuits; press or roll each biscuit to a 4 inch circle. Spoon 1 tablespoon cream cheese mixture onto center of each biscuit. Overlap dough over filling, forming finger-shaped rolls. Place rolls, seam side down, in 2 rows of 10 in prepared pan. Bake for 25 to 30 minutes or until deep golden brown. Cool 3 minutes; turn onto serving plate or waxed paper. Refrigerate any leftovers. Yield: 10 servings.

The ambience of Main Street was beguiling as Ruenell Jarriel was growing up in Denison. Her delightful recollections are shared in verse:

THE OLD DRUGSTORE THRU THE EYES OF A CHILD

Saturdays were so special,
Nearly everyone went to town,
Most to do the shopping,
And some to just hang around.
But high on the list of things to do,
Before the day was done,
Was to stop by the local drugstore,
Cause gosh, it was so much fun.
The jingle of the shop bells,
As the door swung open wide,
Seemed to whisper, "Welcome, Welcome"
As I slowly strolled inside.
Funny how a little girl
Remembers favorite things,
Just thinking back to how things were,
What happiness it brings.
The store was filled with everything
A little one could need,
From tonics for the tummy
To Granny's garden seed.
Bubble gum and funny books,
Jewelry in glass cases,
Perfumes and talcs that smelled so good,
And make-up for our faces.
And for sending cards and letters
To our secret pals and such,
Was the handy little post office there,
Now, that was a special touch!
And about the old man in the pharmacy
With all the good advice,
On how to take the pills he sold,
He was always very nice.
But as I recall, the best of all,
Was the soda fountain there,
A burger and a cherry coke?
Only a pittance fare.
Now, if I could, I know I would,
Go back there for a day,
I'd linger for a little while,
Then I would simply say,
Thanks For The Memories.

Background: Kingston Drug Store, founded in 1892, was one of the most frequented Main Street establishments for over nine decades.

Clickety Clack

In the compact train galley, a steward prepares salad plates with the artistry and skill expected for the luxury meal service in the dining car of the Bluebonnet around 1945.

Named for the state flower of Texas, the Bluebonnet and the famous Texas Special were considered the Katy Line's premier trains for comfort and passenger service.

Soups & Salads

FROM CATTLE TRAILS TO RAILROAD TRACKS, *the transformation focused on rolling Texas land where the Shawnee Trail crossed the Red River and where the Denison railhead would come to be.*

Before the Civil War, the SHAWNEE TRAIL was the main cattle route, crossing the Red River at Rock Bluff and angling northeastward toward the railroad in Sedalia, Missouri.

Trail campfire tales paint images of epic movements of men and cattle. One day around 1870, the Rock Bluff Ferry manager, John Malcolm, heard the thunder and roar of 7,900 head of cattle. At Rock Bluff the terrain formed a natural chute so livestock would hit the water swimming and not mill around at water's edge. The huge herd that day almost dammed the river, but not one head was lost. The last trail ride? In 1871 Sam Vaughan, Donna Hunt's great-grandfather, worked the last big one trailing 1,500 head up the Shawnee Trail.

Texas soldiers returning from the Civil War found the economy bleak, their cattle running wild but multiplied by the millions, and the passage to markets over the Shawnee Trail beset with settlers and progress. At the same time returning Union soldiers found their own cattle depleted by wartime demand for meat.

Enter Joseph G. McCoy, a wheeler-dealer cattle entrepreneur who kept things moving in the quest to make Texas livestock-on-the-hoof available for the dinner platters of beef hungry Easterners. In 1867 McCoy laid out a new cattle trail from Central Texas through Fort Worth crossing the Red River about 35 miles west of Denison. It ended in Abilene, Kansas, the point where McCoy had persuaded the Kansas-Pacific Railroad to extend their rails. It was the McCoy Trail, so most thought.

Then why was it called the CHISHOLM TRAIL? Because Jesse Chisholm had guided wagon trains over part of that route, early drovers literally followed Chisholm's wagon ruts. The biggest year for the Chisholm Trail was 1871 when more than 5,000 cowboys driving 700,000 cattle arrived at the Abilene yards.

The north end of the Shawnee Trail reached the edge of civilization in Kansas and Missouri where a few railroads meandered and terminated. To jump-start southwesterly construction, the government offered to grant great sections of land to the first railroad to reach Indian Territory. This inducement spawned a high stakes three-way race. The winner would have exclusive right to build through the vast wilderness of the Indian Territory.

Deciding to take the gamble, a cadre of daring businessmen hectically amassed money, men and materials. On May 23, 1870, the name Missouri, Kansas & Texas Railway was formally adopted. Intent on extending western frontiers, it is startling to be reminded an established country flourished to the east...with a stock exchange. The Missouri, Kansas & Texas Railway's symbol on the exchange was K-T. The Katy.

Headlong construction drove down The Texas Trail, the name used by northern planners for the Shawnee Trail. Rails were laid on bare ground packed and paved by animal hooves, first by massive migrating buffalo herds, then by countless Texas cattle. With brains and nerve, principal contractor John Scullin supervised men inured to hardship working twenty-fours a day, got along with Indian tribes whose land was traversed, and armed his camp for survival fending off marauding low life.

Relentlessly pushing south, the Katy won the land grant race. Robert S. Stevens, General Manager, telegraphed his bosses, "We've struck the Territory line and are going like hell!". They were headed for the narrow crossing of the Red River into Texas. On December 24, 1872, a tiny woodburning Katy engine triumphantly chugged across the new Red River bridge. Four short miles later, it drew up at a cluster of tents and makeshift structures now called Denison. The Gateway to Texas.

Cabbage Patch Soup

1	pound ground beef	2	teaspoons chili powder
1	large onion, chopped		Garlic powder to taste
1	bell pepper, chopped	1	cup water
¾	cup chopped celery	2	cups chopped cabbage
1	(15 ounce) can tomatoes	1	cup Ranch Style beans

Brown ground beef, onion and bell pepper. Add celery, tomatoes, chili powder, garlic, water, cabbage and beans. Simmer until done. If stock boils down, add a little water. Great with cornbread.

Canadian Soup

¼	cup margarine	1	quart chicken broth
½	cup diced onions	1	quart whole milk
2½	cups shredded carrots	½	teaspoon baking soda
2½	cups chopped celery	1	cup cubed processed cheese loaf
¼	cup flour	1	teaspoon salt
1½	tablespoons cornstarch	¼	teaspoon black pepper

Melt margarine; add onions, carrots and celery. Cook until tender. Add flour and cornstarch; stir until blended. Add chicken broth and milk; stir to make a smooth sauce. Add baking soda and cheese. Season with salt and pepper. Simmer to melt cheese.

Cassoulet

½	pound sausage	1	bay leaf
1	small onion, coarsely chopped	2	cups cooked navy beans
1	clove garlic, finely chopped	¼	cup dry white wine
½	pound ham, cut in ½ inch cubes	2	cups bean liquid or chicken broth
2	tablespoons chopped parsley		

Cook sausage until browned. Add onion and garlic while sausage is browning; drain grease. Add ham, parsley and bay leaf to the sausage. Put navy beans, wine and bean liquid in a 1½-quart casserole. Add all ingredients together and stir. Bake uncovered at 325 degrees for 45 minutes. Yield: 6 servings.

Serve with French bread and a big salad for a great winter supper.

Kay's Italian Chicken Soup

1	large chicken or 5 chicken breasts	½	small head of cabbage, chopped
1	medium onion, sliced	2	medium tomatoes, chopped
1	package dry Italian salad dressing mix	3	baby squash, sliced
3	celery stalks, chopped	3	medium carrots, sliced
1	(8¾ ounce) can shoepeg corn		Salt and pepper to taste

Boil chicken in a large pot with 2½ to 3 quarts water. Add onion and Italian dressing. When meat is thoroughly done, remove from bone and cut into smaller pieces. Return to liquid. Add remaining ingredients and simmer 2 to 3 hours. If stock boils down, add more water.

◷ The Molly Cherry Bed & Breakfast's Cold Fruit Soup

Nestled in a country setting in the city of Denison is THE MOLLY CHERRY, a bed and breakfast inn. In 1890 J. J. Fairbanks, real estate tycoon and gambler, built this lavish Queen Anne Victorian home for his wife, Edith. Beautifully restored features include an ornate hand carved staircase and stained glass double doors nine feet tall. The inn owners also opened The Gandy Dancer, a Victorian tea room on Main Street.

1	cup sour cream	Sliced strawberries
1	(15 ounce) can real cream of coconut	Sliced kiwi
1	(20 ounce) can pineapple tidbits	Sliced bananas
1	cup water	Toasted slivered almonds

Mix first 4 ingredients together in a blender. Garnish with the sliced fruit and toasted almonds. Serve cold!

CLICKETY CLACK

🕐 Good and Quick Gazpacho

1 (26 ounce) can peeled tomatoes
1 cucumber, peeled and chunked
4-5 scallions, including tops, coarsely chopped

2 cloves garlic, crushed, optional
2 teaspoons Worcestershire sauce

Put all ingredients in a blender and mix. Chill if possible. May also be served at room temperature or hot.

🕐 Ham and Potato Chowder

2 tablespoons butter or margarine
1 cup chopped onion
1 cup chopped celery
½ clove garlic, minced
2 cups diced ham (about 1 pound)
2 cups diced raw potatoes

1 bay leaf
¾ teaspoon salt
½ teaspoon dried leaf thyme
½ teaspoon red hot pepper sauce
2 cups water
2 cups milk

Melt butter in a saucepan; add onion, celery, garlic and ham. Cook until onion and celery are tender. Add potatoes, bay leaf, salt, thyme, hot sauce and water. Simmer covered until potatoes are tender, about 20 to 30 minutes. Add milk and heat; do NOT allow to boil. Serve with hot cornbread and a crisp green salad.

Parsnip Soup

2 cups cubed parsnips
½ medium onion, chopped thick
1 large carrot, sliced thick
1 potato, cubed (about 1 cup)
2 cups chicken broth

1 cup milk
½ cup heavy cream
Salt and pepper to taste
¼ teaspoon mace or nutmeg

Cook parsnips, onion, carrot and potato in chicken broth, uncovered, until tender. Puree vegetables and broth; return to saucepan. Add milk and cream, season, heat through.

Jambalaya

1½ pounds chicken strips
½ teaspoon salt
½ teaspoon ground black pepper
1 tablespoon vegetable oil
¾ pound smoked sausage, cut into
   ¼ inch slices
2 medium onions, chopped
1 large green pepper, chopped

1 cup chopped celery
1 clove garlic, minced
2 cups uncooked rice
¼ teaspoon ground red pepper
2½ cups chicken broth
1 cup sliced green onions
1 medium tomato, chopped

Season chicken with salt and pepper; brown in hot oil in a Dutch oven. Add sausage; cook 2 to 3 minutes. Remove chicken and sausage from pan; set aside. Cook onions, green pepper, celery and garlic in same pan over medium heat until tender crisp. Stir in rice, red pepper, broth and reserved chicken and sausage; bring to a boil. Simmer covered for 30 minutes. Stir in green onions and tomato before serving.

Minestrone Cortonese

1 cup white dry beans (or 3 cans
   cooked beans)
2 cups chopped onions
4 cups diced potatoes or 2 cups
   uncooked pasta
1 cup coarsely chopped parsley
2 teaspoons finely minced garlic
2 cups water or chicken broth

2 tablespoons olive oil
2 tablespoons dry basil
   Salt and pepper to taste
1 (28 ounce) can of tomatoes
½ cup washed and shredded
   spinach
6 slices French bread
   Parmesan cheese

Cover beans in water; cook until nearly tender. Add onions, potatoes, parsley, garlic, water or broth, olive oil, basil, salt and pepper to beans; cook until tender crisp. Add tomatoes and enough water or stock to cover vegetables by 1 to 2 inches. When ready to serve, stir in spinach to wilt the leaves. Put a slice of bread into each bowl, pour in soup and top with Parmesan cheese.

Great served over garlic bread.

Soups from these two authentic recipes were offered in the Katy Railroad dining cars, circa 1930. Note the prices on the Special Luncheons menu card!

Old Fashioned Navy Bean Soup

3	slices bacon	1	small green pepper
1	ounce butter	¾	cup Navy beans
1	carrot	1	quart meat stock
1	medium sized onion	1	medium sized potato
1	outside stalk celery	2	tomatoes

Fry bacon for one minute in sauce pan; add one ounce butter and the carrot, onion, celery, and pepper after cutting them in small dices. Cover pan and cook slowly for approximately 10 minutes or until vegetables are soft. Now add Navy beans (after soaking them in cold water for four to six hours). Add meat stock, cook for one hour, and then add raw potato cut in quarter inch dices; add peeled and cut tomatoes. Season to taste until all ingredients are well done. If the soup is too thick, add more stock. Four bouillon cubes to one quart of water may be substituted for the meat stock. If a ham bone is available, it may be cooked with the soup but in this case little salt should be used.

The Katy's Special Onion Soup

6	large onions
¼	pound butter
½	cup flour
1	gallon of rich stock
¼	cup Worcestershire sauce

Cut onions into quarters, and then slice thin cross sections. Sauté in butter to a golden brown. Add the flour to the onion and butter and blend well. Then add the hot stock and let simmer 20 minutes. Season with a bunch of parsley, bay leaves and a touch of garlic. Boil for a few minutes and then remove the bouquet. Season to taste with salt and pepper, and add the Worcestershire sauce. For each portion of soup prepare crouton fried in oil or butter. After soup is poured, place crouton in cup topped with a generous portion of grated Parmesan cheese. Place in hot oven a few minutes just before serving. Yield: 1 gallon.

Black Bean Soup

½-1 pound ground beef
⅓ cup chopped onion
¼ cup diced green pepper
3   (15 ounce) cans black beans,
      undrained

2   (14½ ounce) cans chicken broth
2   tablespoons chopped cilantro
Picante sauce to taste
Grated Cheddar cheese
Sour cream

Brown ground beef with onions and green pepper. Drain grease. Mix all ingredients together and heat. Serve with grated Cheddar cheese and sour cream.

Zesty Zucchini Soup

1   pound Italian bulk sausage
4   cups diced zucchini
2   whole green peppers, diced
2   cups sliced celery
1   cup chopped onion
2   (32 ounce) cans tomato juice

1   teaspoon salt
1   teaspoon basil
1   teaspoon Italian seasoning
1   teaspoon oregano
1   teaspoon sugar
1   teaspoon garlic salt

Brown sausage; drain grease. Add remaining ingredients; cook slowly for about one hour.

Wild Rice and Chicken Soup

1   tablespoon olive oil
2   cloves garlic, finely chopped
1   cup finely chopped carrots
½ cup finely chopped celery
1   cup finely chopped onion
2   (14½ ounce) cans chicken broth
2   cups water

1   (6 ounce) package long grain &
      wild rice, cooked
½ teaspoon ground black pepper
2   cups diced cooked chicken breast
½-1 cup whipping cream, optional
2   tablespoons chopped fresh
      parsley (garnish)

Heat olive oil in a large saucepan. Sauté garlic, carrots, celery and onion until vegetables are soft and transparent. Add broth, water, rice, pepper and cooked chicken. Heat for 10 minutes. If soup becomes too thick, add water to desired consistency. For creamy soup, add whipping cream. Ladle into bowls; garnish with chopped parsley.

Ranch Potato and Bacon Soup

6	strips of bacon	2	cups milk, more if desired
1	medium onion, chopped		Salt and pepper to taste
5	large potatoes, diced in ½ inch cubes	3	tablespoons ranch dressing mix
		1	cup sour cream
4	cups chicken broth	3	tablespoons flour

Cook bacon until crisp. Remove bacon and set aside. Sauté onion in bacon drippings until softened. In a large saucepan combine potato, onion and broth; simmer until potatoes are tender. Mash about half the potatoes to help thicken soup. Add milk (enough for desired consistency), salt, pepper and ranch dressing; heat thoroughly. Crumble bacon; add to mixture and remove from heat. Whisk together sour cream and flour; stir into soup. Heat very gently (do NOT boil).

Irish Potato Chowder

7	tablespoons butter, divided	4	cups vegetable or chicken stock
7	tablespoons flour	5	cups peeled and diced potatoes (about 1¼ pounds)
1	cup chopped onion		
⅔	cup diced carrots	3	cups milk
⅔	cup chopped celery	½	cup sour cream
1	teaspoon dried basil	⅛-¼	teaspoon hot pepper sauce
1	teaspoon dried parsley		Salt and ground white pepper to taste
1	teaspoon freeze-dried chives		

To make roux, melt 5½ tablespoons butter in a small saucepan. Stir in flour until well blended. Cook over low heat for 3 to 5 minutes, stirring often. Remove from heat; set aside. Melt remaining 1½ tablespoons butter in a soup pot. Add onions, carrots, celery, basil, parsley and chives. Cook about 10 minutes. Add stock and potatoes; simmer until potatoes are tender (about 15 to 20 minutes). Stir in milk, return to simmer and whisk in roux until liquid is thickened and smooth. Simmer 10 minutes, stirring occasionally; add sour cream, hot pepper sauce and season to taste with salt and ground white pepper.

Creamy Potato Soup

6	slices bacon	2	(10¾ ounce) cans cream of
1	cup chopped onion		mushroom soup
2	cups cubed potatoes	2	soup cans milk
1	cup water	2	tablespoons parsley, snipped
1	teaspoon salt		

In a saucepan, cook bacon until crisp; set bacon aside. Pour off all but 3 tablespoons fat. Add onion and brown. Add potatoes and water. Cook covered 15 minutes or until potatoes are tender. Stir in salt, soup and milk. Heat but do NOT boil. Garnish with bacon and parsley. Yield: 4 servings. This is a hearty soup.

Turkey Corn Chowder

2	tablespoons butter or margarine	1	teaspoon coarse ground black
2	cups chopped onion		pepper
2	tablespoons flour		Salt to taste
4	cups turkey stock	1	large red or green bell pepper,
2	large potatoes, diced		diced
1	cup milk	1	cup diced turkey
2-3	(10 ounce) packages frozen corn,	3	green onions, sliced
	cooked	1	tablespoon cilantro

Melt butter; add onions and cook until soft, about 10 minutes. Add flour and cook, stirring for another 5 minutes. Add stock and potatoes, continue cooking over medium low heat until potatoes are just tender (12 to 15 minutes). Add milk, corn, coarse ground black pepper and salt. Cook 7 minutes, stirring occasionally. Add bell pepper, turkey and green onions. Adjust seasonings and cook 5 more minutes. Serve immediately, garnished with cilantro.

A Dining Car Menu for a

Spring Brunch Buffet
Bellinis
Cucumber Rounds
Spinach-Ham Rolls
Fruit Salad with Poppy Seed Dressing
Crab-Stuffed Cherry Tomatoes
Rolls
Strawberry Freeze

Cream of Roasted Sweet Red Pepper Soup

8 large sweet red peppers
6 cloves garlic, minced
1 small onion, chopped
3 tablespoons butter or margarine, divided
2 (14½ ounce) cans ready to serve chicken broth
2 cups dry white wine
1 bay leaf
½ teaspoon salt
¼ teaspoon pepper
2 tablespoons all-purpose flour
1½ cups whipping cream
Fresh basil, cut into thin strips, garnish

Place peppers on an aluminum foil-lined baking sheet; broil 5½ inches from heat (with electric oven door partially opened) about 5 minutes on each side or until peppers look blistered. Place roasted peppers in a heavy-duty zip-top plastic bag immediately; seal and let stand 10 minutes. Peel peppers; remove and discard stem and seeds. Set roasted peppers aside.

Cook minced garlic and chopped onion in 1 tablespoon butter in a Dutch oven over medium heat until crisp-tender. Add chicken broth and next 4 ingredients; bring to a boil. Reduce heat; simmer 30 minutes. Pour broth mixture through a large wire-mesh strainer into a large container, reserving solids. Remove and discard bay leaf. Set broth mixture aside.

Using a food processor with knife blade, add reserved solids and roasted peppers to bowl. Process 30 seconds or until mixture is smooth, stopping once to scrape down sides, set pepper puree aside.

Melt remaining 2 tablespoons of butter in a Dutch oven over low heat; add flour, stirring until smooth. Cook 1 minute, stirring constantly. Gradually add broth mixture, cook over medium heat, stirring constantly, until thickened and bubbly (about 3 minutes). Stir in pepper puree. Gradually stir in whipping cream. Cook over low heat until thoroughly heated. Garnish, if desired. Yield: 8 cups.

◑ Shrimp and Corn Chowder

¼ cup chopped green onions
1 clove garlic, minced
⅛ teaspoon cayenne pepper
1 tablespoon butter or margarine
2 (10¾ ounce) cans cream of potato soup

1 (3 ounce) package cream cheese, softened
1½ soup cans of milk
2 cups cleaned raw shrimp
1 (8 ounce) can whole kernel corn, undrained

In a saucepan, cook onions with garlic and pepper in butter until tender. Blend in soup, cream cheese and milk; add shrimp and corn. Bring to a boil; reduce heat. Cover, simmer 10 minutes or until done; stir occasionally. Yield: approximately 7 cups. Can substitute crab meat for shrimp or combine shrimp and crab.

Serve over rice or cook diced potatoes to make broth thicker.

Oyster Stew

1 pint oysters
4 tablespoons butter, divided
¾ teaspoon salt
Pepper to taste

Dash hot pepper sauce
1 pint milk
1 pint light cream
Paprika

Drain oysters; reserve liquor. Melt all but 2 teaspoons of butter over medium heat; add salt, pepper, and hot pepper sauce. Add oyster liquor to butter and seasonings; stir to blend. Add oysters and cook only until edges begin to curl. Stir in milk and cream; bring almost to the boiling point. Serve in hot bowls, top with remaining butter, and sprinkle with paprika.

◑ Cottage Cheese Salad

1 (3 ounce) package strawberry flavored gelatin
1 (8 ounce) can crushed pineapple, drained
16 ounces cottage cheese

4½ ounces frozen whipped dessert topping, thawed
1 (10 ounce) carton frozen strawberries, drained

Mix all ingredients together except gelatin. After mixing, shake dry gelatin in as you mix. Chill or eat immediately. Yield: 8 servings.

Apricot Jello Salad

2 (3 ounce) packages apricot flavored gelatin	2 (4 ounce) jars apricot baby food
1 cup water	1 (20 ounce) can crushed pineapple with juice
⅓ cup sugar	8 ounces cream cheese
1 (14 ounce) can sweetened condensed milk	1½ cups chopped nuts

Bring the first 3 ingredients to a boil. Mix and add the remaining 5 ingredients to gelatin mixture. Spoon into a 9 x 13-inch casserole dish. Chill until firm.

Honey Walnut Fruit Salad

⅓ cup honey	1 (11 ounce) can Mandarin oranges
½ cup mayonnaise	1 cup seedless grapes
½ cup chopped walnuts	1 cup shredded lettuce
3 cored, unpeeled apples, chopped	1 tablespoon lemon juice
2 bananas, peeled and sliced	

Blend honey and mayonnaise until smooth. Toss all ingredients with lemon juice; stir in honey mixture and refrigerate. Yield: 7 cups.

Festive Cranberry Salad

1 (14 ounce) can sweetened condensed milk	2 cups miniature marshmallows
¼ cup lemon juice	½ cup chopped pecans
1 (20 ounce) can crushed pineapple, drained	Red food coloring, optional
1 (16 ounce) can whole berry cranberry sauce	8 ounces frozen whipped dessert topping, thawed

In a bowl, combine milk and lemon juice; mix well. Stir in pineapple, cranberry sauce, marshmallows, pecans, and food coloring, if desired. Fold in whipped dessert topping. Spoon into a 9 x 13-inch baking dish. Freeze until firm, 4 hours or overnight. Cut into squares. Yield: 12 to 16 servings.

Mom's Easy Fruit Salad

2   Red Delicious apples, chopped
2   bananas, diced
1   bunch seedless grapes, halved
2   seedless oranges, sectioned and halved
1   cup small marshmallows

1   stalk celery, chopped
½   cup chopped pecans, optional
½   pint whipping cream
2   tablespoons sugar, optional
½   teaspoon vanilla extract, optional

Place fruit, marshmallows, celery and pecans in a large bowl. Using a separate bowl, beat whipping cream until fluffy; add sugar and vanilla if used. Combine whipped cream with fruit mixture. Refrigerate until cold. Yield: 8 to 12 servings as a side salad.

Orange Cream Fruit Salad

1   (15¼ ounce) can pineapple tidbits, drained
1   (16 ounce) can peach slices, drained
1   (11 ounce) can Mandarin oranges, drained
2   medium firm bananas, sliced

1   medium apple, chopped
1   (3.4 ounce) package instant vanilla pudding mix
1½ cups milk
⅓   cup frozen orange juice concentrate
¾   cup sour cream

In a large bowl, combine fruits and set aside. In a small mixing bowl, beat pudding mix, milk and orange concentrate for 2 minutes. Add sour cream; mix well. Spoon over fruit, toss to coat. Cover and refrigerate for 2 hours. Yield: 8 to 10 servings.

Frozen Pineapple Salad

2   cups sour cream
¾   cup sugar
2   tablespoons lemon juice
⅛   teaspoon salt
1   (8 ounce) can crushed pineapple, drained

¼   cup seedless green grapes and/or
¼   cup maraschino cherries, chopped
¼   cup chopped pecans
1   sliced banana, optional

Combine first 4 ingredients; stir in crushed pineapple. Add remaining ingredients; freeze in oiled muffin tins. Yield: 12 salads.

☽ *Strawberry Ribbon Salad*

1 large box strawberry flavored gelatin
1 cup boiling water
¼ cup cold water or pineapple juice
1 (16 ounce) can crushed pineapple

2 (10 ounce) packages frozen strawberries, thawed
1 cup mashed bananas
1 pint sour cream

Pour boiling water over gelatin; mix well. Add ¼ cup cold water or pineapple juice; cool. Add all other ingredients except sour cream. Pour half of mixture into large bowl or mold and allow to set. Spread one pint of sour cream on congealed gelatin. Pour remainder of gelatin fruit mixture over sour cream. Let set overnight.

Watermelon Salad

6 cups torn mixed salad greens
3 cups seeded, cubed watermelon

½ cup sliced onion
⅓ cup Feta cheese, crumbled

Combine and toss with vinaigrette (recipe follows). Yield: 6 servings.

Watermelon Vinaigrette

2 tablespoons currant jelly
¼ cup pureed watermelon
2 tablespoons wine vinegar

¼ teaspoon garlic pepper
1 tablespoon vegetable oil

Heat jelly in saucepan until just melted; cool. Add watermelon, vinegar, garlic pepper, and vegetable oil. Yield: half cup. Store in refrigerator. Shake before using.

Tangy Strawberry and Cranberry Salad

2 (3 ounce) packages strawberry flavored gelatin
1½ cups boiling water
1 (10 ounce) package frozen strawberries

1 (16 ounce) can whole cranberry sauce
1 (16 ounce) can crushed pineapple, drained
    Pecans, optional
    Mayonnaise, optional

Dissolve gelatin in boiling water. Add remaining ingredients. Mix well; refrigerate.

Strawberry Frozen Salad

1   (8 ounce) package cream cheese, diced
¾   cup sugar
1   (8 ounce) can crushed pineapple, drained

1   package frozen sweetened strawberries
1   banana, diced
1   (12 ounce) frozen whipped dessert topping, thawed

Combine all ingredients; mix well. Place in a 9 x 13-inch pan; freeze until firm. Cut into squares and serve.

Mandarin Orange Salad and Dressing

Dressing
3   tablespoons lemon juice
2   tablespoons sugar
1   clove crushed garlic

1   teaspoon salt
½   cup salad oil

Blend everything but oil; then add oil slowly.

Salad
1   (11 ounce) can Mandarin oranges, drained
¼   cup chopped green or red onion

½   cup toasted almonds
Assorted greens of your choice

Toss oranges and onions with dressing. Serve over greens and sprinkle with almonds.

Black Cherry Salad

1   cup sugar
8   ounces cream cheese softened
½   cup chopped pecans
1   (16 ounce) can black cherries, drained

1   (16 ounce) can pineapple tidbits, drained
8   ounces frozen whipped dessert topping, thawed

Blend sugar and cheese together. Add pecans, cherries and pineapple; mix well. Fold in whipped dessert topping; chill. Yield: 10 to 12 small servings.

May use low fat cream cheese and low fat whipped dessert topping.

Fruit Salad with Poppy Seed Dressing

2 cups blueberries	1 cup strawberry halves
2 kiwi fruit, sliced	1 fresh pineapple, peeled, cored and sliced or 1 (20 ounce) can sliced pineapple, drained and cut in half
2 red apples, sliced	
2 green apples, sliced	
1 bunch seedless green grapes	
1 bunch seedless red grapes	Poppy Seed Dressing, recipe follows

Arrange fruit on a serving platter. Serve with Poppy Seed Dressing. Yield: 12 servings.

Poppy Seed Dressing

¾ cup sugar	½ teaspoon salt
⅓ cup vinegar	1 cup vegetable oil
1½ tablespoons onion juice	1½ tablespoons poppy seeds
1 teaspoon dry mustard	

Combine all ingredients; mix well and chill. Store in refrigerator.

Oriental Chicken Salad

4 cups cooked and cubed chicken breasts	1 (4 ounce) jar pimentos, drained and chopped
2 cups chopped celery	1 (10 ounce) can bamboo shoots, drained
2 (8 ounce) cans sliced water chestnuts, drained	
4 green onions, diced	Dressing, recipe follows

Dressing

1½ cups mayonnaise	2 tablespoons lemon juice
4 tablespoons soy sauce	

Make dressing in advance. Mix rest of ingredients; toss with chicken mixture just before serving.

Chicken Salad with Rice

1 box original wild rice with seasoning package, cooked and cooled
4 cups cooked and cubed chicken breasts
1 cup salad dressing or mayonnaise
½ cup Catalina dressing

½ cup sliced almonds
1 cup chopped celery
2 (11 ounce) cans Mandarin oranges, drained
1 (20 ounce) can pineapple chunks, drained

Mix together first 6 ingredients; chill. Drain fruits and refrigerate; add to chicken mixture just before serving. Yield: 8 to 10 servings.

Sarah's Hot Chicken Salad

2 cups cooked and diced chicken
1 teaspoon salt
1 cup chopped celery
1 small chopped onion
1 cup mayonnaise
1 (10¾ ounce) can cream of mushroom soup

2 tablespoons lemon juice
2 tablespoons chopped pimento
1 cup sliced water chestnuts, drained
½ cup toasted slivered almonds
1 cup crushed potato chips, for topping

Combine ingredients (except for potato chips) in order given. Place in a casserole and top with potato chips. Bake at 350 degrees for 30 minutes. Yield: 6 to 8 servings.

✷☽ Tuna Salad

1 (3 ounce) package lemon flavored gelatin
½ cup mayonnaise-type salad dressing
½ cup unwhipped whipping cream
1 teaspoon grated green pepper
½ pound chopped Cheddar cheese
3 hard boiled eggs, chopped

1 cup hot water
½ teaspoon salt
1 tablespoon grated onion
¾ cup diced celery
1 cup chopped pecans
2 (6 ounce) cans of tuna
Lettuce leaves

Mix all ingredients (except lettuce leaves) together; chill overnight. Serve on lettuce leaves.

Apple Cabbage Slaw

3	tablespoons flour	½	cup vinegar
3	tablespoons sugar	3	tablespoons lemon juice
1	teaspoon dry mustard	5	cups shredded cabbage
½	teaspoon celery seeds	1	medium Red Delicious apple,
1	cup skim milk		diced (do apple last)

Combine flour, sugar, mustard and celery seeds in a saucepan; stir in milk. Cook over medium heat stirring constantly until thickened; remove from burner. Stir in vinegar and lemon juice. Cool to room temperature. Pour vinegar mix over cabbage and diced apple. Toss, cover and chill. Yield: 6 servings.

Japanese Chicken Salad

2	chicken breasts, cooked and shredded	2	tablespoons sesame seeds
1	package Oriental ramen noodles	1	cup sliced almonds
2	tablespoons margarine	1	head of lettuce, chopped fine
		6	green onions, chopped

Dressing

1	seasoning package from the noodles	1	teaspoon salt
2	tablespoons sugar	1	teaspoon seasoned salt flavor enhancer
¼	cup oil	½	teaspoon black pepper
¼	cup rice vinegar		

Crush and brown uncooked noodles in margarine. Set aside to cool. Mix remaining salad ingredients; add noodles. Mix dressing and toss salad just before serving. Yield: 4 servings.

Chicken Pasta Salad

1½	pounds cooked and diced chicken breasts	1½	cups celery slices
1	(7 ounce) box shell macaroni, cooked	1	(11 ounce) can Mandarin oranges, drained
1½	cups sliced green grapes	1	cup mayonnaise
		1	cup whipped dessert topping

Mix several hours ahead all but whipped dessert topping; add just before serving.

Romaine Salad

1-2 bunches Romaine lettuce
6-8 green onions, sliced (green part too)
2   ripe avocados, chopped
¾   cup Parmesan cheese
½   cup cooking oil

⅓   cup fresh lemon juice
    Sprinkle of seasoned salt flavor enhancer
½   teaspoon Beau Monde
    Fresh ground pepper and salt, to taste

In a bowl tear up lettuce; add onions and avocados. Sprinkle Parmesan cheese on top. Add oil, lemon juice and seasonings to a jar; mix well. Pour over salad just before serving.

Sunshine Salad from The Inn of Many Faces

Capturing the charm of bygone days, the INN OF MANY FACES is a bed and breakfast inn in a Queen Anne Victorian mansion built for J. B. McDougall. Plans and components for this impressive home were ordered from a manufacturer, shipped to Denison and assembled over a period of five years from 1892 through 1897. McDougall owned and managed the Denison Opera, the McDougall Hotel at the Depot, a steam laundry and was president of the Denison Electric Light and Power Company.

1   cup rice
1   cup celery slices
2   cups ham cubes
¾   cup green pepper cubed
½   cup carrot slices

½   cup chopped onion
¾   cup mayonnaise
    Salt and pepper to taste
    Lettuce or spinach shredded

Prepare rice according to directions; chill. Combine the first 8 ingredients; mix well. Fold in shredded greens. Yield: 6 to 8 servings.

Lightly Dilled Potato Salad

4 pounds new potatoes, cooked and cut into ¾ inch chunks	1 tablespoon Dijon mustard
2 tablespoons olive oil	½ teaspoon seasoned salt
2 tablespoons cider vinegar	½ teaspoon black pepper
1 cup light mayonnaise	1 cup minced red onion
1 cup plain nonfat yogurt	½ cup minced fresh dill weed

Put potatoes in a large bowl; sprinkle with olive oil and vinegar; toss lightly to coat. Mix mayonnaise, yogurt, mustard, salt and pepper in a bowl. Stir in onion and dill. Pour over potatoes. Toss gently to coat well. Cover and chill! Keeps at least 24 hours.

German Potato Salad

1 pound bacon	2 teaspoons salt
½ cup coarsely chopped onion	½ teaspoon black pepper
3 tablespoons cider vinegar	3 cups cubed, hot, cooked potatoes
3 tablespoons wine vinegar	2 tablespoons finely chopped fresh parsley
1½ teaspoons sugar	
¾ cup water	1 (2 ounce) jar chopped pimentos

Brown bacon until crisp; drain and crumble. Reserve 1 tablespoon grease in skillet; sauté onion until tender. Add vinegars, sugar and water. Cover and heat to boiling; simmer 2 minutes. Add salt, pepper, potatoes, bacon, parsley and pimento. Toss lightly and heat throughout. Serve hot!

Avocado with Warm Tomato Vinaigrette

2 large ripe tomatoes, peeled, seeded and diced	2 tablespoons Dijon mustard
	Salt and pepper to taste
½ cup chopped basil leaves	2 avocados, halved and pitted
4 tablespoons red wine vinegar	Lettuce leaves, torn
½ cup olive oil	Fresh basil leaves, garnish

In a saucepan combine the first 6 ingredients; bring to a simmer. Put avocado halves on individual plates lined with lettuce. Spoon warm dressing over the avocados. Garnish with basil leaf; serve immediately. Yield: 4 servings.

Garden Potato Salad

6	large potatoes (about 3 pounds), cooked, peeled and cubed	6	green onions with tops, sliced
4	hard boiled eggs, sliced	6	radishes, sliced
2	celery ribs, diced	1	teaspoon salt
		½	teaspoon pepper

Dressing

3	eggs, beaten	½	teaspoon dry mustard
¼	cup vinegar	½	teaspoon salt
¼	cup sugar	1	cup mayonnaise or salad dressing

In a large bowl, combine potatoes, eggs, celery, green onions, radishes, salt and pepper; set aside. For dressing, combine eggs, vinegar, sugar, dry mustard and salt in a saucepan. Cook and stir over medium heat until thickened; cool. Stir in mayonnaise; mix well. Pour over potato mixture; toss to coat. Refrigerate for several hours. Yield: 8 servings.

Best Ever Hot German Potato Salad

6	medium red potatoes, diced with skins left on	1	cup sour cream
½	pound smoked bacon, cooked and crumbled	½	cup sugar
		¼	cup vinegar
3	medium onions, peeled and diced	2	tablespoons dried parsley
			Salt and pepper to taste

Place potatoes in pan, cover with water and boil until tender but not waterlogged. Drain well. Let stand in pan to dry a few minutes so when seasonings are added they will soak in. Then place in a large bowl. Fry bacon in a large skillet until crisp. Drain bacon; crumble and set aside. Add onions to bacon drippings; sauté until clear. Stir into the skillet mixture the sour cream, sugar, vinegar, parsley, salt and pepper. Pour over cooked potatoes. Add crumbled bacon and gently turn until well mixed, leaving any loose potato skins in the salad. Delicious at once but flavor is enhanced by a wait.

Broccoli Salad

1 large bunch broccoli or 2 small bunches
½ cup raisins
1 cup sunflower seeds, salted

2-3 slices red onion, for color
½ pound bacon, cooked and crumbled

Dressing
1 cup mayonnaise
¼ cup sugar

2 tablespoons white vinegar

Mix dressing and let sit overnight or for 2 to 3 days. Cut broccoli into bite-size pieces including stems. Toss broccoli, raisins, sunflower seeds, onion and bacon with dressing before serving. May be tossed 1 to 2 hours ahead of time. Yield: 8 to 10 servings.

You may substitute the onion with a diced red bell pepper; use both if desired.

Cornbread Salad

1 (6 ounce) package jalapeño cornbread mix, cook as directed
1 (6 ounce) package regular cornbread mix, cook as directed
1 onion, chopped

1 tomato, chopped
1 bell pepper, chopped
1 large stalk celery, chopped
1 pint mayonnaise

Cool and crumble cornbread; mix all ingredients together. Let sit in refrigerator for 1 hour, or overnight if necessary.

Corned Beef Salad

¾ cup boiling water
1 (3 ounce) package lime flavored gelatin
½ cup whipping cream or frozen whipped dessert topping, thawed

1 cup mayonnaise
1 (12 ounce) can corned beef
1 cup diced cucumber
2 cups diced celery
1 cup diced onions

Add boiling water to gelatin; mix well and cool. Whip cream and mayonnaise together. Add all ingredients to the cooled gelatin. Place in refrigerator and chill until set. Best if prepared the day before.

Cashews and Pea Salad

2 (10 ounce) packages frozen tiny green peas, thawed
2 cups chopped celery
1 cup cashews
½ cup chopped green onion

12 slices bacon, crisply cooked and crumbled
1 cup sour cream
Salt and pepper to taste

Combine peas, celery, cashews, onions and bacon in a large bowl. Add sour cream, salt and pepper. Toss lightly to coat. Cover and chill thoroughly.

Pea and Cheese Salad

1 (10 ounce) package frozen peas
1 cup diced celery
1 tablespoon grated green onions
½ cup chopped sweet pickles
¼ pound diced sharp cheese

¼ pound diced smoked ham
1 cup green grapes, cut in half
½ cup low-fat mayonnaise-type salad dressing
Salt and pepper to taste

Combine all ingredients; toss lightly. Serve on lettuce leaves. Yield: 6 servings.

Perfection Salad

1 tablespoon unflavored gelatin
¼ cup cold water
1 cup boiling water
¼ cup vinegar
1 tablespoon lemon juice
¼ cup sugar

1 teaspoon salt
⅔ cup diced celery
½ cup shredded cabbage
1 green pepper, chopped
2 tablespoons pimento, finely cut

Stir gelatin into cold water and let soak for about 5 minutes. Add boiling water; stir until dissolved. Add vinegar, salt, lemon juice and sugar; mix thoroughly. Put in refrigerator until it starts to set; add vegetables. Pour into a mold; chill until set.

☽ *Vermicelli Salad*

1 teaspoon seasoned salt flavor enhancer	½ cup chopped green pepper
2 tablespoons seasoned salt	½ cup chopped onion
3 tablespoons lemon juice	½ cup chopped stuffed olives or ripe olives
4 tablespoons salad oil	1 (4 ounce) jar pimentos
12 ounces vermicelli	1-1½ cups mayonnaise or salad dressing
1 cup chopped celery	

Mix together the first 4 ingredients. Cook and drain vermicelli; add marinade and marinate overnight. Add chopped ingredients and mayonnaise. Chill and serve.

◷ *Colorful Vegetable Salad*

1 head cauliflower, chopped fine	2 large green peppers, chopped fine
1 (4 ounce) jar pimentos, chopped	1 jar black olives, chopped
	Oil, vinegar, and sugar

Mix together the first 4 ingredients; toss with oil and vinegar with a little sugar.

World War I. The Canteen For the Comfort of Soldier Boys was by the railroad tracks just south of the Katy Depot. This card was postmarked November 2, 1918.

Food rationing during World War I was fairly straightforward. Food Administrator Herbert Hoover launched a national program of voluntary food rationing by instituting wheatless Mondays and Wednesdays, meatless Tuesdays and porkless Thursdays and Saturdays.

A World War I slogan: "Feed a Fighter. Eat only what you need - waste nothing - that he and his family may have enough."

At 11:00 a.m. on November 11, 1918, Hartley Edwards of Denison blew "Taps" on his bugle as the official signal World War I had ended. The bugle is in the Smithsonian.

☽ Marinated Vegetable Salad

1	(16 ounce) can peas, drained	1	green pepper, chopped
1	(16 ounce) can corn, drained	1	stalk celery, chopped
1	(16 ounce) can French-style green beans, drained	1	cucumber, diced
1	(4 ounce) jar pimento	1	cup apple cider vinegar
1	medium red onion, chopped	1	cup sugar
1	carrot, grated	½	cup vegetable oil

Prepare and mix first 9 ingredients as instructed in ingredients list. Combine last 3 ingredients and pour over vegetables; mix well. Chill 24 hours. Drain before serving.

Company Vinaigrette

1	small shallot, peeled and chopped	Salt and pepper to taste
¼	cup balsamic vinegar	Several types of torn lettuce
3	tablespoons light olive oil	leaves
1	tablespoon walnut oil	

Whisk all ingredients, except lettuce, together in a small bowl. Just before serving, toss several different types of lettuce leaves with the dressing.

This salad is delicious topped with one (11 ounce) can of drained Mandarin oranges and ½ cup pecan halves.

Honey Mustard Dressing

¾-1	cup creamy mayonnaise-type salad dressing	2 tablespoons honey
2	tablespoons prepared mustard	1 tablespoon white vinegar
		Salt and pepper to taste

Combine all ingredients; mix well.

This tastes great on spinach salad.

☽ Salad with Baked Goat Cheese

8	rounds Montrachet (goat cheese) or some other soft cheese	1	teaspoon thyme leaves, fresh or dried
½	cup olive oil	¼	teaspoon salt
4	sprigs fresh thyme		Pepper to taste
¾	cup fine white bread crumbs	3	tablespoons balsamic vinegar Torn lettuce leaves

Arrange cheese in a shallow dish. Combine oil and sprigs of thyme, pour over cheese and marinate for several hours or overnight.

Preheat oven to 350 degrees. Combine bread crumbs, thyme leaves, salt and pepper. Roll the rounds of goat cheese in mixture, put them in a baking dish and bake for 15 minutes or until cheese is softened and crumbs are golden. Meanwhile, combine oil from the marinade with the vinegar, and salt and pepper to taste. Pour over greens; toss well. Serve the salad on individual plates with 2 slices of warm goat cheese on the side.

Cauliflower and Lettuce Salad

1	head cauliflower, cut into florets	½	pound bacon, crisply cooked and crumbled
1	head lettuce, torn		
½	medium red onion, diced, optional		

Dressing

2	cups mayonnaise	1	tablespoon sugar
½	cup Parmesan cheese		

Mix dressing several hours ahead. At serving time, add enough dressing to coat salad ingredients.

⏰ Last Minute Corn Salad

3	(10 ounce) cans Mex-i-corn, drained	1	(16 ounce) bottle Catalina salad dressing
		1	(11½ ounce) package corn chips

Combine first 2 ingredients. Stir in corn chips just before serving.

Dinner on Board

A very genteel fishing expedition on the Red River was enjoyed by Dr. and Mrs. Arthur Freels around 1912.
Here the Red River is Texas' northern boundary with Oklahoma, so from their vantage point, the Freelses had a panoramic view of both states.

Main Dishes

Beef Tips

1	envelope dry onion soup mix	1	(4 ounce) can mushrooms, drained
1	(10¾ ounce) can cream of mushroom soup	½	cup dry red cooking wine
		2	pounds lean stew meat

In a slow cooker, place and mix well the first 4 ingredients. Add stew meat and cook on high 5½ to 6 hours. Serve over cooked noodles with a salad and hot French bread. Yield: 6 servings.

On a warm spring Sunday afternoon, Micajah Davis was sitting in a rocking chair on the porch of his log cabin and looking out over his fields. The rolling hills, covered with thicket and brush, were abundant with deer, squirrels, rabbits and other game. Micajah knew how much his daughters, Louisa and Mary Caroline, enjoyed it when his friend, Sam Houston, visited and let them ride this land perched high behind him on his horse.

As Micajah rocked, a band of Indians appeared silently from the woods. Not exactly afraid, but a little uneasy, Micajah sent his two daughters indoors. Their mother, Polly, quickly barred the door.

As the Indians approached, they indicated by hand signs they were hungry. Micajah scooped a dipper full of buttermilk from the churn setting near him on the porch and offered it to the leader. The man tasted it and appeared satisfied it

was good. The hungry Indians, after finishing off the contents of the churn, quietly disappeared into the trees.

Micajah Davis had just hosted Denison's FIRST, LAST, and probably ONLY, BUTTERMILK TASTING SOCIAL.

Micajah, a blacksmith, built his cabin about 1840 on Iron Ore Creek of hand-hewn logs and planks. It is preserved at Frontier Village in Denison.

A Dining Car Menu for a

Pre-Game Spread

Brisket Carbonado
Ranch Style Beans
Garden Potato Salad
Southern Biscuits
Cobbler

Brisket Carbonado

3-4	pound brisket	¼	teaspoon thyme
	Salt and pepper to taste	4	peppercorns
3	medium onions, sliced	1	bay leaf
1	(12 ounce) can beer	¼	cup cold water
2	tablespoons brown sugar	2	tablespoons flour
1	clove garlic, minced		

Season meat with salt and pepper; place in 9 x 13-inch baking dish. Cover with onion slices. Combine beer, brown sugar, garlic, thyme, peppercorns and bay leaf; pour over meat. Cover pan with foil and bake at 350 degrees for 3½ to 4 hours. Remove meat, skim off excess fat. Measure juice to make 1¼ cups liquid. Pour juice into small sauce-pan. Blend ¼ cup cold water and 2 tablespoons of flour; stir into liquid. Stir until bubbly; add salt and pepper. Serve gravy with brisket.

Upside-Down Pizza

1½	pounds ground beef	2	eggs
1	medium onion, chopped	1	cup milk
1	(15½ ounce) jar pizza sauce	1	tablespoon oil
½	teaspoon garlic salt	½	teaspoon salt
¼	teaspoon dried oregano	1	cup flour
8	ounces mozzarella cheese, grated	½	cup grated Parmesan cheese

Preheat oven to 350 degrees. Brown meat and onion; drain. Blend in pizza sauce, garlic salt, and oregano. Put mixture in a greased 9 x 13-inch pan and sprinkle with mozzarella cheese. In a small bowl, mix eggs, milk, oil, salt and flour. Pour over meat mixture and sprinkle with Parmesan cheese. Bake for 30 minutes.

Cavitini

1	pound ground beef	½	cup each of three pastas (such as rigatoni, macaroni, twirls, etc.) cooked, drained and tossed together
1	medium onion, chopped		
1	medium green pepper, chopped		
1	(3½ ounce) package sliced pepperoni	1	(8 ounce) carton small curd cottage cheese
1	(15½ ounce) jar spaghetti sauce	1	(10 ounce) package mozzarella cheese, grated

Cook ground beef, onion and pepper until beef is no longer pink. Add pepperoni just long enough to heat through. Drain mixture; add spaghetti sauce and simmer about 5 minutes. Pour half the cooked pasta into a lightly greased 3-quart casserole. Spoon on half the meat sauce mixture. Spoon all the cottage cheese over the sauce. Sprinkle half the mozzarella cheese over the cottage cheese. Repeat layers, omitting the cottage cheese and ending with the mozzarella cheese. Bake at 350 degrees for 30 to 35 minutes. Yield: 6 to 8 servings.

Lasagna

1	pound ground beef	12	ounces cottage or ricotta cheese
1	teaspoon oil, if needed	1	egg, beaten
1	(20 ounce) can tomatoes	1	teaspoon salt
1	teaspoon parsley flakes	¼	teaspoon pepper
1	teaspoon oregano	1	tablespoon parsley flakes
2	teaspoons salt	1	cup Parmesan cheese
1	(6 ounce) can tomato paste	8	ounces mozzarella cheese, sliced thin
6-8	lasagna noodles		

Brown meat (in oil if needed), drain any grease. Add next 5 ingredients; mix well. Simmer uncovered until thick (about 1 hour); stirring occasionally. While sauce is simmering, cook 6 to 8 lasagna noodles according to directions. Mix well the cottage cheese, egg, salt, pepper, parsley and Parmesan cheese. Set aside in refrigerator. In a lightly sprayed 9 x 13-inch baking dish place a layer of noodles; spread half the cottage cheese mixture; then half of the mozzarella cheese; top with half the sauce. Next, a layer of noodles, remaining cheese mixture, meat sauce and top with remaining mozzarella cheese. Warm in a 350 degree oven for ½ hour or until cheese melts. Let stand for 10 minutes before serving.

No Peek Beef Stew

2 pounds lean beef, cubed	Salt and pepper to taste
2 large potatoes, cubed	Seasoned salt
1 cup sliced carrots	2 tablespoons tapioca
1 cup chopped celery	2 (10 ounce) cans spicy tomato
1 large onion, chopped	juice

In a Dutch oven, mix together all the meat and vegetables and sprinkle with seasonings to taste. Dissolve tapioca in the tomato juice; pour over mixture. Bake at 250 degrees for 5 hours. NO PEEKING! Yield: 6 to 8 servings.

Easy, Meaty Spaghetti Sauce

Julie Nixon Eisenhower, in Denison in 1973 for the unveiling of the Eisenhower statue, looks at the wood burning stove and utensils in the kitchen presided over by

her husband David's great-grandmother, Ida. Julie graciously shared a family favorite recipe, Easy, Meaty Spaghetti Sauce. In her note she wrote:

It is good to learn of the fine work of the Denison Service League. I remember well my visit to Denison in the 1970's. I know it is still a special town.

As a minor footnote of interest, this recipe was given to David's mother by one of his Secret Service agents. The Nixon family had the White House chef prepare this meal often.

Good Luck!

1 (6 ounce) can tomato paste	1 teaspoon chili powder
3 cups tomato juice	1 pound lean ground beef
1 teaspoon sugar	

Brown meat; drain. Add all other ingredients and simmer 45 minutes to an hour. Yield: 5 servings.

Burger and Cabbage Bake

8	cups chopped cabbage, divided	1	teaspoon salt
½	cup chopped onion	¼	teaspoon black pepper
1	cup uncooked rice	1	(27 ounce) can spaghetti sauce
¼	cup bacon drippings	3	cups water
1	pound ground beef	2	tablespoons picante sauce

Place 4 cups of the chopped cabbage in a buttered 9 x 13-inch baking dish. In a large skillet, sauté onion and rice in bacon drippings. Cook until rice is light brown and onion is soft. Spoon over cabbage. Cook meat until no pink remains. Spoon over rice mixture. Sprinkle with salt and pepper. Top with the remaining cabbage. Heat spaghetti sauce, water and picante sauce to boiling. Pour slowly over cabbage. Cover with foil and bake at 400 degrees for 50 to 60 minutes until rice and cabbage are tender. Bake 10 minutes longer after removing foil.

Meat Loaf with Onion Rings

2	slices rye bread	¼	teaspoon black pepper
2	slices white bread	1	teaspoon oregano
¾	cup water	1	(2.8 ounce) can French fried onion rings, divided
1	medium onion, chopped		
1	pound ground beef	2	tablespoons butter
3	tablespoons Parmesan cheese	1	(8 ounce) can tomato sauce, can use ketchup
1	egg, beaten		
1	teaspoon salt		

Pull bread apart into bite-size pieces and place in a large bowl; pour water over bread to soften. Crumble and combine with onion, beef, cheese, beaten egg, salt, pepper, oregano and half the can of onion rings. Mix and shape in loaf, dot with butter if desired. Bake at 350 degrees for 30 minutes. Pour on sauce and sprinkle with extra cheese. Bake 15 minutes more, then add remaining onion rings. Bake 5 more minutes.

If you don't count fat grams, place strips of bacon on top of the loaf; then add the sauce when baking starts. Remove bacon before adding onion rings.

Mushrooms St. Thomas

2   (10 ounce) packages frozen
    chopped spinach
8   ounces sour cream
1   cup shredded Cheddar cheese
1   cup shredded Monterey Jack
    cheese
½   cup grated Parmesan cheese

1   teaspoon salt, divided
1   teaspoon Italian herb seasoning
6-8 medium-size fresh mushrooms,
    sliced
1   pound lean hamburger
½   cup sliced green onions
    Nutmeg to garnish, optional

Cook spinach briefly in hot water; drain well. Mix with sour cream, ½ cup each of
Cheddar, Monterey Jack and Parmesan cheese, ¼ cup onion, ½ teaspoon salt and
Italian seasoning. Sauté beef with ¼ cup onion and remaining salt. Drain any fat or
liquid; mix with the spinach mixture. Place sliced mushrooms in the bottom of a
shallow baking dish. Spoon hamburger and spinach mixture over the mushrooms.
Cover with remaining cheese. Sprinkle lightly with nutmeg, if desired. Cover; bake at
350 degrees for 25 minutes.

Can be made in advance.

Easy Hamburger Stroganoff

1   pound ground beef
1   medium onion, chopped
2   tablespoons all-purpose flour
½   teaspoon salt
½   teaspoon garlic salt
¼   teaspoon pepper

1   (8 ounce) can mushrooms,
    drained
1   (10¾ ounce) can cream of
    chicken soup
8   ounces sour cream
1   (8 ounce) package egg noodles,
    cooked and drained

Cook beef and onion until brown; drain. Stir in flour, salts, pepper and mushrooms;
cook over medium heat 5 minutes, stirring constantly. Add soup; simmer 10 minutes,
stirring occasionally. Stir in sour cream and heat thoroughly. Serve over hot noodles.
Yield: 4 servings.

Tasty Meatloaf

1½ pounds ground round steak
1   cup bread crumbs or 12 crackers
1   onion, chopped
1   egg

½   teaspoon salt
¼   teaspoon pepper
½   cup tomato sauce

Sauce

½   cup tomato sauce
2   tablespoons vinegar
2   tablespoons brown sugar

1   cup water
1   teaspoon prepared mustard

Preheat oven to 300 degrees. Combine meatloaf ingredients; put in a loaf pan and cook until browned. Prepare sauce and pour half over the meatloaf and continue cooking for 30 to 35 minutes. Save some sauce to pour over when eating.

Grilled Beef Tenderloin

1   3 pound beef tenderloin
1   cup dry red wine
½   cup olive oil
1   scallion, minced
1   teaspoon salt
3   garlic cloves, minced
½   teaspoon black peppercorns,
     crushed

½   teaspoon dry mustard
½   teaspoon dried thyme
6   parsley sprigs
1   bay leaf
     Green Peppercorn Butter, recipe
     follows

Mix marinade ingredients and marinate the beef overnight. Grill meat over hot coals, brushing occasionally with Green Peppercorn Butter to desired degree of doneness. Rare to medium-rare is preferable. Slice meat thin and dot slices with additional Green Peppercorn Butter. Yield: 6 servings.

Green Peppercorn Butter

1   stick of softened butter or
     margarine
¼   cup chopped parsley
1   tablespoon green peppercorns

1   teaspoon fresh lemon juice
½   teaspoon Dijon mustard
     Worcestershire sauce to taste

Use food processor with metal blades. Combine all ingredients and process until smooth. Transfer to bowl and chill. Yield: ½ cup.

Teriyaki Kabob - Beef or Shrimp

½   cup soy sauce
2   tablespoons vegetable oil
2   tablespoons mirin, sweet
     vermouth or sherry
2   tablespoons finely chopped green
     onion
1   tablespoon brown sugar
2   teaspoons minced or grated fresh
     ginger

1   teaspoon minced or pressed garlic
     Black pepper as desired
1¼ pounds medium shrimp, peeled
     and deveined OR 1¼ pounds
     steak, sirloin or London broil,
     thinly sliced or cubed for kabob
     Steamed rice

Combine first 8 ingredients in a large bowl. Add shrimp or steak; stir to coat meat. Let sit in refrigerator about 20 minutes for shrimp or 1 hour for steak. Remove meat from marinade and sauté in wok or skillet, or skewer to grill. Cook until shrimp are opaque and steak is cooked to desired doneness. Boil marinade in a saucepan; pour over meat before serving. Serve over steamed rice.

In the restored dining room, General Ike Eisenhower displays pictures of his birthplace. The paintings of the white clapboard gabled house beside the railroad tracks were done by Dr. Clifford Mott, a distinguished Denison artist. Miss Jennie Jackson remembers the Eisenhowers as neighbors when Ike was born October 14, 1890, rocking him as an infant. Her memories led to correspondence with the family and the preservation of the home place. Others pictured are Ralph Geisenhoner and General Walton Walker.

History honors Eisenhower as the World War II Supreme Commander of the Allied Forces in Europe and later as President of the United States.

Crock Pot Spaghetti

1 pound ground beef	¼ teaspoon black pepper
1 tablespoon instant onion	1 (8 ounce) can tomato sauce
1 teaspoon salt	1 (4 ounce) can mushrooms
½ teaspoon garlic powder	3 cups tomato juice
½ teaspoon dry mustard	4 ounces dry spaghetti, break into
¼ teaspoon mace	4 to 5 inch pieces
¼ teaspoon allspice	

Brown ground beef in skillet, drain and place in a crock pot. Add all ingredients except spaghetti; stir well. Cover and cook on low 6 to 8 hours or high for 3½ hours. Turn to high during last hour and stir in spaghetti.

Stroganoff Superb

2 pounds sirloin steak or beef tenderloin	¼ cup ketchup
1 pound fresh mushrooms, sliced	2 small cloves garlic, crushed
1 cup minced onion	2 teaspoons salt
¾ cup butter or margarine	⅓ cup flour
2 (10½ ounce) cans beef bouillon, divided	2 cups sour cream
	Oven Easy Rice, recipe follows

Cut meat into bite-size pieces. In skillet or blazer pan of chafing dish, cook and stir mushrooms and onion in butter until onion is tender; remove mushrooms and onion. In same skillet brown meat lightly on both sides. Set aside ¾ cup bouillon; add remaining bouillon, ketchup, garlic and salt to skillet; stir to mix. Cover and simmer 15 minutes. Blend reserved bouillon and the flour; stir into meat mixture. Add mushrooms and onion. Heat to boiling, stirring constantly; boil 1 minute. Stir in sour cream; heat. Serve over rice. Yield: 6 servings.

Oven Easy Rice

3 cups boiling water	1½ teaspoons salt
1½ cups uncooked regular rice	

Heat oven to 350 degrees. Mix ingredients thoroughly in a 1½-quart casserole or an 8 x 11-inch baking dish. Cover dish tightly with casserole lid or aluminum foil. Lid or foil cover must be tight enough to prevent escape of steam. Bake 25 to 30 minutes, or until liquid is absorbed and rice is tender. Fluff and spoon into bowl to serve. Yield: 6 servings.

Spaghetti Alla Bolognese

¼ pound bacon, minced	1 tablespoon tomato paste
¾ pound ground round	Salt and freshly ground black
¼ pound ground veal	pepper
1 medium onion, thinly sliced	½ cup canned tomatoes
1 carrot, thinly sliced	¼ pound fresh mushrooms, coarsely
1 stalk celery, diced	chopped
1 clove garlic, minced	Hot cooked spaghetti, drained
2 cups beef stock	

Fry bacon in a large skillet until crisp. Pour off all but 1 tablespoon of fat. Add ground round and veal, onion, carrot, celery and garlic. Cook over low heat, stirring occasionally, until meat is brown. Add beef stock; simmer 30 minutes. Stir in tomato paste; add salt and pepper to taste; cover. Simmer 1 hour; stir in tomatoes and mushrooms; simmer uncovered for 15 minutes. Serve sauce over hot spaghetti. Yield: 4 to 6 servings.

Fried Venison with Pan Gravy

2 pounds venison steak, thinly sliced	4 tablespoons pan drippings
	3 tablespoons flour
½ cup flour	2¼ cups milk
1 teaspoon salt	1 teaspoon salt
¼ teaspoon pepper	½ teaspoon pepper
½ cup oil	

Pound steak until ¼ inch thick. Cut into small pieces. Combine flour, salt and pepper and coat steaks on both sides. In a heavy skillet, heat oil and sauté steaks on medium to high heat 5 minutes on each side. Remove from skillet and keep warm. Pour off all but 4 tablespoons of pan drippings. Blend in 3 tablespoons flour, stirring constantly, scraping cooked juices on bottom of pan until bubbly. Stir in milk, salt and pepper. Continue cooking over medium heat, stirring and scraping bottom and sides until gravy thickens and bubbles for 1 minute. Yield: 6 to 8 servings.

For a hearty breakfast serve these steaks with eggs, biscuits and Bloody Mary's. This is a traditional chicken fried recipe and works well with turkey breasts or round steaks.

Venison Chili

4	pounds venison	1	(28 ounce) can tomatoes
¼	cup oil		Dash of hot pepper sauce
6	large onions, chopped	1	(4½ ounce) can green chiles
2-4	minced garlic cloves	2	(10¾ ounce) cans beef broth
1	teaspoon ground cumin	2	cups water
1	teaspoon oregano	2	tablespoons cornmeal for thickening
	Salt and pepper		
3	tablespoons chili powder	½	pound pinto beans, cooked

Brown meat in oil. Lower heat; add onions and garlic. Stir occasionally until onions are translucent. Add cumin, oregano, salt, pepper and chili powder. Stir to coat meat with seasonings. Add tomatoes, hot pepper sauce, green chiles, beef broth and water; bring to a boil. Reduce heat and simmer. Cook 1½ hours. Add cornmeal for thickening and precooked pinto beans. Yield: 8 servings.

Venison Stew

3-4	pounds venison	1	teaspoon mixed herbs (thyme, marjoram, basil)
¼	cup flour	1	teaspoon dried parsley
3	tablespoons bacon drippings or cooking oil	1	large onion, sliced
1½	cups hot water	1½	teaspoons salt
1½	cups red wine		Black pepper to taste
2	cloves garlic, chopped	4	carrots, peeled and quartered
	Hot pepper sauce to taste	4	potatoes, peeled and quartered
	Cayenne pepper to taste	1	cup mushroom pieces

Cut sinews and bones from venison. Cut meat into bite-size pieces; dredge in flour. Brown venison in hot bacon drippings. Add hot water, wine, garlic, hot pepper sauce, cayenne, herbs, parsley, onion, salt and pepper. Cover and bring to a boil. Reduce heat; simmer about 2 hours. Add carrots and potatoes, cover and simmer for 1 hour. Add a little water if needed. Add mushrooms during the last 15 minutes. Yield: 8 servings.

Roast Ducklings with Wild Rice Stuffing

4 cups boiling water	1¾ teaspoons salt
1 cup uncooked wild rice	¼ teaspoon black pepper
2 ready-to-cook ducklings, 4 to 5 pounds each	½ cup chopped onion
	½ cup chopped celery
2 (4½ ounce) jars whole mushrooms, drained, reserve liquid	¼ cup butter or margarine
	½ cup coarsely chopped Brazil nuts
3 beef bouillon cubes	¼ teaspoon marjoram
1 cup long grain white rice	½ cup honey

Pour boiling water over wild rice; cover and let stand 20 minutes; drain. Wash ducklings; dry thoroughly. Fasten neck skin to back with skewers. Lift wing tips up and over back for natural brace. Add hot water to reserved mushroom liquid to measure 3 cups. Add bouillon cubes to this liquid in a large skillet; heat until bouillon cubes dissolve. Add white and wild rice, salt and pepper; stir until mixed. Heat mixture to boiling; reduce heat and cover. Simmer about 14 minutes, or until rice is tender. Fluff rice with fork; cover and steam 5 minutes. Stir onion and celery in butter; cook until onion is tender. Stir onion mixture, mushrooms, nuts and marjoram into rice mixture; toss lightly. Heat oven to 325 degrees. Stuff body cavity of each duckling with rice mixture. Do not pack. Secure openings with skewers and string. Roast ducklings 2 to 2½ hours. Brush with honey during last 15 minutes. Yield: 6 to 8 servings. Serve with Cranberry Frost.

Cranberry Frost
Divide 1 quart lemon sherbet among 8 small glass cups or footed goblets; freeze until serving time. Just before serving, pour 1 quart cranberry cocktail over sherbet. Yield: 8 servings. Excellent with Roast Ducklings.

Southwest Duck or Dove

Fillet the breast of a fresh pintail, mallard, teal, canvasback, wood duck, or dove. Apply a layer of hot sliced jalapeño peppers to the rib side of the fillets. Fold the fillets together and wrap with peppered bacon held in place with a toothpick. A few jalapeño peppers are placed under the bacon wrap. The juice in the jalapeño jar can be sprinkled on the fillet and it is ready to cook. Cook over a mature fire of pure Mesquite charcoal coals for 15 to 20 minutes. Ten minutes for doves.

Birds should be very close to the coals and absolutely NO air allowed into the cooker to support a flame. DO NOT OVERCOOK! Serve hot!

Chicken and Pasta Primavera

8 ounces vegetable flavored corkscrew pasta	1 teaspoon dried parsley flakes
4 tablespoons olive oil	1½ cups broccoli florets
1 small onion, chopped	1½ cups baby carrots
2 cloves garlic, minced	4 ounces mushrooms, sliced
4 boneless, skinless chicken breasts, cut into strips	½ cup white wine
1 teaspoon dried basil	¼ teaspoon white pepper
	¾ cup grated Parmesan cheese

Cook pasta according to package directions; drain and set aside. Heat olive oil in a large skillet until hot; add onion, garlic and sliced chicken. Cook over medium heat until chicken is almost done. Add basil, parsley, broccoli, carrots; cook 2 minutes. Add mushrooms and cook 1 minute; stir occasionally. Add wine and pepper; bring to a boil. Cover, reduce heat, and simmer 3 minutes or until vegetables are tender. Add mixture and Parmesan cheese to pasta; stir well. Serve immediately. Yield: 4 servings.

Basil Grilled Chicken

¾ teaspoon coarse ground pepper	1 tablespoon grated Parmesan cheese
4 skinless chicken breast halves	¼ teaspoon garlic powder
⅓ cup butter or margarine, melted	⅛ teaspoon salt
¼ cup chopped fresh basil	⅛ teaspoon pepper
½ cup butter or margarine, softened	Fresh basil sprigs, optional
2 tablespoons minced fresh basil	

Press ¾ teaspoon pepper into meaty sides of chicken breast halves. Combine ⅓ cup melted butter and ¼ cup chopped basil; stir well. Brush chicken lightly with melted butter mixture. Combine ½ cup softened butter, 2 tablespoons basil, Parmesan cheese, garlic powder, salt, and pepper in a small bowl. Using an electric mixer, beat on low speed until mixture is well blended and smooth. Transfer to a small serving bowl; set aside.

Grill chicken over medium coals 8 to 10 minutes on each side, basting frequently with remaining melted butter mixture.

Serve grilled chicken with basil-butter mixture. Garnish with fresh basil sprigs, if desired. Yield: 4 servings.

Chicken Shrimp Casserole

3   cups cooked and cubed chicken
2   cups cooked and deveined shrimp
3   cups mayonnaise
4½ (10¾ ounce) cans cream of
        mushroom soup
3   cups chopped celery
1   cup minced green onions
2   cups sliced water chestnuts

Garlic powder to taste
Lemon pepper to taste
Seasoned salt flavor enhancer to
    taste
3   (3 ounce) cans Chinese noodles
3   (2 ounce) packages of sliced
        almonds

Combine all but the noodles and almonds. Fold in Chinese noodles and top with sliced almonds. Bake at 375 degrees for about 40 minutes or until bubbly.

Chicken Tetrazzini

1   (3½ to 4 pound) chicken
1   large onion, chopped
½   teaspoon garlic powder
1   package spaghetti
1   (10¾ ounce) can tomato soup

1   (10¾ ounce) can cream of
        mushroom soup
1   can English peas, drained
¼   pound American cheese, grated

Stew chicken until tender; remove chicken, reserving stock. When chicken has cooled, remove skin, bone and cut into bite size pieces. Simmer onion and garlic in chicken stock for 15 minutes. Add spaghetti and cook until tender; drain. Add chicken and soups to spaghetti; lightly mix in peas and cheese. Heat, but do not boil.

Broccoli and Chicken Lasagna

1   (10¾ ounce) can cream of
        mushroom soup
¾   cup sour cream
¼   teaspoon thyme
2   cups chicken, cooked and cubed
6   lasagna noodles, cooked and drained

1   (10 ounce) package chopped
        frozen broccoli, cooked
1   (12 ounce) package shredded
        Cheddar cheese
Salt and pepper to taste or any
    other seasonings of choice

Mix soup, sour cream, thyme and any seasonings of choice; add chicken and combine. In a lightly sprayed 8 x 12-inch baking dish, layer with 3 lasagna noodles, half the chicken mixture, half the broccoli, and half the cheese. Repeat; noodles, chicken mixture, broccoli and cheese. Bake at 350 degrees for 25 to 30 minutes until bubbly and cheese melts.

Patty's Paprika Chicken

8-10 boneless, skinless chicken
    breasts
½   cup margarine
    Salt and pepper
    Paprika

1   (10¾ ounce) can cream of
    mushroom soup
8   ounces sour cream
1   (2.8 ounce) can French fried
    onion rings, divided

Place chicken in a lightly sprayed 9 x 13-inch baking dish. Dab chicken with butter; sprinkle with salt, pepper and paprika. Bake covered at 350 degrees for 40 minutes. Remove from oven. Drain broth into a large bowl. Add mushroom soup, sour cream, and half of the onion rings. Mix together and pour over chicken. Sprinkle again with paprika. Put remaining onion rings on top of chicken. Bake uncovered at 350 degrees for 20 minutes.

Dave Cowen's Baked Chicken Breasts

4   ounces chipped beef
8   boneless, skinless chicken breasts
8   strips bacon
1   cup sour cream

1   (10½ ounce) can cream of
    mushroom soup
¼   cup white wine

Line the bottom of a greased or sprayed 9 x 13-inch baking dish with chipped beef. Top with chicken; cover with bacon. Make a sauce with remaining ingredients; pour on top. Bake at 375 degrees for 1 hour. Yield: 8 servings.

⧗ Chicken Divan

2   (10 ounce) packages frozen
    broccoli
2   cups chicken, cooked and cubed
2   (10¾ ounce) cans cream of
    chicken soup
1   teaspoon lemon juice
1   cup mayonnaise

1   teaspoon curry
1   teaspoon lemon pepper
1   cup or more grated Cheddar
    cheese
1   recipe cornbread mix, cooked and
    crumbled

Cook and drain broccoli. Put in a greased 9 x 13-inch baking dish. Place chicken over broccoli. Mix soup, lemon juice, mayonnaise, curry and lemon pepper. Pour over chicken. Sprinkle with cheese. Top with cornbread crumbs. Bake at 350 degrees for 30 minutes. If made ahead, refrigerate and put cornbread mix over just before cooking. Yield: 10 servings.

Chicken Crisp

2	cups chicken, cooked and cubed	1/4	cup chopped onion
1	cup chopped celery	2	(10¾ ounce) cans cream of
1	(5 ounce) can sliced water		mushroom soup
	chestnuts	1	(3 ounce) can chow mein noodles
½	cup chicken broth	1	teaspoon salt free all natural
1	tablespoon lemon pepper		seasoning blends

Mix all ingredients and place in a greased casserole. Bake at 350 degrees for 30 minutes. Yield: 6 to 8 servings.

Easy Chicken Casserole

4	boneless, skinless chicken breasts	1	(8 or 9 ounce) jar marinated
1	box chicken flavored rice		artichoke hearts, drained,
	vermicelli mix		reserve juice
		¾	cup mayonnaise
		⅛	teaspoon curry, optional

Cook chicken; cut into cubes and set aside. Prepare chicken flavored rice vermicelli mix according to package directions; set aside. Combine artichoke juice, mayonnaise and curry. Put all ingredients together; mix well. Bake at 375 degrees for 45 minutes.

Full bodied? French roast? Decaf? Vanilla bean? Cappuccino? No, none of these. It's the tantalizing aroma of freshly roasted coffee wafting across downtown from the Waples-Platter roasting plant installed in 1907.

Begun in 1871 as a commissary at the railroad construction site on the Red River, Waples-Platter moved into Denison with the train.

Waples-Platter prospered to become one of the Southwest's leading grocery wholesalers. Denison's Waples Memorial Methodist Church is named for one of its founders.

Coffee testing room circa 1920.

Five Quick Chicken Meals

Sauté skinless chicken breasts in a nonstick skillet in 1 tablespoon of olive or canola oil for 8 to 10 minutes or until brown. Prepare one of these 5 sauces in the same skillet and serve on top or place chicken in skillet for a few minutes with sauce.

Provençal
Over medium heat, in 1 teaspoon oil, cook 1 medium chopped onion until tender. Stir in 1 (14½ ounce) can chunky tomatoes with olive oil, garlic and spices; ½ cup pitted ripe olives cut in half, 1 tablespoon drained capers, and ¼ cup water. Cook 1 minute or until heated through.

Salsa
Over medium heat, stir 1 (15 ounce) can of black beans, rinsed and drained; 1 (10 ounce) jar thick and chunky salsa; 1 (8½ ounce) can whole kernel corn, drained; 2 tablespoons chopped cilantro and ¼ cup water. Cook 1 minute to heat through.

Creamy Mushroom
Over medium heat, in 1 teaspoon of oil, add 10 ounces of sliced mushrooms, 1 medium chopped onion and ¼ teaspoon salt; cook until golden and tender. Reduce heat to low and stir in ½ cup light sour cream and ¼ cup water; heat through.

Chinese Ginger
Over medium heat, in 1 teaspoon oil, cook 1 medium-sized red pepper, thinly sliced, until tender crisp. Stir in ½ cup water, 2 tablespoons soy sauce, 2 tablespoons seasoned rice vinegar, and 1 tablespoon grated, peeled ginger root. Boil 1 minute. Sprinkle with chopped green onions.

Dijon
Over low heat, stir ½ cup light evaporated milk or light cream, 2 tablespoons Dijon mustard with seeds, and ¾ cup seedless red or green grapes, cut in half. Cook 1 minute to blend flavors and thicken sauce slightly. Serve with small clusters of grapes.

It has been said the real heroine of the first decade (1900-1910) lived not in romantic fiction but in the American kitchen; and she, too, had her hero—it was Sears, Roebuck & Co.

Jenn's Chicken Artichoke Sauce on Pasta

3	tablespoons olive oil	2	tablespoons capers, drained
1	pound boneless, skinless chicken breasts, cut in strips	1	tablespoon lemon juice
½	cup chopped shallots	¼	teaspoon black pepper
2	tablespoons flour	1	(14 ounce) can artichoke hearts, drained and quartered
1½	cups chicken broth or stock	¼	pound snow peas, cut in slivers
1	cup dry white wine		Pasta, cooked

In a medium size skillet heat oil over medium-high heat. Add chicken and sauté until lightly browned. Reduce heat to medium-low and add shallots; sauté 2 minutes. Sprinkle flour over the chicken and shallots, stirring constantly until flour is well blended. Add chicken broth and wine. Cook and stir until thickened. Add capers, lemon juice, pepper, artichoke hearts and snow peas; cook for 3 minutes. Serve over hot pasta. Yield: 4 to 6 servings.

Favorite Chicken Casserole

6	tablespoons shortening	½	cup almonds, toasted
6	tablespoons flour	3	tablespoons minced parsley
1½	teaspoons salt	2	tablespoons cooking sherry
	Dash of pepper	6-8	ounces medium noodles, cooked and drained
½	teaspoon celery salt		
2	cups chicken stock	2	cups cooked and diced chicken
1	cup evaporated milk, scalded	½	cup grated cheese
1	(6 ounce) can mushrooms		

Make a cream sauce of shortening, flour, salt, pepper, celery salt, stock and milk. Add mushrooms, almonds, parsley and sherry. Alternate layers of noodles, chicken and sauce in buttered casserole. Cover with cheese and bake at 375 degrees for 20 to 30 minutes. Yield: 6 to 8 servings.

Baked Sesame Chicken

¼	cup melted butter	3	tablespoons sesame seeds
½	cup milk	1½	teaspoons salt
1	large egg, slightly beaten	1	teaspoon lemon pepper
½	cup flour	¼	teaspoon baking powder
¼	cup chopped almonds	4	skinless chicken breasts
¼	cup paprika		

Place melted butter in a 9 x 13-inch baking dish; set aside. Combine milk and egg in a shallow dish; mix well. Combine flour and next 6 ingredients in a bowl; mix well. Dip chicken pieces in egg mixture. Dredge in flour mixture. Place chicken in prepared pan. Bake uncovered at 400 degrees for 50 to 55 minutes or until tender. Yield: 4 servings.

🕐 Chicken Delight

8	boneless, skinless chicken breasts	1	can whole cranberries
1	(8 ounce) bottle Russian salad dressing, more if desired	1	package instant onion soup (may use less, to taste)

Mix dressing, cranberries and soup in a saucepan and cook until hot. Place chicken in a lightly sprayed 9 x 13-inch baking dish. Pour hot mixture over chicken. Bake uncovered at 350 degrees for 1 hour.

♥ Honey Basil Chicken

1	cup raspberry vinegar	2	tablespoons minced fresh basil
3	tablespoons Dijon mustard	½	teaspoon dried thyme
2	tablespoons low sodium soy sauce		Pinch of black pepper
2	tablespoons honey	4	boneless, skinless chicken breast halves

In a shallow baking dish mix the first 7 ingredients. Add chicken; turn to coat all sides. Allow to marinate at room temperature for 15 minutes. Transfer chicken to a grill or broiling rack; reserve the marinade in a quart saucepan. Grill or broil chicken for 7 to 10 minutes on each side, or until done. While chicken is cooking, boil marinade until reduced by half. Pour marinade over chicken when done.

Boys will be boys. And boys do play pranks. Sometimes those pranks take more work than a real job.

It took the boys at the Oak Grove school one whole Sunday afternoon. They picked not-quite-ripe wild persimmons from a plentiful supply, squeezed the juice from them, and liberally laced it into the Communion juice to be used at the church service at their school that night.

According to Glen Blankenship, one of the culprits, the congregation duly partook of the concoction. When they rose for the final hymn, their lips were too puckered to sing.

♥ Chicken Noodle Casserole

1 cooked and cutup chicken	1 cup sour cream
1 (10¾ ounce) can cream of chicken soup	1 package egg noodles, cooked and drained
1 (10¾ ounce) can cream of mushroom soup	Salt and pepper to taste
4 ounces cream cheese	Cheddar cheese

Mix the first 7 ingredients together. Top with Cheddar cheese and bake at 350 degrees for 20 to 30 minutes or until bubbly.

This is also good with reduced or no fat ingredients.

Chicken and Broccoli Roll-Ups

1 (10¾ ounce) can cream of chicken soup	1 cup shredded Cheddar cheese, divided
1 cup milk	1 cup or a 2.8 ounce can French fried onion rings, divided
2 cups shredded chicken	8 (7 inch) flour tortillas
1 (10 ounce) package frozen chopped broccoli, cooked and drained	

Combine soup and milk in a bowl. Combine chicken, broccoli, ½ cup cheese and ½ can onion rings. Stir in ¾ cup of soup mixture into chicken mixture. Divide mixture evenly into tortillas. Roll up and put seam side down into lightly greased 9 x 13-inch baking dish. Pour remaining soup mixture over top and bake covered at 350 degrees for 35 minutes. Top with remaining cheese and onion rings; cook uncovered 5 minutes longer.

Chicken Fettuccine Supreme

¼ cup butter or margarine
1¼ pounds boneless, skinless
    chicken breasts, cut into ¾ inch
    pieces
3 cups sliced fresh mushrooms
1 cup chopped green onions
1 small sweet red pepper, cut into
    thin strips
1 clove garlic, crushed

½ teaspoon salt
½ teaspoon pepper
10 ounces uncooked fettuccine
¾ cup half and half
½ cup butter or margarine, melted
¼ cup chopped fresh parsley
¼ teaspoon salt
¼ teaspoon black pepper
1 cup grated Parmesan cheese

Melt ¼ cup butter in a large skillet; add chicken pieces and cook until browned. Remove chicken; set aside; reserve pan drippings. Add mushrooms and next 5 ingredients to pan drippings in skillet; sauté until vegetables are tender. Add chicken; reduce heat, cook 15 minutes or until chicken is done and mixture is thoroughly heated. Set aside; keep warm. Cook fettuccine according to package directions, omitting salt; drain. Place fettuccine in a large bowl. Combine half and half, ½ cup melted butter, parsley, ¼ teaspoon salt and ¼ teaspoon pepper; stir well. Add half and half mixture to the fettuccine; toss gently to combine. Add chicken mixture and Parmesan cheese to fettuccine; toss gently to combine. Serve immediately. Yield: 6 servings.

The Gandy Dancer's Chicken Ritz

1 (10¾ ounce) can cream of
    mushroom soup
1 (10¾ ounce) can cream of
    chicken soup
16 ounces sour cream
1 cup cooked rice
1 can sliced water chestnuts,
    drained

1 teaspoon lemon juice
    Coarse ground pepper to taste
2-3 cups cooked and cubed chicken
    breasts
2 tubes round buttery crackers,
    crushed
1½ sticks margarine, melted
    Poppy seeds

Mix soups, sour cream, rice, water chestnuts, lemon juice and coarse ground pepper to taste. Line chicken in the bottom of a greased baking dish. Pour soup mixture over chicken. Spread with crushed crackers. Melt butter; drizzle over top. Sprinkle with poppy seeds. Bake at 350 degrees for 30 minutes. Yield: 8 to 10 servings.

Chick and Chips

1 (10¾ ounce) can cream of chicken soup	1 (15 ounce) can mixed vegetables, drained or 1 (1 pound) package frozen vegetables, cooked and drained
½ cup milk	
1 cup cooked and cubed chicken	
1¼ cups crushed potato chips, divided	

Mix soup and milk thoroughly and pour into a lightly greased or sprayed 1-quart casserole. Add chicken, 1 cup potato chips and mixed vegetables; mix well. Sprinkle top with remaining ¼ cup of potato chips. Bake at 375 degrees for 25 minutes.

Lemon Butter Chicken Breasts

6 boneless, skinless chicken breast halves	Lemon pepper to taste
½ cup flour	½ cup butter
	2 tablespoons lemon juice

Pound chicken to ¼ inch thickness. Dredge chicken in flour; liberally sprinkle each side of chicken with lemon pepper. Sauté chicken in butter about 15 minutes until lightly browned. Leaving chicken in skillet, stir in lemon juice and increase heat to deglaze pan. Stir liquid, scraping particles from bottom of pan. Yield: 4 to 6 servings.

Lemon Grilled Chicken

½ cup lemon juice	⅛ teaspoon pepper sauce
½ cup butter, melted	1 broiler or fryer quartered
½ teaspoon crushed thyme leaves	Salt and pepper to taste

Combine lemon juice, butter, thyme and pepper sauce in a small bowl. Sprinkle chicken with salt and pepper. Place chicken, bone side down on grill over hot coals. Brush with basting sauce. Grill for 40 minutes, turning once. Baste frequently with sauce. Can be served with extra sauce.

☽ Chicken Marinade

½	cup corn oil	2	cloves garlic, minced
⅓	cup soy sauce	½	teaspoon ground ginger
¼	cup lemon juice	¼	teaspoon black pepper
2	tablespoons yellow mustard	3	pounds chicken parts

Combine first 7 ingredients; mix well. Marinate chicken for several hours or overnight. Braise on grill. Turn and brush often. Cook at least 45 minutes or until done.

Matterhorn Chicken

4	boneless, skinless chicken breasts	3	eggs, beaten
1	(8 ounce) package mozzarella cheese, shredded		Bread crumbs
			Cooking oil

Flatten boneless chicken breasts; sprinkle shredded mozzarella cheese in middle of chicken. Roll up; secure with toothpicks. Dip chicken in beaten eggs; then in bread crumbs. Brown in oil on each side. Place in an ungreased baking dish uncovered; bake at 400 degrees for 20 minutes.

🕐 Linda's Chicken and Rice

1	medium sized onion, diced	1	(10¾ ounce) can cream of chicken soup
1	green pepper, diced		
2	tablespoons butter or margarine, melted	1	(12 ounce) can chicken, drained
1	small jar pimentos, drained and chopped		Processed cheese loaf, to taste
			Cooked rice

Sauté onion and green pepper in a little butter or margarine. Add pimentos and cream of chicken soup. Add canned chicken and processed cheese loaf to taste; may need to add a little milk. Serve over rice.

Chicken with Mushrooms

4 pounds boneless, skinless chicken breasts	1½ cups chicken broth
½ cup flour	1 tablespoon lemon juice
½ teaspoon salt	½ cup white wine
½ teaspoon pepper	Dash of nutmeg
3 tablespoons butter	Salt and pepper to taste
3 tablespoons olive oil	1-2 tablespoons chopped fresh
1 pound fresh mushrooms, sliced	parsley, garnish

Rinse chicken pieces under cold, running water; dredge in a mixture of flour, salt and pepper. In a large skillet, melt butter and olive oil over medium heat. Sauté chicken pieces until golden brown. Reduce heat; continue to simmer for 30 to 40 minutes, turning occasionally. Remove chicken from skillet; place on a platter to keep warm in a 250 degree oven while you make the sauce. To the same skillet, add mushrooms (and a little extra butter, if needed); sauté for 5 minutes. Add chicken broth, lemon juice and white wine. Boil vigorously for 3 to 4 minutes. Scrape any bits of the browned chicken and mushrooms from the sides and bottom of the pan. Lower heat; add nutmeg, salt and pepper to taste; pour over chicken and top with parsley. Sauce and chicken can be stored separately in the refrigerator for up to 2 days.

Chicken Pie

Pastry for double pie shell	¾ cup sliced celery
1 cup shredded Cheddar or colby cheese	1½ teaspoons lemon juice
1 tablespoon flour	½ cup mayonnaise
½ cup toasted slivered almonds	¼ teaspoon poultry seasoning
1½ cups cooked and cubed chicken or turkey	Salt and pepper to taste

Make pie shell. Roll out half and cover the bottom of a 1½ or 2-quart casserole dish. Toss cheese with flour. Combine with almonds, chicken and the next 4 ingredients. Mix well and place in pastry lined casserole dish. Roll out remaining dough; place over chicken filling. Pierce dough to allow steam to escape while baking. Bake at 400 degrees for 30 to 35 minutes or until crust is golden brown.

Spaghetti with Chicken and Artichokes

6	ounces spaghetti	2	cups cooked and diced chicken
6	slices bacon, crisply cooked and crumbled	1	cup frozen green peas
		1	teaspoon dried oregano leaves
1	(6 ounce) jar marinated artichoke hearts	1/4	teaspoon salt
		1/4	teaspoon pepper
1	medium onion, diced	8	ounces sour cream

Cook spaghetti; drain. Cook bacon, remove and cool; reserve drippings and add drained marinated oil from artichokes into the 10-inch skillet. Cut artichoke hearts in cubes and reserve. Cook diced onions in marinated oil until tender. Stir in hearts, chicken, peas, bacon, oregano, salt and pepper. Cook and stir until hot. Stir in sour cream; toss with spaghetti. Yield: 4 servings.

As I rode the trail, I kept wonderin' how far to that spring I heered so much about. Dang Texas sun! It's sure 'nuff hotter'n I heered. Reckoned Old Duke was thirstier'n me, so I climbed down out of the saddle and stood in the shade - fannin' Duke and me with my old hat and sayin' a prayer. I took the reins and started walkin' and lo and behold! There, not fifty yards ahead, was that blessed spring. Sand Springs! Thank you, Lord!

As early as 1840 prospectors, wagon train masters and settlers camped at Sand Springs where the strong currents of water, icy cold and pure, bubbled up at the foot of a rocky bluff. The sandstone of the bluff's face was an invitation to all to carve their names or to leave a message.

The spring was put on the map in 1857 as a regular stop for the Southern Overland Mail Coaches of John Butterfield as they traveled from St. Louis to San Francisco. The bluff, today at Waterloo Lake, still bears the weathered carvings of the tired and weary travelers who came and lingered long enough to carve their names for all to see.

Margaret's Chicken Spaghetti

1	pound boneless, skinless chicken breasts	2	(10¾ ounce) cans cream of mushroom soup
4	cups water	2	cups grated Cheddar cheese
2	onions, quartered	1	(8 ounce) can tomato sauce
3	stalks celery, thickly sliced	1	(3 ounce) jar green olives, sliced, drained
3	carrots, chopped		
3	tablespoons Worcestershire sauce	2	(4½ ounce) jars button mushrooms, drained
1	teaspoon black pepper		
	Dash of salt		Black pepper
1	bay leaf		Paprika
1	(6 ounce) package spaghetti		Whole olives, garnish

In a large covered Dutch oven bring chicken, water, onion, celery, carrots, Worcestershire sauce and spices to a boil. Cover; simmer on low heat 20 to 25 minutes until chicken is cooked through. Remove chicken to platter; allow to cool. Remove bay leaf and discard. When chicken has cooled, cut into bite-size pieces; set aside. Do NOT remove cooked vegetables from broth. Bring chicken broth to a boil; add spaghetti and cook until tender; drain.

To cooked spaghetti, stir in chopped chicken, soup, 1 cup cheese, tomato sauce, olives and mushrooms. Stir and toss until all ingredients are evenly blended. Pour into a large greased or sprayed casserole and cover with remaining cheese. Sprinkle with pepper and paprika. Garnish with whole olives. Bake at 350 degrees for 15 minutes until cheese is melted and slightly brown on top.

🕐 Walnut Chicken

¼	cup soy sauce	¼	cup oil
¼	cup beer	⅓	cup sliced green onions
½	teaspoon ground ginger	1	cup sliced mushrooms
1	clove garlic, minced	1	cup broken walnuts
1	pound boneless, skinless and cubed chicken breasts		

Combine soy sauce, beer, ginger, garlic and chicken in a bowl. Marinate 30 minutes. Heat oil in wok; add chicken and soy mixture. Stir-fry until chicken is cooked and soy mixture begins to coat chicken, about 5 minutes. Add green onions, mushrooms and walnuts. Cook 3 minutes, tossing.

Herbed Lamb

1 leg of lamb, about 6 pounds	¼ cup chopped green onions with
4-5 cloves garlic	tops
2 teaspoons salt	2½ tablespoons lemon juice
2½ teaspoons oregano	2 tablespoons butter
½ teaspoon pepper	2 tablespoons flour
1 cup claret wine or dry red wine	

Cut deep slits in lamb, about 2 inches apart, over entire surface. Crush garlic, mix with salt, oregano, and pepper. Press mixture evenly into all slits in meat. Place meat on rack in pan with fat side up. Do not cover. Roast at 325 degrees for 30 to 35 minutes per pound for medium. If using a meat thermometer, roast meat to 175 degrees for medium or 180 degrees for well done. Combine wine, green onions, and lemon juice; reserve half of this basting mixture for the gravy. Baste lamb often with remaining half of mixture. When meat is done, put on warm platter, skim fat off juices, reserving one cup. Melt butter and blend in flour. Stir in reserved wine mixture and meat juices. Cook and stir until thickened. Serve sauce separately.

Ham Loaf

1 (20 ounce) can pineapple slices, drained, reserving juice	¼ teaspoon salt
	¼ teaspoon pepper
3 tablespoons butter	1 cup milk
¾ cup brown sugar, divided	2 eggs, slightly beaten
1½ pounds ground pork	¼ teaspoon dry mustard
1 pound ground smoked ham	2 tablespoons vinegar
1 cup fresh bread crumbs	2 tablespoons pineapple juice

Sauce

Whipping cream, whipped   Horseradish

Preheat oven to 350 degrees. Arrange pineapple in the bottom of a 9-inch loaf pan. Melt butter; mix with ¼ cup brown sugar. Spread on top of pineapple. Mix meats thoroughly in a large bowl. Mix in bread crumbs, salt and pepper. Stir milk and eggs together; combine with meat mixture. Pack this mixture in pan. Combine remaining brown sugar with mustard and stir into vinegar and pineapple juice. Pour this syrup over meat; bake 1 hour. Turn loaf upside down in roasting pan; pour off about half the liquid. Put back in oven; bake 30 minutes, basting occasionally to give loaf a good glaze. Turn out on platter. For sauce, combine whipped cream and horseradish to taste. Yield: 6 generous servings.

Sausage Rice Casserole

1	large chopped onion	1	cup chopped celery
1	pound ground sausage	1	cup hard rice
4½	cups water	1	package dry chicken noodle soup mix
1	teaspoon salt		

Sauté onion in a lightly greased frying pan; remove. Brown sausage in frying pan; drain grease. Reserve meat and onion. In a sauce pan, simmer remaining ingredients for 10 minutes. Mix with meat and onion and place in a 2-quart casserole. Bake covered at 325 degrees for 1 hour. Uncover for last 10 minutes to brown.

German Sausage
with Red Cabbage and Apples

4	tablespoons bacon drippings	2	tablespoons malt vinegar
2	tablespoons brown sugar	½	teaspoon caraway seeds
1	small onion, chopped		Salt and black pepper to taste
4	cups shredded red cabbage	6	links German sausage
2	tart apples, sliced		Water or red wine, optional

Heat drippings in a large skillet; add sugar and stir until brown. Add onion; cook slowly until golden. Add remaining ingredients; place sausage on top of cabbage. Cook slowly 45 minutes to 1 hour. Add a little water or red wine as needed to keep from sticking. Yield: 6 servings.

May substitute with green cabbage but use ¼ cup sugar and 1 tablespoon vinegar.

Pork Tenderloin

4	tablespoons honey	1	tablespoon brown mustard
2	tablespoons brown sugar	2-3	pound prepared pork tenderloin
2	tablespoons cider vinegar		

Combine first 4 ingredients; mix well. Then coat tenderloin with sauce. Roast at 375 degrees for 30 to 40 minutes per pound or until 160 degrees on a meat thermometer. Slice thin and serve. May serve the sweet sauce over the sliced meat if desired.

Pork St. Trenton

6	tablespoons butter or margarine, divided	4	cups beef broth
3	garlic cloves, minced	1	teaspoon salt, divided
2	tablespoons sliced green onions	½	teaspoon ground black pepper
4	small mushrooms, sliced	2	pounds pork tenderloin
1	cup port wine	½	teaspoon cracked pepper
½	cup red currant jelly		Fresh rosemary sprigs for garnish

Melt 2 tablespoons butter in a large skillet over medium heat; add garlic, green onions, mushrooms and sauté for 2 minutes. Add wine, stirring to loosen particles. Cook 10 minutes or until reduced by half. Stir in jelly, beef broth, ½ teaspoon salt and ground black pepper. Cook 10 to 15 minutes or until sauce is reduced by half and coats a spoon. Remove from heat; stir in 2 tablespoons butter. Pour through a fine wire-mesh strainer into a bowl; keep warm. Wipe skillet clean with a paper towel.

Cut pork into 1 inch thick slices; sprinkle slices with remaining ½ teaspoon salt and cracked pepper. Melt remaining 2 tablespoons butter in skillet over medium high heat; add pork and cook 1 to 2 minutes on each side or to desired degree of doneness. Serve with sauce. Garnish, if desired. Yield: 6 servings.

❊ Sausage and Zucchini or Squash Dish

1	pound hot sausage	2	eggs, slightly beaten
1	clove garlic, washed and minced	½	cup milk
5	medium squash, chunked and cooked	½	cup bread crumbs
		½	teaspoon oregano
½	cup Parmesan cheese		

Brown sausage with garlic; drain. Mix with remaining ingredients and pour into a casserole dish. Bake at 325 degrees for 30 minutes until browned. Freezes well.

☽ Savory Pork Chops

3 cloves of garlic, mashed	1½ cups dry white wine
½ teaspoon salt	1½ cups beef broth
½ teaspoon thyme	5 tablespoons tomato paste
⅛ teaspoon pepper	3 tablespoons minced parsley
8 loin pork chops 1 inch thick	1 tablespoon Dijon mustard
3 tablespoons butter	⅓ cup grated sour pickles
1 small onion, finely chopped	3 tablespoons butter, softened
2 cloves of garlic minced	

Combine first 4 ingredients; rub mixture into both sides of pork chops. Place in a plastic bag and refrigerate overnight. Grease a large oven proof skillet. Wipe garlic mixture from the chops and brown them in the skillet on 1 side only for 15 minutes over moderate heat. Preheat oven to 350 degrees. Turn chops over and transfer skillet to oven. Bake uncovered for 20 minutes. While chops are baking, melt 3 tablespoons butter in a saucepan. Add onion and 2 cloves garlic and sauté until onion is limp. Add wine, broth, tomato paste, parsley and mustard to onion mixture. Bring to a boil and continue to cook until sauce is slightly thickened. Stir in grated pickle. Remove chops from oven and place on a large platter. Skim grease from the pan juices. Pour onion sauce into skillet and heat sauce, stirring up the brown bits from bottom of skillet. Return chops to pan; heat and spoon sauce over them. Remove chops to a platter, swirl butter into sauce and pour over chops. Yield: 8 servings.

Domaine Denison Cabernet Sauvignon was first bottled in 1988 by Dr. Roy Renfro's Red River Valley Vineyards, Inc., to promote Denison's wine heritage. It has won honors in many private taste testings as well as a gold and a silver rating at the Lone Star Wine competition.

Grandmother Vivienne's Crabmeat Casserole

1	onion, chopped	1	(4 ounce) packet saltine crackers, crushed, divided
3	tablespoons bacon drippings		
2	cloves garlic, crushed	1	cup cream or half and half
1	pound of crabmeat, canned or fresh	½	cup melted butter
			Salt and pepper to taste (may add cayenne pepper to taste)

Mix all ingredients together reserving enough crushed crackers to sprinkle on top. Pour in a greased casserole dish. Sprinkle with reserved crushed crackers. Bake at 350 degrees for 20 to 30 minutes.

Stuffed Flounder

2	cups cooked shrimp or crabmeat	2	teaspoons chopped chives
2	eggs	1	tablespoon flour
1	cup cream	4	tablespoons sherry
2	tablespoons butter	4	(¾ pound) flounders
½	cup mushrooms		Butter

Mix shrimp, eggs and cream together. Melt butter, add mushrooms and chives; sauté until soft. Add flour and cook until bubbly. Add shrimp mixture, sherry and cook until thick. Slit flounder along the back bone and cut the flesh of the fish away from the bone but leave intact. Spoon as much stuffing into the slit as possible. Top with butter and bake at 300 degrees for 30 minutes, or until done.

🕐 Salmon Patties

1	(15 ounce) can salmon	½	cup flour
1	egg	1½	teaspoons baking powder
⅓	cup minced onion		Oil for frying

Drain salmon; set aside 2 tablespoons of juice. Mix salmon, egg and onion until sticky. Stir in flour; add baking powder to reserved juice and mix. Form into patties and fry until golden brown.

116

Salmon Loaf

1	(16 ounce) can salmon, drained	½	cup chopped onion
½	cup salad dressing	¼	cup chopped green pepper
1	cup cream of celery soup	1	tablespoon lemon juice
1	egg, beaten	1	teaspoon salt
1	cup dry bread crumbs		

Mix all ingredients and bake in a greased loaf pan at 350 degrees for 1 hour and 10 minutes. Serve with cucumber sauce; recipe follows.

Cucumber Sauce

¼	cup salad dressing	¼	cup chopped cucumbers
½	cup sour cream		

Mix all ingredients and serve. Yield: 6 servings.

"Soda pop" has long been one of Denison's industries. Pop? The pop came not from the soda water but from bottling it.

Red River Bottling Co. drinks had no corks or metal cans, so until 1912 the lids were glass stoppers with a spring and a large hook on the top. The bottles were capped using a "foot-stomper" machine needed to slam the crowns down in the bottle, hence the popping sound.

Red River pop was priced at 24 bottles for sixty-five cents. Soft drink giant, Dr. Pepper, came to town in 1929 and purchased Red River. In their advertising, the "Dr." suggested a drink of his soda pop at 10, 2, and 4 o'clock would be beneficial. A "new" bottle is held by Fred Harvey who managed the Dr. Pepper Co. when it was in Denison.

🕐 Best Baked Fish

4-6 fish fillets	Salt and pepper to taste
⅓ cup melted margarine	2 cups finely crushed cracker crumbs

Place fish, melted margarine, salt and pepper in a bowl; mix until coated. Place cracker crumbs in a large plastic bag. Add fish and shake well. Place fillets in a greased, shallow, oblong baking pan. Bake at 350 degrees for 30 to 35 minutes. Simply delicious.

Angling in magnificent Lake Texoma is a far cry from the days of the Indians and pioneers who depended on fish from the Red River for sustenance.

From dramatic rocky cliffs to sandy beaches to tree-shaded coves, Lake Texoma backs up behind Denison Dam with 580 miles of shoreline and a pool level of 89,000 surface acres of water at depths to ninety feet. The huge earthen dam was completed across the Red River by the U. S. Army Corps of Engineers in 1944.

To catch a fish dinner, you might go after black bass, sand bass, crappie, bluegill, catfish or the famed striped bass which came from ocean waters to Lake Texoma. Lots of big fish tales abound including a record monster blue catfish weighing 118.5 pounds.

Along with the great fishing, water sports and camping, boats of all kinds and sizes ply Texoma's water. The Texoma Lakefest Regatta has grown from local sailors racing to raise money for disadvantaged children to a three day mega-event ranking in the top five charitable sailing regattas in the nation.

Shrimp Bake

1 small green pepper, chopped	1 (10¾ ounce) can cream of
1 cup chopped celery	mushroom soup
½ cup chopped onion	1 teaspoon salt
1 (11 ounce) can mushrooms,	1 cup mayonnaise
reserve half the liquid	3 cups cooked rice
¾ cup milk	1 cup grated Cheddar cheese
	2 cans shrimp, drained

Mix all ingredients together, EXCEPT grated cheese and shrimp, and refrigerate until the next day. The next day, add shrimp to mixture. Bake at 350 degrees for 45 to 65 minutes. Sprinkle cheese on top for last 10 minutes of baking.

Instead of shrimp, use 1 can of drained tuna OR 1 can salmon.

Sweet and Sour Shrimp

1½ pounds raw medium shrimp, shelled	3 tablespoons cornstarch
¼ cup peanut or soy oil	3 medium onions made into shells by cutting onions into sections and separating the layers
¼ teaspoon salt	
⅛ teaspoon coarse ground black pepper	1 large green pepper, cut in pieces
4 tablespoons dark brown sugar	1 cup canned pineapple chunks, drained but reserve 1 tablespoon of liquid
½ cup cider vinegar	
2 tablespoons tomato ketchup	White rice
3 tablespoons soy sauce	

Heat oil in a large skillet with cover; add salt and pepper. Quickly sauté shrimp until lightly browned. With a slotted spoon remove shrimp; keep warm. Meanwhile, in a sauce pan, mix brown sugar, vinegar, ketchup, soy sauce, and cornstarch blended with a little water. Bring to a boil, stirring constantly. Cook about 2 minutes. (If desired, some of the juice from the pineapple can also be added, but do not use more than 1 tablespoon.) Pour sauce into a skillet, add onion, green pepper and pineapple; mix thoroughly but carefully. Cover and cook over low heat 15 minutes. About 5 minutes before serving, add shrimp and mix well. Cover again and simmer. Serve hot with individual bowls of steamed white rice.

Louisiana Style Baked Shrimp

¾	pound shrimp (approximately 20, shelled)	⅛	teaspoon cayenne pepper
3	tablespoons unsalted butter	1	teaspoon minced garlic
1	teaspoon chili powder	2	teaspoons Worcestershire sauce
1	teaspoon freshly ground black pepper	2	tablespoons dry red wine
		¼	teaspoon salt
			Crusty bread (Italian or French)

Preheat oven to 400 degrees. Arrange shrimp in a baking dish just large enough to hold them in one layer. In a small saucepan, combine butter, chili powder, black pepper, cayenne, garlic, Worcestershire sauce, wine and salt. Bring to a boil and pour over the shrimp. Bake for 8 to 10 minutes or until the shrimp are just firm and serve with crusty bread as an accompaniment. Yield: 2 servings.

Can easily be doubled or tripled. May be used as an appetizer.

Shrimp Imperial

¼	cup butter	½	cup sliced mushrooms
¾	cup chopped green pepper	3	tablespoons chopped pimento
½	cup minced onion	1	tablespoon finely chopped parsley
3	tablespoons flour	1	tablespoon horseradish
1	teaspoon salt	1	teaspoon Worcestershire sauce
½	teaspoon black pepper	1½	pounds cooked shrimp
1	cup evaporated milk		Grated Cheddar cheese
1	cup water		Thin bread slices
2	egg yolks, slightly beaten		

Melt butter; add onion, pepper and cook until tender. Blend in flour, salt and pepper. When this bubbles, add evaporated milk and water; bring to a boil. Add 3 tablespoons of this mixture to the egg yolks; add this to original mixture. Add mushrooms, pimento, parsley, horseradish and Worcestershire sauce. Add 1½ pounds cooked shrimp. When serving, top with grated Cheddar cheese. Serve in Toast Cups.

Toast Cups

Cut crusts from thin slices of bread. Lightly brush both sides of bread with melted butter. Press into muffin pans. Toast in oven at 325 degrees until lightly browned.

This Texas Gran Vin Brut, Cuvee T. V. Munson, champagne from a limited release of 1200 bottles by Moyer Wines in 1991 salutes the legendary Denison horticulturist.

The Dallas Opera annually honors an outstanding American wine maker with the T. V. Munson Award. The Texas Wine and Grape Grower Association similarly recognizes an exemplary Texas viticulturist.

Swordfish Supreme

4	(6 to 8 ounce) swordfish steaks, 1 inch thick	1	tablespoon lemon juice
1	teaspoon salt	1	teaspoon crushed chervil leaves
¼	teaspoon black pepper		Avocado Sauce, recipe follows
¼	cup butter or margarine, melted		Lemon wedges, garnish

Sprinkle fish with salt and pepper. Combine butter, lemon juice and chervil. Place steaks on a lightly greased grill 4 inches from medium coals. Grill 10 minutes on each side, brushing frequently with butter mixture. Serve steaks with Avocado Sauce and lemon wedges. Yield: 4 servings.

Avocado Sauce

1	small ripe avocado, peeled and pitted	1	teaspoon lemon juice
⅓	cup sour cream	¼	teaspoon salt
			A few drops of hot pepper sauce

Mix all ingredients in a blender or beat with rotary beater until smooth. Serve with swordfish steaks.

Crevette a la Friloux

Broiled Shrimp

2-3 pounds clean, fresh shrimp in shell	1-2 tablespoons black pepper
¼ cup salt	1-2 tablespoons mustard powder
1 pound sweet cream butter	1 dash of red pepper, optional
1-2 cups Worcestershire sauce	Garlic powder or fresh garlic, to taste

Soak shrimp in ¼ cup of salt dissolved in ½ gallon of cold water for one hour or so. Drain shrimp; do NOT rinse. Place shrimp flat in bottom of a deep dish or pan for broiling. Mix remaining ingredients together; heat and stir well. Then pour heated mixture over shrimp. Broil 3 to 4 minutes on each side. Check often. Shrimp will be bright pink when done. Do NOT overcook! Pour remaining liquid into bowls and serve for dipping shrimp. Peel and eat. Serve with hot French bread and a garden green salad. THEN ENJOY!

These World War II ration coupon books belong to the family of Betty Turner of Denison.

Almost everything Americans really liked to eat was strictly rationed by a system that drove housewives and grocers crazy. Red stamps were surrendered for meat, butter, fats, cheese, canned milk and canned fish. Blue stamps were for canned fruits, vegetables and related items. Sugar, coffee, shoes, tires and gasoline had their own special stamps.

Victory gardens were encouraged, even replacing flower beds. The speed limit was 35 mph to conserve tires and gasoline in pre-war cars. Bacon drippings and grease were turned in for use in producing explosives.

Everyone cooperated in "the war effort", a time when citizens sacrificed and worked for the national good.

Side Tracks

*T*he Annie P. is the only steamboat to navigate the Red River as far north as Denison. Her 1905 voyage set off a flurry of excited interest in navigation of the Red River from New Orleans to Denison. Discussion revived when the Denison Dam was constructed but never came to fruition.

Side Dishes

Irish Potatoes

1½ pounds potatoes, cut into 2 inch chunks	⅔ cup milk
1½ cups chopped cabbage	2 tablespoons margarine
⅓ cup finely chopped green onions	1 teaspoon salt
2 cups boiling water	½ teaspoon black pepper

Put potatoes in cold water and bring to a boil. Boil for 5 minutes; add cabbage and cook 10 minutes. Put green onions in a sieve, pour boiling water over them; drain. Mix onions, milk, margarine, salt and pepper; bring to a boil. Drain potatoes and cabbage. Beat on low speed. Add milk mixture and beat until light and fluffy.

Mattie Barrett's eighty-four years have witnessed many changes in Denison. Asked about old-time recipes, she responded:
I BET YOU NEVER COOKED A CHICKEN WITH THE FEATHERS ON!

When Mattie was young, her family had to be working in the fields by sun-up. Breakfast was fixed in a large black kettle over an open fire in the yard, then lunch was left cooking in the embers.

Baked chicken for lunch: Shoot a chicken; remove its innards. Stuff cavity with garlic, onions and herbs if you can find some. Pour water on the ground and make mud. Cover the chicken well with mud, then bury in the coals left from the fire. When you come back at noontime, peel off the skin, also removing mud and feathers. The lightly browned chicken meat will be delicious.

While this recipe reflects Denison's rich culinary heritage, it was deemed prudent to forego kitchen testing.

Mattie's father always said a blessing before meals: "For all we eat, for all we are, for all we have everywhere, we thank Thee, Father."

A Dining Car Menu for   *Casual Dining on the Deck*

Spinach Spread & Crackers
Basil Grilled Chicken
Parsley Rice
Avocado with Warm Tomato Vinaigrette
Oreo Cookie Dessert

🕐 Hash Brown Casserole

2 pounds frozen hash brown potatoes	1 (10¾ ounce) can cream of mushroom soup
¼ cup chopped onion	1 teaspoon salt
10 ounces grated Cheddar cheese	½ teaspoon black pepper
½ cup melted margarine	1 cup sour cream

Thaw potatoes; mix all ingredients together. Spray a 9 x 13-inch casserole generously with a nonstick cooking spray. Bake at 350 degrees for 1 hour and 15 minutes.

🕐 Kay's Potatoes

8-10 medium potatoes, boiled and grated	8 ounces sour cream
10 ounces Cheddar cheese, grated	3 tablespoons milk
1 diced onion	Salt and pepper to taste

Thoroughly mix all ingredients, either by hand or mixer, as you would mashed potatoes. Pour into a lightly greased deep baking dish, cover with foil and bake at 300 degrees for 30 minutes.

◷ Hash Brown O'Brien

1	tablespoon minced onion	1	cup milk
2	teaspoons minced green pepper	½	cup shredded sharp Cheddar cheese
2	tablespoons melted butter		
2	tablespoons flour	2	teaspoons minced pimento
½	teaspoon salt	1	(12 ounce) package frozen shredded hash browns, thawed
¼	teaspoon dry mustard		
	Dash black pepper	¼	cup shredded Cheddar cheese

Preheat oven to 400 degrees. Sauté onion and green pepper in butter. Combine flour, salt, mustard and pepper. Stir into butter mixture; cook and stir 1 minute. Add milk; cook until thickened. Stir in cheese and pimento; blend well. Separate potatoes into 4 sections. Arrange in an 8-inch square baking dish. Spoon cheese sauce over potatoes. Sprinkle ¼ cup cheese over potatoes. Bake covered for 30 minutes. Uncover and bake 5 to 10 minutes until brown and bubbly. Yield: 4 to 6 servings.

NO MORE TEARS! To keep onions from burning your eyes - place them in the freezer for 20 minutes before using.

Crispy Potatoes

4	large potatoes, unpeeled	½	cup melted butter
	Salt and lemon pepper to taste	1	cup grated Parmesan cheese

Cut potatoes in ⅛ inch slices. Arrange in a single layer on cookie sheets. Season to taste. Pour melted butter over potatoes and top with cheese. Bake at 350 degrees for 45 minutes or until crisp. Yield: 6 servings.

Scottish Skillet Potatoes

2	tablespoons margarine or butter	1½	teaspoons salt
6	medium potatoes, thinly sliced (about 4 cups)	¼	teaspoon pepper
		¼	cup snipped parsley
2	medium onions, sliced	¾	cup water

Heat butter or margarine in a 10-inch skillet until hot. Layer half each of the potato and onion slices in skillet. Sprinkle with half each of the salt, pepper and parsley. Repeat; add water. Cover and simmer over low heat until potatoes are tender and liquid is absorbed, about 30 minutes. (Add more water if necessary) Yield: 6 servings.

Fabulous Potatoes

2 pounds frozen hash brown
   potatoes, thawed
½ cup butter or margarine, melted
1 teaspoon salt

2 cups grated Cheddar cheese
½ cup chopped onion
2 cups sour cream
1 (10¾ ounce) can cream of
   chicken soup

Mix all ingredients together. Place in a buttered casserole and bake at 350 degrees for 45 minutes. Yield: 12 servings.

Katy's famous Texas Special train, inaugurated in 1948, offered premier service and comfort aboard a diesel powered all streamlined marvel.

For train and people watchers, a popular pastime, Jack Maguire claims the highpoint of the day was greeting the northbound Texas Special as it arrived

in Denison about dusk. By then the Pullman coach lights would be on and dinner service begun in the diner. The tables with white linen tablecloths and napkins, candles, fresh flowers, gleaming silver and jacketed waiters were fascinating to spectators outside.

Hi-Ho Hash Browns

3 (12 ounce) packages frozen hash
   brown potatoes, thawed
½ cup melted butter
½ cup chopped onions
1 teaspoon salt
16 ounces sour cream

1 (10¾ ounce) can cream of
   mushroom or chicken soup
10 ounces grated American cheese
¼ cup additional butter, melted for
   cracker crumbs
2 cups crushed round buttery
   crackers

Mix well all ingredients, except the ¼ cup additional butter and cracker crumbs. Place in a greased 9 x 13-inch baking dish. Mix the ¼ cup melted butter with the cracker crumbs and sprinkle over potato mixture. Bake at 350 degrees for 45 minutes.

Crusty Potato Cake

6   medium baking potatoes, thinly
    sliced
1   teaspoon salt

Pepper
⅓   cup margarine or butter, melted

Arrange a layer of potato slices in bottom of a generously greased 9-inch pie plate. Sprinkle with small amount of salt and a dash of pepper. Repeat until all potatoes have been layered, sprinkling each layer with a small amount of salt and a dash of pepper. Pour margarine over potatoes. Cook at 400 degrees, uncovered, until potatoes are tender, about 50 minutes.

Loosen edge and bottom of potatoes with a wide spatula. Place inverted platter over pie plate; invert potatoes onto platter. Cut into wedges to serve. Yield: 6 servings.

A Taste for Politics: Lyndon B. Johnson
Congressman from Texas 1937–1948

Jack Maguire was a young reporter for the Denison Herald *and the sole occupant of the editorial office late one afternoon in 1940. A tall, curly-headed man came in and announced: "My name is Lyndon Johnson and I'd like to buy somebody a cup of coffee." That cup of coffee began a 33-year friendship.*

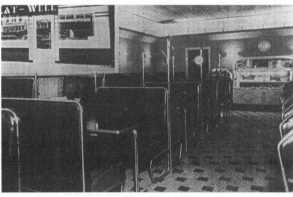

The two walked down the street to the Eat-Well Cafe and talked about "Mr. Sam". Legendary Sam Rayburn served 48 years in Washington, first as a congressman, then as Speaker of the House.

Johnson had come to Denison to board the Katy Railroad's Texas Special. He knew "Mr. Sam" planned to be on that train for Washington. Johnson wanted those two nights and a day on the Pullman to visit with the man who would so significantly influence his life on the way to the Presidency.

Lemon Herb Potatoes

6   small baking potatoes
1/3 cup chopped onions
1   clove garlic, minced
2   tablespoons margarine
1/2 cup hot skim milk
1   teaspoon grated lemon zest

1/8 teaspoon ground white pepper
1   tablespoon chopped fresh dill or
     1 teaspoon dried dill weed
1   tablespoon finely chopped parsley
     Paprika

Bake potatoes until done. While cooling enough to handle, sauté onions and garlic in margarine until tender. Cut a slice from top of each potato; carefully remove insides. Mash potatoes and beat in onion mixture, hot milk, lemon zest and pepper. Add dill and parsley. Fill potato skins with mashed potato mixture; sprinkle with paprika. Bake at 400 degrees about 30 minutes or until lightly browned. Yield: 6 servings.

Rosy Potatoes

6   carrots
6   potatoes
3   cloves of garlic, chopped

Melted butter
Salt and pepper to taste
Milk, optional

Peel and slice carrots and potatoes; cover with water; add chopped garlic and boil for 20 minutes or until done. Drain; save cooking liquid; mash vegetables, adding back cooking liquid or use enough milk instead to make moist mashed potatoes. Add melted butter, salt and pepper to taste.

Snowy Mashed Potato Casserole

4   pounds potatoes (12 medium)
1   cup sour cream
8   ounces cream cheese
2   teaspoons salt
1/8 teaspoon black pepper

1   clove garlic, crushed
1/4 cup chopped chives
1/2 teaspoon paprika
1   tablespoon butter or margarine

Cook potatoes in boiling salted water in a large kettle for 15 minutes or until tender; drain. Put potatoes in a large mixing bowl, add sour cream, cream cheese, salt, pepper and garlic. Beat at high speed until smooth and light. Stir in chopped chives. Pour into a greased 10 cup baking dish; sprinkle with paprika and dot with butter. Bake at 350 degrees for 30 minutes or until lightly golden and heated through. Yield: 12 servings.

The Adolphus Hotel Scalloped Potatoes

4	baking potatoes	½	cup half and half
½	ounce butter	1	pint heavy cream
½	clove garlic, finely minced		Salt, pepper and nutmeg to taste
3	eggs		

Peel and thinly slice potatoes. Butter bottom of a 5-inch square baking pan. Sprinkle with garlic. Layer potatoes in pan evenly and press down firmly. Pan should be ½ full. Combine eggs, half and half and cream; beat until smooth. Season with spices; pour over potatoes until pan is ¾ full. Cover with foil; bake at 225 degrees about 3 hours, until tender. Remove foil; bake at 325 degrees about 15 minutes until top is golden brown.

Ivy Blue Bed and Breakfast
Scalloped Potatoes

Southern hospitality at the IVY BLUE, a bed and breakfast inn, recreates turn of the century charm and pleasure. The lovely Victorian home, built in 1899 for Dr. Julian C. Fields, features south-facing windows in every room. Original stained glass windows and historical reproductions of fine wall coverings and fabrics reflect the careful restoration.

6-8	potatoes, peeled and sliced	4	green onions, chopped
1	(10¾ ounce) can cream of mushroom soup	½	stick of butter
1	cup Cheddar cheese	16	ounces sour cream
			Grapenuts

Cook potatoes until soft but NOT mushy; drain. In a pan, melt soup, cheese, onions and butter. After sauce is melted, turn heat off and add sour cream; mix well. Spray a 9 x 13-inch pan with a nonstick cooking spray; layer potatoes in pan. Pour sauce over potatoes. Top with a sprinkling of grapenuts. Bake at 325 degrees for 1 hour.

Pommes Anna

1 cup melted butter, divided
4 white potatoes, peeled, sliced and placed in water
1 acorn squash, halved, seeded, peeled and sliced
1 butternut squash, halved lengthwise, seeded, peeled and sliced

3 Granny Smith apples, cored, peeled, and sliced
1 teaspoon dried thyme
Salt and pepper to taste

Completely cover bottom of pan with some of the butter. Pat and dry potatoes with paper towels. Place a layer of potatoes in concentric circles on bottom of pan. Follow with other vegetables and apples sprinkling with thyme, butter, salt and pepper between each layer. Mound layers high; weight down with a heavy skillet or other oven safe object. Bake at 375 degrees until golden brown, approximately 1 hour. Let cool a little; pour off excess butter. Invert onto a platter. Yield: 6 to 8 servings.

Sweet Potato and Apple Casserole

3 thinly sliced medium sweet potatoes
2 large thinly sliced Rome apples
2-4 cups miniature marshmallows, according to preference
¾ cup sugar

1 teaspoon salt
1 teaspoon cinnamon
2 tablespoons corn starch
½ cup water
4 tablespoons margarine or butter

Spray a 9 x 13-inch baking dish with a nonstick cooking spray. Spread half the potatoes in the dish. Top with half the apples, then 1 cup of the marshmallows. Repeat layers. Combine sugar, salt and cinnamon; sprinkle on top. Dissolve corn starch in ½ cup of water; pour over casserole. Dot with butter. Cover with foil; bake at 350 degrees for 1 hour. Yield: 8 to 10 servings.

Savory Mashed Yams with Apple

4	medium yams, cooked and peeled		Dash of onion salt
6	tablespoons butter or margarine, divided	⅛	teaspoon ground thyme
			Pepper to taste
2	tablespoons chopped parsley	1	tablespoon lemon juice
¾	teaspoon salt	1	medium tart apple

Mash yams with 4 tablespoons butter, parsley, seasonings and lemon juice. Turn into a 9-inch pie plate; spread evenly. Cut apple into thin wedges; sauté in remaining butter for one minute. Arrange apple slices on yams. Pour melted butter on top. Bake at 375 degrees for 15 minutes.

Sweet Potatoes with Apples

3	medium size sweet potatoes (about 1 pound)	1	tablespoon plus 1 teaspoon margarine, divided
2	sweet apples	⅓	cup light brown sugar
			Pinch of nutmeg

Peel and slice sweet potatoes ¼ inch thick. Core and thinly slice apples. Preheat oven to 375 degrees. Grease a large pie pan with 1 teaspoon of margarine. Lay sweet potato and apple slices in the pan in a circle, alternating and overlapping the slices. Mix brown sugar and nutmeg together; sprinkle over potatoes and apples; dot with the remaining margarine. Cover with aluminum foil; bake for 35 minutes. Uncover; bake for 10 to 15 minutes longer or until potatoes are tender.

🕐 Parsley Rice

2	cups cooked rice	1	pound grated cheese
1	cup milk	1	egg, slightly beaten
2	tablespoons margarine	1	cup chopped fresh parsley
1	tablespoon garlic powder	¼	cup oil

Mix all ingredients; bake at 375 degrees for 30 minutes.

Sweet Potato Casserole

3 cups mashed sweet potatoes or 1 (23 ounce) can of yams	½ cup butter
1 cup sugar	⅓ cup milk
1 teaspoon vanilla extract	2 eggs, beaten

Combine all of the above ingredients; mix well.

Topping:

½ cup packed brown sugar	2½ tablespoons butter
¼ cup flour	½ cup chopped nuts

Mix well; sprinkle on potatoes. Bake at 350 degrees for 30 to 40 minutes.

Cashew Rice Pilaf

⅓ cup chopped onion	½ teaspoon salt
¼ cup butter, melted	½ cup chopped cashews
2 cups chicken broth	¼ cup chopped fresh parsley
1 cup long grain rice, uncooked	

Sauté onion in butter in a large skillet over medium high heat. Stir constantly until tender. Add chicken broth, rice and salt. Bring to a boil. Cover, reduce heat, and simmer 25 minutes or until rice is tender and liquid is absorbed. Remove from heat, and stir in cashews and parsley. Yield: 6 servings.

Baked Rice

4 tablespoons unsalted butter	1 sprig fresh tarragon
2 shallots, peeled and minced	3 cups chicken stock
2 cups long grain rice	2 tablespoons fresh tarragon leaves
Zest of 2 lemons	Salt and pepper to taste

Preheat oven to 400 degrees. Melt butter in a medium casserole and sauté shallots until tender, 3 to 4 minutes. Add rice and cook until translucent. Stir in half the lemon zest, tarragon sprig and stock. Cover casserole, place in oven and bake until liquid is absorbed and rice tender, about 20 to 25 minutes. Stir in remaining lemon zest and tarragon leaves. Season to taste.

German Sweet Rice

1	cup long grain white rice	Cinnamon
2	cups milk (at least)	½ stick margarine
	Sugar	

In a large saucepan over medium heat cook long grain white rice according to package directions. As water is absorbed, add milk. Continue adding milk as needed while cooking; stir frequently. Takes about 2 cups or more. Cook for 30 to 45 minutes or until done. Pour in serving bowl. Sprinkle top with sugar and cinnamon. Melt ½ stick margarine in skillet until browned. Pour over top. Although sweet, serve as a side dish. Yield: 4 to 6 servings.

Green Rice Casserole

1 cup shredded Monterey Jack cheese
1 cup ricotta cheese, optional
1 cup mayonnaise
½ teaspoon garlic salt
¼ teaspoon black pepper

3 cups cooked rice
1 (10 ounce) package frozen chopped broccoli, thawed and drained
1 cup frozen English peas, thawed
¼ cup sliced green onions

Combine first 5 ingredients. Stir in cooked rice. Add remaining ingredients. Spoon into a lightly greased 2-quart casserole. Bake uncovered at 375 degrees for 20 minutes.

Cornbread Dressing

1 cup chopped onion
1 cup chopped celery
½ cup margarine
1 cornbread recipe, cooked and crumbled
1 small can biscuits, cooked and torn
2 (15 ounce) cans chicken broth

1 chopped apple
1 teaspoon sage
2 boiled eggs
1 can mushrooms, drained
Salt and pepper
Parsley

Cook onion and celery in margarine. Combine all ingredients. Will look like thick cake batter, a little thicker than cornbread batter. Pour into a sprayed or greased 9 x 13-inch baking dish. Bake at 350 degrees for 1 hour or until slightly brown. Yield: 12 to 15 servings. Can be halved to serve fewer people.

🕐 Squash Dressing

2-3 cups yellow squash, cubed
    (crookneck variety)
1 small onion, diced
2 cups crumbled corn bread
2 tablespoons butter or margarine,
    melted

1 (10¾ ounce) can cream of
    chicken soup
1 teaspoon poultry seasoning
    (marjoram, thyme, sage)
Salt and pepper to taste

Cook squash and onion in enough water to simmer, about 1½ cups, until tender. Drain; reserving 1 cup of liquid. Mix all ingredients lightly; place in a 2-quart buttered casserole. Bake at 350 degrees for 30 minutes or until light golden brown. Yield: 6 to 8 servings.

🕐 Pineapple and Cheese Casserole

1 (20 ounce) can pineapple tidbits,
    drained
1 cup grated Cheddar cheese
3 tablespoons flour

½ cup sugar
½ cup butter, melted
1 tube round buttery crackers

Mix pineapple tidbits with the Cheddar cheese. Mix flour and sugar together and add to pineapple mixture. Put in casserole and melt ½ cup butter and pour over top with crushed crackers. Bake at 350 degrees for 30 minutes.

☽ Green Beans

⅓ pound bacon
1 medium onion, chopped
1 tablespoon dry mustard
2 tablespoons vinegar

½ cup brown sugar
Salt and pepper to taste
2 (14½ ounce) cans cut green beans
Juice from one can of the beans

Fry bacon until crisp; remove bacon, crumble and set aside. Sauté onion in bacon drippings. Add dry mustard, vinegar, brown sugar, salt, pepper, and juice from one can of beans. Mix together and pour over beans. Top with chopped bacon. Let sit overnight. Heat and serve.

Marinated Green Beans

2 cups sugar
1 cup apple cider vinegar
½ cup salad oil
1 green pepper, chopped
1 small onion, chopped

2 (14½ ounce) cans cut green beans, drained
2 (8¼ ounce) cans sliced carrots, drained
Salt and pepper to taste

Mix sugar, vinegar, and salad oil together until sugar is dissolved. Add green pepper, onion, beans, and carrots. Season with salt and pepper to taste. Let sit several hours to marinate.

☽ Marinated Asparagus

⅔ cup white vinegar
½ cup sugar
½ teaspoon salt
1 teaspoon whole cloves

3 sticks cinnamon
1 tablespoon celery seeds
½ cup water
3 tall cans of asparagus, drained

Bring all ingredients EXCEPT asparagus to a boil and pour over asparagus. Cover; refrigerate overnight or 12 to 24 hours. Serve cold.

Good for picnics, family meal or ladies' luncheon.

◔ Asparagus and Pea Casserole

1 (15 ounce) can asparagus, drained
1 (17 ounce) can small peas, drained
1 (10¾ ounce) can mushroom soup

1 (8 ounce) can chopped water chestnuts, drained
1½ cups sharp Cheddar cheese, shredded
1 cup bread crumbs

Mix all ingredients EXCEPT bread crumbs. Pour into a 9 x 11-inch buttered dish. Top with crumbs. Bake at 325 degrees until cheese is melted and top is brown, about 20 to 25 minutes.

Good for ladies' luncheon.

🕐 Asparagus in White Wine Au Gratin

2 pounds fresh asparagus	Salt and pepper to taste
6 tablespoons butter or margarine	⅓ cup Parmesan cheese
¼ cup dry white wine	

Remove tough ends of asparagus; cook in salted water until crisp tender. Place in casserole. Melt butter; combine with wine and pour over asparagus. Add salt and pepper. Sprinkle with cheese. Bake at 425 degrees about 10 minutes.

Corn-Onion Bake

3 eggs, separated	1 (14¾ ounce) can cream style corn
2 teaspoons sugar	1 (2.8 ounce) can French fried
1 teaspoon salt	onion rings, divided
¼ teaspoon pepper	

Beat egg yolks until thick and lemon colored. Add next 4 ingredients and blend well. Stir in 1 cup French fried onions. Fold in stiffly beaten egg whites. Pour mixture into a 1½-quart ungreased casserole dish. Bake, uncovered, at 350 degrees for 30 minutes or until firm. Top with remaining onions and bake 5 minutes longer. Serve immediately. Yield: 8 servings.

Broccoli and Corn Casserole

1 (16 ounce) can cream style corn	2 tablespoons butter
1 (10 ounce) package frozen chopped broccoli, cooked and drained	½ teaspoon salt Dash of black pepper
1 beaten egg	¼ cup cracker crumbs, about 6 crackers
1 teaspoon minced onion	1 tablespoon butter, melted
½ cup cracker crumbs, about 12 crackers	

Combine corn, broccoli, egg, minced onion, ½ cup cracker crumbs, 2 tablespoons butter, salt and pepper. Pour into a 1-quart casserole. Combine ¼ cup cracker crumbs and butter. Sprinkle on top of casserole. Bake, uncovered, at 350 degrees for 35 to 40 minutes.

Corn Rice Casserole

1	small onion, chopped	1	(2 ounce) jar pimentos, drained and chopped
1	small green pepper, chopped		
¼	cup margarine	1	(8 ounce) box processed cheese loaf, partially melted
2	(15¼ ounce) cans whole kernel corn, drained	2	cups cooked rice
			Salt and pepper to taste

In a large skillet, sauté onion and green pepper in margarine. Pour into a large casserole dish. Add remaining ingredients, stirring until well mixed. Bake at 350 degrees for 20 minutes.

Heavenly Corn

2	(10 ounce) packages whole kernel corn	¼	teaspoon seasoned salt flavor enhancer
½	pint whipping cream	6	teaspoons sugar
1	cup milk		Pinch of cayenne pepper
1	teaspoon salt	2	tablespoons melted butter
		2	tablespoons flour

Put all ingredients except butter and flour into a pan. Bring to a boil and simmer for 5 minutes. Blend butter and flour; mix with other mixture to thicken. Can be served as is or can be put in oven with cheese or bread crumbs on top. Yield: 8 servings.

Corn Casserole

½	stick margarine	¼	cup evaporated milk
8	ounces cream cheese		Cayenne pepper to taste
1	(14¾ ounce) can cream style corn	¼	teaspoon garlic powder or to taste
2	(15¼ ounce) cans whole kernel corn, drained	1	(4½ ounce) can chopped green chiles

Melt butter and cream cheese. Add remaining ingredients; mix well. Pour into baking dish and bake at 350 degrees for 30 minutes.

Zesty Black-Eyed Peas

2	(16 ounce) cans black-eyed peas, rinsed and drained	1	(4 ounce) jar diced pimentos, drained
1	cup chopped celery	1	(8 ounce) bottle Italian salad dressing
1	green pepper, chopped		Lettuce leaves
1	large tomato, peeled and chopped	3	slices bacon, cooked and crumbled
1	clove garlic, minced		
2	green onions, sliced		
1	(4 ounce) jar sliced mushrooms, drained		

Combine first 9 ingredients in a large bowl; toss. Cover and chill at least 8 hours (stir occasionally); drain. Spoon into a lettuce lined bowl. Garnish with bacon. Yield: 8 servings.

Tuscan White Beans with Sage

3-4	slices bacon	1-2	teaspoons rubbed sage
1	small onion, sliced	2	(16 ounce) cans small white navy beans, rinsed & drained
3	cloves garlic, crushed		

In a skillet, fry bacon until crisp. Remove and cool; then crumble. In bacon drippings, sauté onion, garlic and sprinkle with sage. Add bacon crumbles and beans. Stir and heat through. Yield: 6 servings.

🕐 Spinach and Garlic Sauté

2	tablespoons unsalted butter	1	pound fresh spinach, trimmed, washed and well drained
1	clove garlic, peeled and minced		Salt and pepper to taste

Melt butter in a large frying pan over medium heat. Add garlic and cook for 2 minutes. Add spinach and sauté over high heat until wilted. Remove from heat. Season and serve at once.

❄ *Broccoli Rice Casserole*

2 cups instant rice	1 (4 ounce) jar of pimentos
1 stick butter or margarine	1 (4 ounce) can sliced water
2 (10 ounce) packages chopped	chestnuts, diced
broccoli	½ pound grated Cheddar cheese,
2 (10¾ ounce) cans cream of	divided
mushroom soup	Salt and pepper to taste
½ onion, grated	

Cook rice according to directions on box. Add one stick of butter or margarine to cooked rice; stir until melted. Cook broccoli 5 minutes; drain well. Mix cooked rice, broccoli, soup, onion, pimentos, water chestnuts, ¼ pound grated cheese, salt and pepper. Place in large greased casserole dish. Top with remaining cheese. Bake at 350 degrees for 30 minutes. This dish freezes well.

Fried Rice

1 cup cooked rice, cooled	1 clove garlic, crushed
6 tablespoons vegetable oil	3 scallions, chopped
2 eggs, slightly beaten	Salt to taste
2 tablespoons soy sauce	1½ cups roast pork, chopped, cooked
¼ teaspoon seasoned salt flavor	shrimp or lobster
enhancer	

Sauté rice in vegetable oil for 3 to 4 minutes. Add eggs and stir until blended with rice, leaving little pieces discernible. Lower heat; add remaining ingredients. Cook, stirring occasionally until brown. When ready to serve, heat through. Yield: 4 servings.

◷ *Broccoli or Spinach Casserole*

2 (10 ounce) packages frozen	1 (2.8 ounce) can French fried
broccoli or spinach	onion rings
1 (10¾ ounce) can cream of	Salt and pepper to taste
mushroom soup	1 stick melted margarine
8 ounces cream cheese, softened	Baked cheese snack crackers

Cook vegetables as directed. Heat soup and cream cheese; mix all together, including onion rings. Add salt and pepper to taste. Pour into a greased or sprayed 2-quart casserole. Top with butter and cracker crumbs. Bake at 350 degrees for 20 minutes.

Broccoli Soufflé

1 tablespoon flour
1 tablespoon butter, melted
2 cups cream or evaporated milk
½ teaspoon salt

½ cup mayonnaise
2 cups cooked broccoli, mashed or finely chopped
3 eggs, well beaten

Preheat oven to 375 degrees. Make white sauce of flour, butter, cream and salt. While still warm, add mayonnaise. Combine with broccoli. Add beaten eggs to mixture. Pour into a well buttered 9- inch square baking dish. Place in a pan of hot water and steam bake for 55 minutes. Yield: 9 to 10 servings. This dish is not temperamental! It will not fall and may be cut into squares to serve.

◔ Wonderful Red Cabbage

7 cups red cabbage, sliced
6 slices bacon
3 tablespoons flour
3 tablespoons brown sugar

¾ cup water
⅔ cup vinegar
Salt and pepper to taste
1 small white onion, sliced

Boil cabbage for 7 minutes; drain. Fry bacon; drain and crumble. Add flour and sugar to bacon grease; stir until smooth. Add water, vinegar, salt and pepper to taste; cook until thick. Add onion, bacon and cabbage; heat through.

Bill and George Blankenship and Dick and Grady Hart grew up in what became one of the finer residential neighborhoods of Denison. Ernest Fritts planted many acres of cantaloupes and watermelons in the same area. And, yes, the boys regularly pillaged the patches.

Trying to protect his crop one year, Mr. Fritts told the boys he would GIVE each of them one watermelon and two cantaloupes if they would promise to leave his fields alone. Accepting the offer, the enterprising boys immediately opened a stand to sell their produce. Sales were so good they soon had only one cantaloupe left to sell.

A woman stopped to buy. Grady (or was it Dick?) held the cantaloupe up for her inspection. "Oh," she said, "I really wanted a bigger one!" The crafty little Hart boy hid the cantaloupe under the stand and a few minutes later brought up the same cantaloupe. "How about this one?" he asked. "Oh, yes," the lady answered. "That's perfect. I think I'll take both of them!!"

Herbed Spinach Casserole

1   (10 ounce) package frozen,
    chopped spinach
1   cup cooked rice
1   cup shredded Cheddar cheese
2   eggs, slightly beaten
2   tablespoons melted butter or
    margarine

⅓   cup milk
2   tablespoons chopped onion
½   teaspoon Worcestershire sauce
¼   teaspoon ground thyme
    Salt and pepper to taste

Cook and drain spinach. In a bowl, mix spinach with remaining ingredients. Pour
into a greased or sprayed casserole and bake at 350 degrees about 25 minutes or until
knife comes out clean. May add additional cheese on top prior to baking.

Fruit Stuffed Acorn Squash

2   small acorn squash
1   cup boiling water
1   medium chopped apple
¼   cup orange juice

1   tablespoon brown sugar
1   teaspoon margarine, melted
¼   teaspoon nutmeg
½   teaspoon cinnamon

Cut squash in half and remove seeds. Place cut side down in shallow baking dish with
boiling water. Cover, bake at 350 degrees for 35 to 45 minutes until tender; drain.
Mix remaining ingredients and spoon into squash halves. Cover and bake 15 minutes.

The Best Squash Soufflé

2   pounds squash (yellow or
    zucchini), peeled and cubed
1   onion, sliced
3   tablespoons butter or margarine
3   eggs, beaten

1   (10¾ ounce) can cream of
    mushroom soup
¾   teaspoon salt
½   teaspoon black pepper
    Parmesan cheese
    Round buttery crackers, crumbled

Cook squash and onion until tender. Drain and mash with butter. Fold in remaining
ingredients. Place in a buttered casserole; top with cracker crumbs and Parmesan
cheese. Bake at 300 degrees for 30 minutes. Yield: 6 to 8 servings.

Poppy Seed Zucchini

¼ cup butter
4   cups sliced zucchini
⅓ cup chopped onion
½ cup sour cream

1   teaspoon salt
2   teaspoons paprika
2   teaspoons poppy seeds

Melt butter, add zucchini and onion. Cover and cook until tender. Mix remaining ingredients. Stir gently into squash mixture and heat through. Do not boil. Yield: 4 servings.

Baked Fresh Vegetable Medley

3-4 carrots, sliced
3   each yellow squash and zucchini, sliced
4   tablespoons margarine
¼ cup chopped onion
2   stalks celery, sliced

8   mushrooms, sliced
1   (14½ ounce) can diced tomatoes, drained
8   ounces Monterey Jack cheese, grated
    Salt and pepper to taste

Prepare vegetables; steam carrots for 15 minutes, add squash and steam 15 minutes more. Drain; set aside and cool. Sauté onion and celery with sliced mushrooms in margarine. Combine all vegetables; mix well. Put into a greased or sprayed baking dish and sprinkle with Monterey Jack cheese. Bake at 350 degrees for 20 minutes.

Cranberries A la Brandy

4   cups fresh cranberries
2¼ cups sugar, divided

¼ cup brandy

Put cranberries into a shallow pan and sprinkle with 2 cups sugar. Bake at 350 degrees for 30 minutes; stir occasionally. Remove from oven and stir in brandy and ¼ cup sugar; chill. Serve with turkey, ham, or pork.

Zucchini Pie

4 cups thinly sliced zucchini (unpeeled)	¼ teaspoon garlic powder
1 cup chopped onion	½ teaspoon basil leaves
½ stick butter or margarine	¼ teaspoon oregano
2 tablespoons parsley flakes	2 eggs, beaten
½ teaspoon salt	2 cups shredded mozzarella cheese
½ teaspoon black pepper	1 (8 ounce) can Crescent dinner rolls

Cook zucchini and onion in butter until tender, about 10 minutes. Stir in spices. Blend eggs and cheese in a large bowl; stir in vegetable mix. Make pie crust with rolls. Pour vegetable mix in evenly. Bake at 375 degrees for 18 to 20 minutes. Let stand 10 minutes before serving.

Line an 8 x 12-inch baking dish with dinner rolls and add 1 pound of browned sausage, crumbled and drained. Pour vegetable and egg mixture over sausage. Remaining instructions are the same.

◷ Squash Casserole

3 pounds yellow squash, sliced	1 (4 ounce) jar chopped pimentos
2 medium onions, chopped	1 stick margarine, melted
1 (10¾ ounce) can cream of chicken soup	1 (8 ounce) package cornbread dressing mix
8 ounces sour cream	2 cups Cheddar cheese, grated
1 (8 ounce) can water chestnuts, drained	Salt and pepper to taste

Cook squash with onion in small amount of water until done; drain. Combine soup, sour cream, water chestnuts and pimento. Gently fold in cooked squash. Drizzle melted margarine over dressing mix. Put half of dressing mix into a greased or sprayed 9 x 13-inch baking dish. Spread squash mixture over crumb mixture. Sprinkle with grated cheese. Put remaining dressing mix on top. Bake at 350 degrees for 30 minutes.

Zucchini Jack Casserole

4	eggs	1	(7 ounce) can green chiles, sliced
½	cup milk	16	ounces shredded Monterey Jack cheese
1	teaspoon salt		
2	teaspoons baking powder	2	pounds zucchini, sliced crosswise about ¼ inch thick (about 7 cups)
3	tablespoons flour		
¼	cup parsley		
1	clove garlic, minced	1	cup seasoned croutons
1	small onion, chopped	3	tablespoons melted butter

Beat together the eggs, milk, salt, baking powder and flour. Combine parsley, garlic, onion, green chiles and cheese; add to egg mixture. Layer sliced zucchini into a 9 x 13-inch greased baking dish. Pour egg mixture over zucchini. Toss 1 cup of seasoned croutons and 3 tablespoons melted butter; sprinkle on top. Bake at 350 degrees for 35 minutes or until set. Let stand 10 minutes before serving.

Vegetable Casserole

½	cup diced onion	1	cup white shoepeg corn, well drained
½	cup diced celery		
½	cup diced green pepper	1	(14½ ounce) can French-style green beans
1	cup sour cream		
	Dash of pepper (NO salt)	1	(10¾ ounce) can cream of celery soup

Mix together and place in greased casserole.

Topping

1	stick margarine, melted	1	(10 ounce) box baked cheese snack crackers, crumbled

Mix together and spread on top of vegetable mixture. Bake at 375 degrees for 45 minutes. Yield: 12 servings.

⊙ Baked Mixed Vegetable Casserole

2 pound bag of frozen mixed vegetables	1½ cups mayonnaise
1 onion, chopped	1 roll crumbled round buttery crackers
1 cup chopped celery	1 stick melted margarine
4 tablespoons margarine	1½ cups sharp Cheddar cheese

Cook vegetables per instructions on bag; drain. Sauté onion and celery in margarine; add to cooked mixed vegetables. Stir in mayonnaise. Put into a greased or sprayed 9 x 13-inch baking dish. Top with crackers. Drizzle with one stick melted margarine; sprinkle 1½ cups shredded cheese. Bake at 350 degrees for 20 to 30 minutes until heated through and cheese melts.

⊙ Roasted Mixed Vegetables

2 pounds assorted fresh vegetables (potatoes, carrots, zucchini, green and red peppers, broccoli, cauliflower) cut into 1 inch chunks or strips	2 tablespoons olive or vegetable oil
	1 envelope (or less) herb flavored recipe soup mix

Toss all ingredients in a bowl or plastic bag. Put into a greased or sprayed 9 x 13-inch baking dish. Bake at 450 degrees for 20 to 30 minutes or until tender. Yield: 6 servings.

Noodles Romanoff

8 ounces egg noodles, cooked	½ teaspoon salt
2 tablespoons butter	½ teaspoon Worcestershire sauce
1 cup ricotta cheese	Dash hot pepper sauce
8 ounces sour cream	1 cup Parmesan cheese
1 teaspoon minced dried onions	

Over medium heat, melt butter. Add ricotta cheese, sour cream, dried onion, salt, Worcestershire and hot pepper sauce. Mix well. Pour over noodles and sprinkle with Parmesan cheese. Bake at 400 degrees for 10 minutes.

Confetti Pepper Relish

2	sweet red peppers, seeded and chopped	1	jalapeño pepper, chopped
2	green peppers, seeded and chopped	½	cup white vinegar
1	large onion, chopped	½	cup sugar
		¼	teaspoon salt

Combine red and green peppers, onion and jalapeño pepper in a large pot; add boiling water to cover mixture. Let stand 5 minutes; drain. Combine vinegar, sugar and salt; bring to a boil until sugar dissolves; stir occasionally. Add to pepper mixture; pour in glass jar or jars. Chill and serve. Yield: 1 quart. Will last approximately 2 to 3 weeks in the refrigerator.

Herb Butter

½	cup butter, softened	2	tablespoons chopped parsley
1	tablespoon lemon juice	1	tablespoon chopped chives
½	teaspoon salt	½	teaspoon tarragon leaves
⅛	teaspoon pepper		

Cream butter. Beat in the rest of ingredients until smooth. Chill. Serve on grilled steak.

Strawberry Butter

¾	cup frozen strawberries, thawed and drained	1	cup butter, softened
		3	tablespoons confectioner's sugar

Mix ingredients in blender until smooth; chill. Serve with warm bread or rolls.

Wine Butter

1	tablespoon minced green onion	2	teaspoons chopped parsley
1	cup dry red wine		Salt and pepper to taste
½	cup butter, softened		

Cook onion and wine in small saucepan until the liquid is reduced to ¼ cup. Remove from heat; cool. With beaters, cream butter and parsley. Gradually beat in the wine mixture. Season to taste with salt and pepper; chill. Serve on grilled steak.

Onion Preserves

2	tablespoons unsalted butter	4	teaspoons dark brown sugar
3	tablespoons olive oil	⅛	teaspoon balsamic vinegar
2	onions, peeled, halved and thinly sliced lengthwise	⅓	cup dry red wine
			Salt and pepper to taste

Heat butter and oil in a heavy skillet and cook the onions over low heat until softened but not browned, approximately 20 minutes. Sprinkle with brown sugar. Lower heat and cook until evenly browned. Stir in vinegar and wine; simmer until liquids are completely absorbed. Season to taste. Delicious served with roasts and pork tenderloin.

A visual essay: the inside of the Safeway grocery store in 1935, from an undated clipping from **The Denison Herald**.

Sugar Bottom

*S*outh of Denison's Main Street where the railroad crossed Armstrong Avenue, Sugar Bottom was a tight knit neighborhood renowned for its independence and civic pride. What a name! And plenty of versions of how it came to be:

- A farmer wrecked his wagon loaded with barrels of sugar, spilling the sweet stuff all over the street.
- A Katy train pulling sugar-filled tank cars derailed at the Armstrong Avenue crossing, dumping the sugar on the tracks.
- At a dance one night, the floor was unwaxed, so sugar was spread on the floor allowing the dancers' feet to slide over the surface.
- Sweet water flowed in a creek just to the east of Armstrong Avenue.
- A madam named Sugar operated a brothel on the east side of the street. Cowboys coming into town liked to go down to the bottom land to see Sugar.
- A grocer named Gideon Stephens had a run-in with some Huckleberry Gang toughs from Skiddy Street. One night they broke into his store and rolled several wooden barrels of sugar outside, letting them smash on the roadway.

Which is the real story? Ah, sweet mystery.

Desserts

Old Fashioned Apple Crisp

4	cups sliced sweet apples, peeled or unpeeled	¼	cup water
1	teaspoon cinnamon	¾	cup sifted flour
½	teaspoon salt	1	cup sugar
		⅓	cup butter

Place apples in a buttered 6 x 10-inch baking dish. Sprinkle with cinnamon, salt and water. In a bowl mix until crumbly the flour, sugar and butter. Spread mixture over apples. Bake at 350 degrees for 40 minutes. Yield: 6 servings. Serve warm with cream, whipped cream or ice cream.

Arrena picked up a bucket on her way to the spring not far from her door. Having water so near was a real blessing. In 1866 she and her husband, John Kinsey Miller, bought 500 acres of the surrounding land.

When Arrena reached the spring, she discovered an Indian with a broken leg. Overcoming her knowledge of Indian scares, she quickly tore strips from her apron and bound his leg. When she went to get help, the Indian slipped away.

After the first fall cold snap, Arrena and John found a dressed deer hanging from a nail on their porch with a piece of Arrena's apron tied around it's leg. The Indian knew the age old way of saying thank you: a gift of food.

In 1872, the Denison Town Company purchased enough Miller acreage for a city. The Millers generously donated land for downtown Forest Park, every church in town and the first free graded public school in Texas.

Miller and his sons built their two room dogtrot house of oak logs over a stone cellar with gun ports for defense in Indian attacks.

Cheryl's Apple Torte

Pastry

½ cup margarine, softened
⅓ cup sugar

¼ teaspoon vanilla extract
1 cup flour

Cream margarine and sugar in a small bowl. Stir in vanilla and flour; mix well. Spread in bottom and 2 inches up the sides of a well greased springform pan.

Filling

1 (8 ounce) package cream cheese, softened
¼ cup sugar

1 egg
½ teaspoon vanilla extract

Combine cheese and sugar. Add egg and vanilla; mix well. Spread filling evenly over pastry.

Apple Topping

4 cups peeled and sliced apples
⅓ cup sugar

½ teaspoon cinnamon
½ cup chopped pecans

Place apples in a dish with sugar and cinnamon; stir to coat. Spoon topping over filling. Sprinkle with nuts. Bake at 425 degrees for 10 minutes. Reduce to 400 degrees and bake 25 minutes more. Cool before removing from pan.

Stern-looking ladies of the Denison Women's Christian Temperance Union gathered one warm day in the late 1890's to dedicate this water fountain in honor of Mrs. Sarah Acheson. Erected on the corner of Main and Rusk, it was expected to provide alternate refreshment to the flourishing saloon trade. In 1926 the fountain was moved to Forest Park but its whereabouts today is a mystery.

☽ Cappuccino Torte

Scrumptious! This recipe may be involved but is WELL WORTH it and lives up to the promise of its name.

Crust
4	whole graham crackers	¼	cup sugar
½	cup chopped walnuts, about 2 ounces		Pinch of salt
½	cup blanched slivered almonds, about 2 ounces	5	tablespoons unsalted butter, melted and cooled

Preheat oven to 350 degrees. Butter a 10-inch diameter springform pan with 2¾ inch high sides. Grind graham crackers to crumbs in processor. Add nuts, sugar and salt; chop coarsely using on/off turns. Add butter and process until crumbs are evenly moistened. Press crumbs into bottom of prepared pan. Bake until edges begin to brown, about 15 minutes. Cool.

Fudge Layer
2	cups whipping cream	2	tablespoons light corn syrup
1	pound semisweet chocolate, finely chopped	1	stick unsalted butter, cut into 8 pieces, room temperature

Bring cream to boil in heavy medium saucepan. Reduce heat to low. Add chocolate; stir until melted. Remove from heat. Mix in corn syrup. Add butter one piece at a time; stir until smooth. Cool to lukewarm, stirring occasionally. Pour fudge into cooled crust. Refrigerate until firm, about 2 hours.

Cappuccino Buttercream Layer
2½	cups golden brown sugar, firmly packed, about 1¼ pounds	4	ounces unsweetened chocolate, chopped, melted, cooled to lukewarm
½	cup water		Coffee Whipped Cream, recipe follows
6	egg yolks		
3	sticks unsalted butter, cut into 12 pieces, room temperature	2	ounces semisweet chocolate, grated
1	tablespoon expresso powder dissolved in 1 teaspoon hot water		Chocolate shavings, optional
			Chocolate coffee bean candies, optional

Cook sugar and water in heavy medium saucepan over very low heat, stirring until sugar dissolves (avoid scraping sides of pan). Increase heat to medium; boil 2 minutes. Meanwhile, beat yolks in heavy-duty mixer at high speed until thick. With mixer running, gradually pour boiling syrup into yolks (do NOT scrape saucepan). Continue to beat until yolk mixture is cool, about 15 minutes. Reduce mixer speed to

Cappuccino Torte continued

medium. Mix in butter 1 piece at a time. Add expresso mixture, then melted chocolate. Spread buttercream over chilled fudge layer. Cover pan loosely with waxed paper. Refrigerate overnight.

Coffee Whipped Cream

1¼ cups chilled whipping cream,
    divided
2 teaspoons instant expresso
    powder

½ teaspoon vanilla extract
2 tablespoons powdered sugar

Combine 1 tablespoon whipping cream, expresso powder and vanilla in a small bowl; stir until powder dissolves. Beat remaining cream in large bowl until beginning to thicken. Mix in coffee mixture and powdered sugar. Beat whipping cream mixture to firm peaks.

Make this a day in advance so the cake has time to set for easier slicing, but add whipped cream and garnish on the day it is served.

Run a small sharp knife around sides of springform pan to loosen torte. Carefully release pan sides. Spread most of Coffee Whipped Cream neatly over top and sides of torte. Press grated chocolate around sides. Transfer to serving platter. Transfer remaining cream to pastry bag fitted with medium star tip. Pipe cream in rosettes around top edge of torte. Garnish with chocolate shavings and coffee bean candies if desired. Can be prepared 6 to 8 hours ahead; refrigerate. Let stand 1 hour at room temperature and serve.

⧖ *Peach Mousse*

1 cup sliced peaches
⅓ cup sugar
3 tablespoons honey

Dash of salt
1 teaspoon almond extract
1 pint whipping cream, whipped

Combine all ingredients except cream in mixing bowl and place in refrigerator. When thoroughly chilled, fold whipped cream into peach mixture. Put into pie plate, cover with foil and freeze.

A Dining Car Menu for an

A Dining Car Menu for an

Elegant Bridal Shower

Calla Lily Sandwiches
Fresh Berry Tartlets
Chocolate Truffles
Sweet Ravioli
Curried Chicken Balls
Cocktail Puffs
Almond Punch

🕐 Aunt Mary's Baked Apples

5	cooking apples	½	cup bread crumbs
½	cup cranberries	1	teaspoon cinnamon
½	cup chopped walnuts		Zest of 1 lemon
½	cup brown sugar	5	tablespoons unsalted butter

Preheat oven to 375 degrees. Wash and core apples; remove ½ inch from the bottom of each so they sit flat in a roaster. Combine all other ingredients. Stuff apples with filling, generously mounding on top. Bake for 25 to 30 minutes, or until filling is cooked and bubbly.

Banana Pudding Supreme

8	ounces cream cheese, softened	1	(8 ounce) carton frozen whipped dessert topping, thawed
1	(14 ounce) can sweetened condensed milk	4	bananas, sliced
2	cups milk	1	(12 ounce) box vanilla wafers
1	(6 ounce) package instant vanilla pudding mix		

Cream the cheese until smooth; stir in sweetened condensed milk. Mix 2 cups milk with the pudding mix; stir into first mixture. Fold in ¾ of the whipped dessert topping. Layer pudding, cookies, and bananas in a dish. Top with remaining topping; chill. Yield: about 12 servings.

⧗ Creamy Mocha Frozen Dessert

2	teaspoons instant coffee granules	2	(8 ounce) packages cream cheese, softened
1	tablespoon hot water		
1	cup cream-filled chocolate cookie crumbs	1	(14 ounce) can sweetened condensed milk
¾	cup chopped pecans, divided	½	cup chocolate-flavored syrup
¼	cup melted butter or margarine	8	ounces frozen whipped dessert topping, thawed

In a small bowl, dissolve coffee granules in hot water; set aside. In another bowl, combine cookie crumbs, ½ cup pecans and butter; pat into the bottom of a 9 x 13-inch baking pan. In a mixing bowl, beat cream cheese until light and fluffy. Blend in coffee mixture, milk and chocolate syrup. Fold in whipped dessert topping; spread over crust. Sprinkle remaining pecans on top; freeze. Yield: 24 servings.

🕐 Frozen Raspberry Dessert

Crust

2	cups crushed chocolate wafer cookies	¼	cup sugar
⅓	cup melted margarine		Fudge or chocolate ice cream sauce

Mix first 3 ingredients well. Reserve ¼ cup for topping. Press remaining ingredients in a 9 x 13-inch pan. Drizzle fudge or chocolate ice cream sauce on crust as desired. Refrigerate 15 minutes.

Filling

1	(12 ounce) package frozen raspberries without syrup	1	pint raspberry sherbet, softened
1	quart vanilla ice cream, softened	8	ounces frozen whipped dessert topping, thawed

Chop raspberries while still frozen in a nut chopper. Divide in half, return one half to freezer for use at another time. Spoon vanilla ice cream over crust; carefully smooth out. Spoon raspberry sherbet over ice cream then swirl gently with a knife. Top with chopped raspberries and gently press raspberries into sherbet. Return to freezer for 15 minutes or longer. Top with whipped dessert topping. Sprinkle remaining crumbs on top and return to freezer. Remove from freezer 15 minutes before slicing. Yield: 15 to 20 servings.

Oreo Cookie Dessert

18-20	chocolate sandwich cookies	2	small cans evaporated milk (1¼ cups)
1	stick butter, softened and divided	8	tablespoons cocoa
½	gallon vanilla ice cream, softened	2	tablespoons vanilla extract
2	cups sugar	8	ounces frozen whipped dessert topping, thawed
			Chopped nuts

In a food processor, mix cookies and ½ stick butter. Press into a buttered 9 x 13-inch pan; freeze. Spread ice cream on cookie crust and return to freezer until ice cream hardens. While ice cream is re-freezing, in a saucepan, mix together the sugar, evaporated milk, cocoa and remaining butter. Boil 3 to 4 minutes, stirring constantly. Remove from heat; add vanilla and cool. Spread over ice cream and freeze. When frozen, top with whipped dessert topping and nuts. Remove from freezer 10 minutes before serving.

Angel Pineapple Cake

1	package one-step angel food cake mix	1	(20 ounce) can crushed pineapple, do NOT drain
			Powdered sugar, optional

Stir first 2 ingredients together (do NOT beat); mix well. Bake in a tube pan according to directions on box. Cool; sprinkle with powdered sugar. Must use a ONE-STEP cake mix. Quick and Easy.

Heavenly Delight

1½	cups flour	2	(3.4 ounce) packages instant chocolate pudding
1½	cups margarine, softened	1	(3.4 ounce) package vanilla pudding
1	cup chopped nuts		
8	ounces cream cheese	4½	cups milk
1	cup powdered sugar	1	carton whipped dessert topping
1	cup frozen whipped dessert topping, thawed	1	chocolate bar, grated

Preheat oven to 325 degrees. Mix flour, margarine and nuts together and press into a 9 x 13-inch baking dish. Bake for 20 minutes; cool. Mix cream cheese, powdered sugar and whipped dessert topping together and pour over the first layer when cool. For third layer, mix puddings with milk and pour on top. Top with 1 carton whipped dessert topping and grated chocolate bar.

⌛ *Strawberry Freeze*

1 cup all-purpose flour	1 cup sugar
½ cup chopped pecans	2 teaspoons fresh lemon juice
¼ cup firmly packed brown sugar	2 egg whites
½ cup butter or margarine, melted	1 cup whipping cream, whipped
1 (10 ounce) package frozen	Sliced fresh strawberries,
strawberries, thawed	optional

Combine flour, pecans, brown sugar and butter in an 8-inch square baking pan; stir well. Bake at 350 degrees for 20 minutes, stirring occasionally; cool. Combine strawberries, sugar, lemon juice and egg whites in a large mixing bowl; beat at high speed with mixer 10 to 12 minutes or until stiff peaks form. Fold in whipped cream. Press about two-thirds of crumb mixture into a 9-inch springform pan; spoon in strawberry mixture. Sprinkle remaining crumbs on top; freeze until firm. Garnish with fresh strawberries, if desired. Yield: 8 to 10 servings.

Strawberries Romanoff

¼ cup sugar	2 tablespoons orange flavored
¼ cup orange flavored liqueur	liqueur
4 cups whole strawberries, hulled	⅛ teaspoon ground cinnamon
1 cup whipping cream	⅓ cup sour cream
2 tablespoons sugar	3 tablespoons chopped pistachios
	or toasted almonds

Combine ¼ cup sugar and ¼ cup orange flavored liqueur in a large bowl; stir until sugar dissolves. Add strawberries; toss gently and set aside. Beat whipping cream until foamy; gradually add 2 tablespoons sugar, 2 tablespoons orange flavored liqueur and cinnamon, beating until soft peaks form. Fold in sour cream. Spoon strawberries and syrup into serving dishes. Top each with a dollop of cream mixture; sprinkle with nuts. Yield: 8 servings.

The party was picture perfect. On a sunny May afternoon in 1985, Dr. and Mrs. Calixto Romero welcomed 600 guests to their Spanish style mansion.

Distinguished guest of honor was Dr. Christian Bernard, pioneer South African heart surgeon, whose mission was to make arrangements to perform the first piggy-back heart transplant. Denison patient Lyndle Hill traveled to South Africa for the trailblazing surgery.

For the caterers, Alonzo and Carrie Cole, this particular party holds a place of pride in their repertoire. Alonzo says, "It was through 'Miss Betsy' Munson that I got to do a lot of parties in the private homes of most of Denison's aristocrats". Their party foods and smiling service were impeccable.

**On the leafy terrace overlooking the pool,
Drs. Calixto Romero, Fernando Soto, Mario Bonilla,
and Christian Bernard visit with Alonzo Cole.**

◷ Dede's Delight

1 angel food cake, torn into pieces	2 packages frozen blackberries,
12 ounces frozen whipped dessert	thawed
topping, thawed	

Mix whipped dessert topping and blackberries together; fold in cake. This is an excellent low-fat dessert.

Taste berries. If tart, sprinkle with a little sugar or sweetener.

Milky Way Cake

8 (1⅞ ounce) Milky Way bars	1 teaspoon vanilla extract
½ cup butter	1¼ cups buttermilk
2 cups sugar	½ teaspoon baking soda
½ cup butter	3 cups flour
4 eggs	1 cup chopped pecans

Preheat oven to 325 degrees. Place candy bars and ½ cup butter in saucepan over low heat and melt, stirring constantly; cool. Cream sugar and ½ cup butter. Add eggs, one at a time, beating well after each addition. Add vanilla. Combine buttermilk and soda; add to creamed mixture alternately with flour. Stir in melted candy bars and chopped pecans. Pour into a greased and floured tube pan. Bake for 1 hour and 20 minutes. Let cool in pan 1 hour. Remove to wire rack.

Icing

2½ cups sugar	1 (6 ounce) package semisweet
½ cup butter	chocolate pieces
1 cup evaporated milk	1 cup marshmallow cream

Combine sugar, butter and milk; cook over medium heat to soft ball stage. Remove from heat; add chocolate pieces and marshmallow cream. Mix well; spread on cake.

***Nick, John, George and Phil with
Mama Lena and Papa Joe Ciaccio***

Mama Lena Ciaccio promised to make an altar in honor of San Guiseppe, or St. Joseph, if her four sons returned from World War II. Of her nine children, Nick, John, George and Phil were in the service at the same time.

Thankfully her prayers were answered and the altar was built across one end of the dining room. For the celebration, Mama Ciaccio added fennel seed to her finely textured bread dough, then formed loaves and circles for baking. Since St. Joseph was a carpenter, in his honor she fashioned extra loaves shaped as hammers, saws and other carpentry tools. When all was blessed by the parish priest, family and friends had a joyful feast.

Old Fashioned Applesauce Cake

Loreen Bledsaw Miller kept this family recipe because of the delightful memories it brought back, as well as unsurpassed delicious taste. Before there were refrigerators, or even much ice available in homes, her mother would make this cake around Thanksgiving time and keep it until Christmas. The trick was to let the fresh cake dry, then wrap it in heavy material and get it up in a dry place. By Christmas it would be the "most wanted" dessert.

2 cups sifted flour	½ cup shortening or margarine
1 teaspoon salt	2 cups sugar
1 teaspoon baking soda	2 eggs, unbeaten
1 teaspoon cinnamon	1 cup cold applesauce
½ teaspoon ground cloves	¾ cup raisins or chopped dates
½ teaspoon nutmeg	½ cup chopped pecans

Preheat oven to 350 degrees. Grease two 8 or 9-inch pans and line bottom with wax paper. Sift all dry ingredients, except sugar; set aside. Mix shortening, sugar and eggs in a large mixing bowl 2 minutes on medium speed. Add applesauce, raisins or dates, nuts and sifted ingredients. Beat 2 more minutes at same speed. Pour in pans; bake about 55 minutes or until done.

Caramel Icing

3 cups sugar, divided	¼ cup butter
2 cups whole milk	1 teaspoon vanilla extract

In a heavy saucepan, heat 1 cup sugar; stirring constantly until melted. Add milk, rest of sugar, and butter; stir until melted again. There will be many crystals. Boil until this forms a soft ball in cold water. After boiled, add vanilla and beat until of spreading consistency. Spread over layer and entire cake quickly. Allow to cool completely. The icing forms a crust over the cake so that it can be wrapped for a month, allowing all the taste to permeate throughout.

Angel Food Cake

12 egg whites at room temperature	1½ cups sugar
1½ teaspoons cream of tartar	1 cup sifted cake flour
¼ teaspoon salt	1½ teaspoons vanilla extract

Beat egg whites until foamy. Add cream of tartar and salt; beat until soft peaks form. Add sugar, 2 tablespoons at a time, beating until stiff peaks form. Sprinkle flour over egg white mixture, ¼ cup at a time; fold in carefully. Fold in vanilla extract. Pour batter into an UNGREASED 10-inch tube pan; spread evenly. Bake at 375 degrees for 30 to 35 minutes or until cake springs back when lightly touched. Invert pan; cool 40 minutes. Loosen cake from sides of pan using a narrow metal spatula; remove from pan.

Washington Apple Cake

3 eggs	½ teaspoon salt
1 cup cooking oil	1 teaspoon vanilla (or rum) extract
2 cups sugar	1 cup chopped nuts (walnuts or
2 cups all-purpose flour	pecans)
2 teaspoons cinnamon	4 cups chopped, pared tart apples
1 teaspoon baking soda	

Preheat oven to 350 degrees. Beat eggs with mixer until thick and light. Combine oil and sugar; pour into eggs while mixing on medium speed. Stir together flour, cinnamon, baking soda and salt; add to egg mixture with vanilla. Beat to mix. Stir in nuts and apples. Pour into a greased 9 x 13-inch pan. Bake for 1 hour or until toothpick comes out clean. Spread with cream cheese icing.

Cream Cheese Icing

2 (3 ounce) packages cream cheese, softened	1-2 cups powdered sugar
	1 teaspoon lemon juice
¼ cup melted butter	

Beat softened cream cheese until fluffy; add melted butter and beat in powdered sugar and lemon juice. Spread over cooled cake.

This cake can also be covered with aluminum foil as soon as you take it out of the oven. Will stay very moist and can be served with a rum sauce instead of icing.

Caramel Raisin Rum Sauce

3 tablespoons butter	½ cup whipping cream or half and half
1 cup firmly packed light brown sugar	½ cup golden raisins
	2-3 tablespoons dark rum

Melt butter in a saucepan; add sugar and cream. Stir over low heat until sugar dissolves. Add raisins and rum; stir well. Yield: 1½ cups.

Need a recipe for Frog on Toast? A Cold Catsup recipe calling for a cupful of nasturtium seed? Instructions for treating nervous prostration? How to whiten the face and remove wrinkles?

Martha Platt White, who settled in Denison just after 1900, had these plus hundreds of recipes, from practical to elegant, in her 1915 The Housekeeper's Handy Book. This book, treasured by great-granddaughter Jane Ellen Myers, includes a poem beginning:

We may live without poetry, music and art;

We may live without conscience, and live without heart,

We may live without friends, we may live without books;

But civilized man cannot live without cooks.

Original German Cheese Cake Pie

Filling

16 ounces cream cheese, softened	2 eggs
¾ cup sugar	2 graham cracker pie shells
1 teaspoon vanilla extract	

Mix first 3 ingredients; add eggs. Pour into pie shells. Do NOT preheat oven. Bake at 350 degrees for 20 minutes. Turn oven off; remove pies and cool 15 minutes.

Top Layer

2 pints sour cream	1 can cherry pie filling, optional
½ cup sugar	

Mix sour cream and sugar; spread carefully on top of pies. Bake at 450 degrees for 5 minutes. Cool and refrigerate at least 3 hours before serving. Best when baked the day before. Use cherry pie filling for topping.

This recipe was acquired in Germany in the mid-1950s. It was made with German cheeses which cannot be bought in local grocery stores. However, the Philadelphia cream cheese is a good substitute.

Chocolate Praline Cake with Broiled Icing

Cake

1	cup buttermilk	2	cups sifted all-purpose flour
1	stick butter	1	teaspoon baking soda
2	cups light brown sugar	3	tablespoons cocoa
2	eggs	1	tablespoon vanilla extract

Grease and flour a 9 x 13-inch pan. Preheat oven to 350 degrees. In a small saucepan, warm buttermilk and butter (DO NOT SCALD). Pour liquid into a mixing bowl. Add brown sugar and eggs; beat well. Sift dry ingredients; slowly add to mixture. Stir in vanilla. Pour into pan; bake for 25 minutes or until done. Prepare icing and spread on cake.

Icing

1	stick butter	½	cup whipping cream or evaporated milk
1	cup light brown sugar, packed	1	cup chopped pecans

Combine all ingredients in a saucepan. Gradually bring to a slow boil. Cook for several minutes until mixture begins to thicken. Spread mixture over top of warm cake. Place cake 4 inches below broiler burner. Broil until icing bubbles and turns golden (1 to 2 minutes). Serve plain or with whipped cream.

Carrot Cake

2	cups sugar	2	teaspoons baking soda
1½	cups oil	1	teaspoon salt
4	eggs	2	teaspoons cinnamon
2	cups flour	3	cups finely grated carrots

Preheat oven to 325 degrees. Mix sugar, oil and eggs until thoroughly blended. Sift together flour, baking soda, salt and cinnamon. Add to first mixture; beat until smooth. Stir in carrots. Pour into 3 greased cake pans. Bake for 30 minutes. Prepare frosting and spread on cake.

Frosting

8	ounces cream cheese, softened	1	stick butter
2½	cups sifted powdered sugar	2	teaspoons vanilla extract

Combine ingredients until smooth; frost cake.

Miss Bessie's Chocolate Cake

2 sticks margarine, softened	⅓ cup cocoa
2 cups sugar	1 small can coconut
4 eggs	1 cup chopped pecans
1½ cups all-purpose flour	2 cups tiny marshmallows

Grease and flour a 9 x 13-inch pan. Preheat oven to 350 degrees. Cream margarine and sugar until fluffy; add eggs and mix well. Add flour, cocoa, coconut and pecans. Pour into pan; bake for 30 minutes. Turn oven off. Cover cake with marshmallows; put back into oven to melt marshmallows while oven cools. Take out and thoroughly cool cake. Cover marshmallow layer with icing; cut into squares to serve.

Icing

⅓ cup cocoa	⅓ cup evaporated milk
1 teaspoon vanilla extract	1 box white powdered sugar
½ cup margarine	

Beat with electric mixer until spreadable. Add more milk if necessary. Frost cake.

Oatmeal Cake

1½ cups water	2 eggs, beaten
1 cup 3 minute oatmeal	1 teaspoon baking soda
1 stick margarine, softened	1 teaspoon cinnamon
1 cup light brown sugar	1⅓ cups sifted flour
1 cup granulated sugar	

Preheat oven to 375 degrees. Bring water to a boil; mix with oatmeal and margarine. Cover, remove from heat and let stand. In another bowl mix remaining ingredients. Add to first mixture and mix well. Bake for 25 minutes in a 9 x 13-inch ungreased pan.

Frosting

1½ sticks margarine, melted	1 cup chopped pecans
1 cup granulated sugar	1 cup coconut
¾ cup evaporated milk	2 teaspoons vanilla extract
¾ cup regular milk	

Over low heat, stirring constantly, cook first 4 ingredients until mixture starts to thicken. Then add remaining 3 ingredients; mix well. Pour over cake while still warm.

Orange Slice Cake

1 cup shortening or butter	1 teaspoon vanilla extract
2 cups sugar	1 teaspoon butter flavoring
4 eggs, beaten	1 pound orange slice candy, chopped
3½ cups flour	
1 cup buttermilk	1 (3½ ounce) can angel flake coconut
2 teaspoons orange rind	
1 teaspoon baking soda	2 cups chopped pecans
1 teaspoon baking powder	

Preheat oven to 325 degrees. Cream shortening and sugar together. Beat and add eggs one at a time. Add remaining ingredients; mix well. Bake in a lightly greased and floured tube or Bundt pan at 325 degrees for 2 hours.

Topping

2 cups powdered sugar	1 (3½ ounce) can angel flake coconut
1 cup orange juice	
1 teaspoon orange rind	

Mix powdered sugar and orange juice. Then add orange rind and coconut; mix all together. Pour on cake while still hot. Let stand until cool.

Pineapple Cream Cake

1 box white cake mix (pudding in mix) plus ingredients for preparation	1 (4 ounce) box instant vanilla pudding plus ingredients for preparation
1 cup sugar	1 cup sour cream
1 (20 ounce) can crushed pineapple, drained	1 (12 ounce) carton frozen whipped dessert topping, thawed
	⅓ cup toasted coconut

Prepare cake according to directions; bake in a 9 x 13-inch pan. While cake is cooling, heat sugar and pineapple in a small saucepan until sugar is dissolved. Pour over cake. Prepare pudding as directed on box. Add sour cream to pudding mixture. Refrigerate mixture for 15 minutes. Pour over cake. Spread whipped topping over top and sprinkle with coconut. Refrigerate. Yield: 12 servings.

To toast coconut, bake at 425 degrees for 5 minutes.

Blackberry Jam Cake

1	cup sugar	½	teaspoon nutmeg
¾	cup margarine	1	teaspoon cinnamon
3	eggs, well beaten	½	teaspoon allspice
3	tablespoons sour cream	1½	cups flour
1	teaspoon baking soda	1	cup blackberry jam

Preheat oven to 350 degrees. Grease and flour a 10-inch tube pan. Cream sugar and margarine together; add well beaten eggs, sour cream and baking soda. Slowly add spices and flour; mixing well. Stir in jam last. Bake for 25 to 30 minutes.

German Chocolate Cake

1	(4 ounce) package German chocolate	1	teaspoon vanilla extract
½	cup hot water	2½	cups cake flour
1	cup shortening	½	teaspoon salt
2	cups sugar	1	teaspoon baking soda
4	egg yolks, unbeaten	1	cup buttermilk
		4	egg whites, stiffly beaten

Grease and flour three 9-inch cake pans. Preheat oven to 350 degrees. Melt chocolate in water; cool. Cream sugar and shortening; add egg yolks one at a time; beat after each yolk. Add chocolate and vanilla. Add flour, salt and baking soda alternately with buttermilk to cake mixture. Fold in egg whites. Bake for 35 to 40 minutes. Cool in pans 10 minutes. Remove from pans and let cool completely on wire racks. Prepare filling and spread on layers and top of cake.

Filling for German Chocolate Cake

1	cup sugar	1	(12 ounce) can evaporated milk
1	tablespoon flour	½	teaspoon vanilla extract
3	egg yolks, beaten	1	cup coconut
1	stick butter or margarine	1	cup chopped nuts

Cook first 6 ingredients in a double boiler until thick. Add coconut and nuts.

Jane's Italian Cream Cake

1	stick margarine	1	cup buttermilk
½	cup vegetable oil	1	teaspoon vanilla extract
2	cups sugar	1	small can angel flake coconut
5	egg yolks	½	cup chopped pecans
2	cups flour	5	egg whites, stiffly beaten
1	teaspoon baking soda		

Grease and flour three 8-inch round cake pans. Preheat oven to 350 degrees. Cream margarine and oil; add sugar, beat until smooth. Add egg yolks; beat well. Combine flour and baking soda; add to creamed mixture alternately with the buttermilk. Add vanilla, coconut and pecans to batter. Fold in egg whites. Pour batter into pans. Bake for 25 minutes. Cool in pans for 10 minutes. Remove to racks and cool completely. Prepare frosting and spread on cake.

Cream Cheese Frosting

8	ounces cream cheese, softened	½	teaspoon vanilla extract
½	stick margarine, softened	½	cup chopped pecans
½	bag or 1 pound box powdered sugar	1	small can coconut

Beat cream cheese and margarine until smooth. Add sugar; mix well. Add extract; beat until smooth. Spread on bottom and second layer; sprinkle with pecans and coconut. Frost top layer; sprinkle with coconut.

Over-Under Cake

1½	cups angel flake coconut	1	stick of butter or margarine
1	cup chopped nuts	8	ounces cream cheese, softened
1	box German chocolate cake mix, plus ingredients for preparation	1	box powdered sugar

Preheat oven to 350 degrees. Grease and flour a 9 x 13-inch pan and sprinkle with the first 2 ingredients. Mix the German chocolate cake mix according to directions and pour over coconut and nuts. Melt butter and cream cheese; beat in powdered sugar. Drizzle over cake mix. Bake for 45 to 50 minutes.

Plum Cake

2 cups sugar	1 teaspoon cinnamon
2 cups flour	3 eggs
½ teaspoon baking soda	1 cup oil
½ teaspoon salt	2 teaspoons red food coloring
1 teaspoon baking powder	2 (4 ounce) jars plum baby food
1 teaspoon cloves	

Preheat oven to 350 degrees. Combine dry ingredients. Add eggs, oil, food coloring, and baby food. Pour into a greased and floured Bundt cake pan. Bake for 35 to 40 minutes. Prepare icing and spread on cake.

Icing

8 ounces cream cheese	2 teaspoons vanilla extract
⅔ cup butter	½ cup chopped pecans, optional
1 box powdered sugar	

Cream the cream cheese and butter together. Add powdered sugar, vanilla and pecans. Spread on cake.

Fresh Apple Coconut Cake

2 eggs	1 teaspoon cinnamon
1 cup softened butter or margarine	1 teaspoon salt
1¼ teaspoons baking soda	1 teaspoon vanilla extract
½ cup warm water	2½ cups peeled and chopped apples
2½ cups flour	1 cup flaked coconut
2½ cups sugar	1 cup chopped pecans
1 tablespoon cocoa	

Grease and flour a 10-inch tube pan. Preheat oven to 350 degrees. Beat eggs with butter. Dissolve baking soda in warm water; set aside. Sift together dry ingredients. Add dry ingredients and soda mixture alternately to egg and margarine mixture; beat. Add vanilla, apple, coconut and pecans. Bake approximately 1 hour or until cake leaves sides of pan.

Buttermilk Pound Cake

3 cups sugar	1 teaspoon vanilla extract
1 cup shortening	3 cups flour
6 eggs	½ teaspoon salt
1 tablespoon vanilla butter and nut flavor	¼ teaspoon baking soda
	1 cup buttermilk

Preheat oven to 350 degrees. Blend sugar and shortening. Add eggs, one at a time, blending after each addition. Add vanilla butter and nut flavor and vanilla extract. Sift dry ingredients together; add to first mixture alternately with buttermilk. Begin and end with dry ingredients. Pour batter into a 10-inch tube pan; greased and sugared. Bake about 1 hour and 20 to 30 minutes. When done, wrap with plastic wrap while hot to make the cake moist; cool.

Nannaw's Sog Cake (Raisin Spice Cake)

1 cup raisins	½ teaspoon allspice
1 cup sugar	½ cup raisin juice, from cooked raisins
½ cup shortening	
½ teaspoon baking soda	1½ cups flour
1 teaspoon baking powder	1 egg
1 teaspoon cinnamon	Pinch of salt
1 teaspoon cloves	1½ cups chopped pecans
1 teaspoon nutmeg	

Grease and flour 2 round cake pans. Preheat oven to 350 degrees. Simmer raisins in just enough water to cover until tender. Reserve ½ cup of the liquid in a large bowl; set aside. Cream sugar and shortening. Dissolve soda and all spices in the reserved liquid from raisins. After spices and baking soda are dissolved, add all ingredients to shortening mixture; mix well. Bake for approximately 40 minutes or until inserted toothpick comes out clean. Cool in pans for 10 minutes. Then turn out and cool completely. Prepare frosting and spread on cake.

Frosting

1 stick margarine at room temperature	⅔ box sifted powdered sugar (2½ cups approximately)
	Canned milk, as necessary

Combine margarine with powdered sugar. Add enough canned milk (a little at a time) until desired consistency for spreading on cake.

Bourbon Pecan Pound Cake

With pecan-filled tow sacks at the ready, Kay Crabtree presides over the pecan cracking machine at the Crabtree Pecan Shoppe. Their mechanized process makes short work of a once laborious task.

The Crabtree family owns about 275 acres of pecan orchard east of Denison. When the fall harvest comes in, Cecil and Kay open the shop in town to market their crop and to provide custom cracking and shelling.

Kay's pound cake recipe with bourbon and pecans is a treasure. She says if she had the time to make this cake, she would sell out every day.

Good For The Holidays

½ pound butter	1 teaspoon ground nutmeg
2½ cups sugar	1 cup sour cream
6 eggs	½ cup bourbon
3 cups sifted cake flour	1½ cups coarsely chopped pecans,
2 teaspoons baking powder	dredged in flour
1 teaspoon salt	

Combine butter and sugar in bowl. With electric mixer blend until light and fluffy. Add eggs one at a time, beating constantly. Sift together flour, baking powder, salt and nutmeg. Blend sour cream and bourbon. Alternately add flour and sour cream mixtures to batter; add pecans (see hint below). Grease bottom and sides of tube or Bundt pan. Pour in batter; bake at 325 degrees for about 1 hour and 30 minutes. Test cake frequently after first hour and 15 minutes for doneness. Let cake cool in pan for 15 minutes before turning out on wire rack. Pour glaze over top of warm cake; let dribble down sides.

Dredge nuts in flour (to coat as by sprinkling) to prevent them from sinking to the bottom of the batter.

Glaze
2 cups sifted powdered sugar	2 tablespoons water
1 tablespoon bourbon	

Combine sugar and bourbon. Stir while gradually adding water. Add only enough water to make a pourable glaze without allowing mixture to become too thin.

Pumpkin Pie Cake

1   (1 pound, 13 ounce) can or
    2 (15 ounce) cans of pumpkin
1   (13 ounce) can evaporated milk
3   eggs, slightly beaten
1½ teaspoons cinnamon
¼   teaspoon cloves
½   teaspoon nutmeg

¼   teaspoon ginger
½   teaspoon salt
1   cup sugar
1   box yellow cake mix
1   cup chopped nuts
1   stick butter or margarine, melted

Preheat oven to 350 degrees. Blend together all ingredients except last 3. Pour into a greased and floured 9 x 13-inch pan. Sprinkle evenly with cake mix and nuts; drizzle with butter. Bake for 50 minutes.

22 Minute Cake

2   cups flour
2   cups sugar
1   stick margarine
½   cup shortening
1   cup water
6   tablespoons cocoa

3½ tablespoons evaporated milk
½   cup buttermilk
2   eggs
1   teaspoon baking soda
1   teaspoon vanilla extract

Do NOT use an electric mixer. Preheat oven to 350 degrees. In a large mixing bowl combine flour and sugar. In a saucepan mix margarine, shortening, water and cocoa. Bring mixture to a boil over low heat, stirring constantly. Add to flour and sugar. By hand, stir into the mixture the evaporated milk, buttermilk, eggs, baking soda and vanilla; mix well. Pour into a 9 x 13-inch baking dish which has been lightly sprayed. Bake for approximately 25 minutes. Prepare frosting and pour over cooled cake.

Frosting

1   stick margarine
3   tablespoons cocoa
⅓   cup milk

1   box powdered sugar
1   cup chopped pecans
1   cup coconut, optional

Bring first 3 ingredients to a boil; add powdered sugar, pecans and, if desired, coconut. Pour over cooled cake.

Turtle Cake

Cake
1 German chocolate cake mix	¾ cup melted margarine
1 large can evaporated milk	

Middle Layer
1 pound caramels	1 cup chopped nuts
⅓ cup milk	1 cup milk chocolate chips

Preheat oven to 350 degrees. Mix and pour half the batter in a greased and floured 9 x 13-inch pan. Bake for 15 minutes. Melt caramels in milk. Add caramel mixture, nuts and chocolate chips over cooked batter. Pour rest of the cake mixture over middle layer. Bake 15 more minutes on top rack. Frost if desired.

German Chocolate Brownies

⅔ cup butter or margarine	4 eggs
1 (4 ounce) package German sweet chocolate	1½ cups all-purpose flour
2 cups sugar	1 cup chopped nuts
2 teaspoons vanilla extract	½ cup flaked coconut

Preheat oven to 350 degrees. Grease and flour a 9 x 13-inch baking pan. In a saucepan, combine butter or margarine and chocolate. Stir constantly over medium low heat 10 to 12 minutes or until melted. Cool 10 minutes. Stir in sugar and vanilla; add eggs, one at a time, beating well with a spoon after each addition. Stir in flour, nuts and coconut; beat well. Pour into prepared pan. Bake for 35 to 40 minutes or until a wooden pick inserted in center of brownies comes out clean. Cool in pan on rack. Cut in squares while warm, but do not remove from pan until completely cool. Store completely cooled brownies in baking pan covered with foil.

Easy Microwave Melting: heat chocolate and butter for 2 minutes or until almost melted; stir halfway through heating time. Stir until completely melted. If more melting is needed, heat at 10 second intervals.

Double Chocolate Brownies

⅔ cup butter
1½ cups sugar
4   tablespoons water
2   (12 ounce) packages semisweet
    chocolate chips, divided
1   tablespoon vanilla extract

4   eggs
1½ cups flour
½   teaspoon baking soda
½   teaspoon salt
1   cup chopped nuts

Preheat oven to 325 degrees. In a saucepan, bring butter, sugar and water to a boil, remove from heat. Add 1 package chocolate chips and vanilla; stir until smooth. Transfer to a large mixing bowl; add eggs one at a time, stirring well after each. Gradually stir in flour, baking soda and salt. Let mixture cool a bit, then stir in the last package of chocolate chips and nuts. Spread into a greased baking pan (jelly-roll size is best). Bake for 30 to 35 minutes. Cool completely before cutting. Yield: approximately 30 (2½ x 2½ inch) brownies.

❄ Heavenly Brownies

2   sticks margarine or butter
4   tablespoons cocoa
4   eggs
2   cups sugar
1½ cups flour

2   cups chopped pecans
    Pinch of salt
2   teaspoons vanilla extract
1   large bag of small marshmallows

Icing
6   tablespoons butter
1   (5½ ounce) can evaporated milk

6   cups powdered sugar (1½ boxes)
¾   cup cocoa
    Pinch of salt

Preheat oven to 350 degrees. In a saucepan melt butter and add cocoa. Beat eggs and add sugar. Combine with butter and cocoa. Add flour, pecans, salt and vanilla; mix well. Bake in 2 greased 8-inch square pans or one lasagna pan for 25 minutes; test for doneness. While brownies are baking, mix all icing ingredients and heat over boiling water or in microwave. When brownies are baked, remove from oven and cover top with marshmallows, then pour the hot icing over all. Cool and cut into squares. Can be frozen.

Brown Sugar Brownies

2	squares unsweetened chocolate	⅛	teaspoon salt
¼	cup butter	½	cup flour
1¼	cups brown sugar	½	cup chopped nuts
2	eggs	1	teaspoon vanilla extract

Preheat oven to 300 degrees. In a large saucepan, melt chocolate and butter over low heat. Remove from heat; add sugar, eggs, salt, flour, nuts and vanilla. Stir until well mixed. Spread evenly in a 9-inch square pan. Bake about 1 hour.

Chocolate Walnut Crumb Bars

1	cup (2 sticks) softened butter	14	ounces sweetened condensed milk
2	cups all-purpose flour		
½	cup granulated sugar	1	teaspoon vanilla extract
¼	teaspoon salt	1	cup chopped walnuts
12	ounces semisweet chocolate morsels, divided		

Preheat oven to 350 degrees. Beat butter in a large mixing bowl until creamy. Beat in flour, sugar and salt until crumbly. With floured fingers, press 2 cups crumb mixture into bottom of a greased 9 x 13-inch baking pan; reserve remaining mixture. Bake for 10 to 12 minutes or until edges are golden brown. Warm 1½ cups morsels and sweetened condensed milk in small heavy saucepan over low heat; stir until smooth. Stir in vanilla; spread over hot crust. Stir walnuts and remaining morsels into reserved crumb mixture; sprinkle over chocolate filling. Bake for 25 to 30 minutes or until center is set. Cool in pan on wire rack.

Pat's Date Nut Bars

¾	cup sifted flour	1	cup chopped, pitted dates
1	cup sugar	1	cup chopped nuts
1	teaspoon baking powder	3	eggs, well beaten
¼	teaspoon salt		Powdered sugar

Preheat oven to 325 degrees; grease a 9-inch square pan. Sift flour with sugar, baking powder and salt. Stir in dates, nuts and eggs. Spread evenly in pan, bake for 35 to 40 minutes until brown. Cool; cut into bars. Sift powdered sugar over bars.

Neiman Marcus Bars

1	box lemon cake mix	1	cup angel flake coconut
1	stick margarine, softened	1	box powdered sugar
2	eggs	8	ounces cream cheese
1	cup chopped pecans	2	eggs

Preheat oven to 350 degrees. Mix well the first 3 ingredients; add pecans and coconut. Pat this mixture into a greased 9 x 13-inch pan. Mix the next 3 ingredients together well; pour over first mixture. Bake for 40 minutes. Cool and cut.

Apricot Sticks

¾	cup sugar	¼	teaspoon baking soda
1	stick margarine	1	(16 ounce) jar apricot preserves
¼	teaspoon salt	2	egg whites
2	egg yolks	¼	cup sugar
1	teaspoon vanilla extract	1	cup chopped pecans
2	cups flour		Powdered sugar

Cream together sugar, margarine and salt. Add egg yolks, vanilla, flour and baking soda. Pat into a well-greased cookie sheet. Spread apricot preserves over the batter. Beat egg whites with ¼ cup sugar until stiff. Spread over preserves and sprinkle with chopped pecans. Bake at 350 degrees for 30 to 35 minutes; cool. Cut into sticks and sprinkle with powdered sugar.

Gingersnaps

¾	cup shortening	¼	teaspoon salt
1	cup sugar	2	teaspoons baking soda
¼	cup light molasses	1	teaspoon cinnamon
1	egg	1	teaspoon cloves
2	cups flour	1	teaspoon ginger
			Sugar

Preheat oven to 375 degrees. Cream shortening and sugar together. Add molasses and egg; beat well. Add sifted dry ingredients; mix well. Roll into small balls; dip into sugar. Place 2 inches apart on greased cookie sheet. Bake for 15 minutes. Yield: 4 dozen.

Molasses Sugar Cookies

¾ cup butter flavor shortening
1 cup sugar
¼ cup molasses
1 egg
2 cups flour
2 teaspoons baking soda

½ teaspoon ground cloves
½ teaspoon ground ginger
1 teaspoon cinnamon
½ teaspoon salt
Sugar

Preheat oven to 375 degrees. Melt shortening and cool. Add sugar, molasses and egg to shortening mixture. Beat well. Sift flour, baking soda, spices and salt together. Add dry ingredients to sugar and egg mixture; mix well. CHILL. Roll into 1 inch balls, then roll in sugar. Place on greased cookie sheets. Bake for 8 to 10 minutes.

Cheesecake Cookies

1 cup flour
¼ cup light brown sugar
1 cup finely chopped pecans
1 stick butter, melted
16 ounces cream cheese, softened
1 cup sugar

1 teaspoon vanilla extract
3 eggs
2 cups sour cream
6 tablespoons sugar
1 teaspoon vanilla extract

Preheat oven to 350 degrees. In a small bowl, mix flour, brown sugar, pecans and melted butter. Press into bottom of a 9 x 13-inch glass baking dish. Bake for 10 to 15 minutes or until brown.

In a medium bowl, beat cream cheese, sugar, and vanilla. Add eggs; beat well. Pour on top of crust. Bake for 20 minutes.

In a small bowl, mix sour cream, sugar and vanilla; pour over baked filling. Bake for 3 to 5 minutes. Cool and refrigerate before cutting into squares. Yield: about 48 squares.

For 124 years, the Hopewell Baptist Church has been an active and progressive force in the Denison community. Founded in 1874 when Denison was still a tough frontier railhead and cattle town, it provided moral and spiritual nourishment for black residents. In 1879 services were held "nearly every evening of the week, commencing about eight o'clock and lasting sometimes until midnight".

Thurgood Marshall spoke at Hopewell in 1950 when they hosted the NAACP regional convention. He would later become the first black U. S. Supreme Court Justice.

Hopewell Baptist ladies, wearing bonnets and hats in honor of Denison's centennial celebration, gather in July, 1972, for their Fifth Sunday Feast, Women's Day.

Cranberry Kuchen

1 egg, beaten	1 cup flour
½ cup sugar	2 teaspoons baking powder
½ cup milk	½ teaspoon salt
2 tablespoons oil	2 cups chopped cranberries
	Crumb topping, recipe follows

Preheat oven to 375 degrees. Combine egg, sugar, milk and oil; add dry ingredients. Mix well. Put in an 8-inch square greased pan. Sprinkle cranberries over batter. Sprinkle crumb topping over all. Bake for 25 to 30 minutes.

Crumb Topping

¾ cup flour	3 tablespoons butter
½ cup sugar	Chopped pecans, optional

Mix all together. Add pecans if desired.

Caramel Graham Crackers

24 cinnamon graham cracker squares, 2½ inch size	½ cup butter
½ cup margarine	1 cup light brown sugar
	1 cup chopped pecans

Preheat oven to 350 degrees. Line a cookie sheet with foil and spray with cooking spray. Cover with a single layer of graham crackers. Mix margarine, butter and sugar in a saucepan; bring to a boil and cook for 2 minutes. Pour mixture over crackers. Sprinkle nuts on top. Bake for 12 minutes. Cut into triangles while warm.

Easy Kolaches

1 cup butter
8 ounces cream cheese
2 cups flour

Apricot preserves or raspberry jam

Glaze
1 cup powder sugar
1 tablespoon water

1 teaspoon vanilla extract

Preheat oven to 400 degrees. Mix butter, cream cheese and flour. Roll into balls. Make well in center of each with thumb. Fill with preserves or jam. Bake on ungreased cookie sheet for 15 minutes. Mix glaze ingredients together. Add glaze after baking, while still warm. Yield: 35 to 40.

Czechoslovakian Cookies

½ pound of butter	2 cups flour
1 cup sugar	1 cup chopped walnuts
2 egg yolks	1 cup strawberry jam

Preheat oven to 325 degrees. Cream butter and sugar; beat until fluffy. Add egg yolks. Gradually add flour and nuts. Spoon ½ the batter into a greased 8-inch square pan. Top with jam. Cover with remaining batter. Bake for 1 hour or until slightly brown.

Other jams may be used if you prefer.

Georgia Candy Cookies

1 cup margarine, softened	1 box confectioners' sugar
1 cup crunchy peanut butter	1 cup chocolate chips
1¼ cups crushed graham crackers	

Mix margarine and peanut butter; add crackers and sugar. Press into a 9 x 13-inch pan. Melt chocolate chips; spread on top. Chill; cut into squares.

Summer's Chocolate Chip Cookies

1 cup brown sugar	1 teaspoon baking soda
1 cup white sugar	2 cups finely crushed potato chips
2 sticks butter or margarine (not low fat)	1 package (more or less according to taste) chocolate chips
2 eggs	1 cup chopped nuts, optional
2 cups flour	2 tablespoons water

Preheat oven to 325 degrees. Cream together first 3 ingredients; beat in eggs. Add flour and baking soda. Mix in rest of ingredients, adding slightly more water if necessary. Put rounded tablespoons of dough on an ungreased cookie sheet; bake until just beginning to brown, about 8 minutes. Cool on cookie sheet for 2 to 3 minutes before removing. To keep these cookies tasting just baked, store them in the freezer.

For variety, use white chocolate chips.

How very nice. Dining car patrons no longer had to shout at their companions. "Almost perfect quiet" resulted from acoustical insulation and dampened vibrations. The Katy Railroad claimed these avant garde innovations on the Texas Special and Bluebonnet provided travelers through Texas and Oklahoma the maximum in comfort. And at no extra cost!

Neiman Marcus Chocolate Chip Cookies

2 cups butter
2 cups sugar
2 cups light brown sugar
4 eggs
2 teaspoons vanilla extract
5 cups oatmeal
4 cups flour

1 teaspoon salt
2 teaspoons baking powder
2 teaspoons baking soda
2 (12 ounce) packages chocolate chips
18 ounces grated Hershey bars
3 cups chopped nuts

Preheat oven to 375 degrees. Cream butter, sugar and brown sugar. Add eggs and vanilla to the creamed mixture. Place oatmeal in a blender and blend to a fine powder. Combine the blended oatmeal, flour, salt, baking powder and baking soda. Gradually add to creamed mixture. When fully mixed, add chocolate chips, grated chocolate bars and chopped nuts. Roll into balls and place 2 inches apart on a cookie sheet. Bake for 6 to 10 minutes.

Sugar Cookies

½ cup butter
¾ cup sugar
1 egg
1½ teaspoons vanilla extract

1½ cups flour
1 teaspoon baking powder
¼ teaspoon salt

Preheat oven to 350 degrees. Cream butter and sugar; beat in egg and vanilla. Sift together flour, baking powder and salt. Stir into creamed mixture. Chill 1 hour. Roll on floured board. Cut dough with cookie cutters; place on lightly greased baking sheet. Bake for 6 to 8 minutes.

Frosting

1 pound box powdered sugar
4 tablespoons melted butter
1 teaspoon vanilla extract

2-3 tablespoons milk
Food coloring

Mix thoroughly one-third of powdered sugar with melted butter. Gradually add rest of sugar, vanilla and milk. Tint with food coloring. Spread on cooled cookies.

A Prize Winning Chocolate Chip Cookie

1 cup butter flavor shortening	1 teaspoon baking soda
1 cup granulated sugar	1 teaspoon vanilla extract
1 cup firmly packed brown sugar	½ teaspoon salt
1 cup all-purpose flour	2 cups quick cooking oats,
1 cup whole wheat flour	uncooked
2 eggs	1 cup semisweet chocolate chips
2 tablespoons milk	1 cup finely chopped pecans

Preheat oven to 350 degrees. Combine shortening, both sugars, both flours, eggs, milk, baking soda, vanilla and salt in a large bowl. Beat at low speed of electric mixer until well blended. Stir in oats, chocolate chips and nuts with a spoon. Drop by heaping tablespoonfuls 3 inches apart onto an ungreased baking sheet. Bake for 13 to 15 minutes or until golden brown. Cool 1 minute on baking sheet before removing to a flat surface. Yield: 3 dozen cookies.

Peppernuts

2 cups shortening	2 teaspoons baking soda, dissolved
1¼ cups sugar	in a little hot water
1 cup brown sugar	1 teaspoon nutmeg
¾ cup sweet cream	1 teaspoon salt
1 cup dark corn syrup	Flour
3 tablespoons anise seed	

Preheat oven to 400 degrees. Cream shortening; add both sugars. Add rest of ingredients. On a bread board, with your hands, work in enough flour to make a stiff dough. For ease in rolling, chill dough about 2 hours. Roll into a tube shape with a diameter about the size of a nickel; slice. Put on a greased cookie sheet. Bake about 4 to 5 minutes; will burn easily.

From **The Denison Daily News,** *April 30, 1874: A well dressed, matronly looking lady walked into a saloon the other day, laid her muff on the counter and took out a pair of spectacles. The bartender promptly informed her that no Bible reading would be in order there! Reaching down into her dress pocket, the woman produced a flat bottle and coolly called for a pint of whiskey—much to the relief of the bartender.*

Sweet Ravioli

1 cup butter or margarine, softened	2½ cups all-purpose flour
⅔ cup sugar	¼ teaspoon baking soda
1 egg, beaten	⅛ teaspoon salt
1 teaspoon grated lemon rind	½ cup raspberry preserves
1½ teaspoons vanilla extract	Sifted powdered sugar
¼ teaspoon almond extract	

Preheat oven to 350 degrees. Beat butter with an electric mixer at medium speed; gradually add sugar, beating well. Add egg, lemon rind and extracts; mix well. Combine flour, baking soda and salt; add to creamed mixture and mix well. Divide dough in half. Roll each portion of dough between 2 sheets of wax paper to a 12 inch square. Chill at least 1 hour.

Remove one portion of dough from refrigerator; remove top piece of wax paper and cut dough into 1½ inch squares. Place ¼ teaspoon raspberry preserves in center of half of squares; brush edges of filled squares with water. Place unfilled squares over filled squares; press edges to seal. Cut an X on top of each. Repeat with remaining dough and preserves. Place cookies on greased cookie sheet and bake for 9 to 11 minutes or until edges are lightly browned. Remove from oven; cool on baking sheets 4 to 5 minutes. Transfer cookies to wire racks and cool completely. Sprinkle with powdered sugar. Yield: 4 dozen.

☽ Eclair Pie

2 (3.4 ounce) packages instant French vanilla pudding	8 ounces whipped dessert topping
	Graham crackers
3½ cups milk	

Mix pudding and milk together. Fold in the whipped dessert topping. Cover the bottom of a 9 x 13-inch dish with graham crackers; layer with pudding mix; repeat, ending with graham crackers. Pour chocolate topping on top of crackers and refrigerate overnight.

Chocolate Topping

2 packages pre-melted chocolate, or 2 squares unsweetened chocolate, melted	2 teaspoons vanilla extract
	2 teaspoons light corn syrup
	3 tablespoons milk
3 tablespoons softened margarine	1½ cups powdered sugar

Mix in sequence and pour on top of crackers. Yield: 16 to 18 servings.

⌛ *Fresh Berry Tartlets*

2 (3 ounce) packages cream cheese, softened	½ cup ground almonds
⅔ cup butter or margarine, softened	Crème Fraîche, recipe follows
2½ cups all-purpose flour	Fresh raspberries, blueberries and sliced strawberries

Preheat oven to 450 degrees. Using knife blade in food processor bowl, add first 4 ingredients; process until mixture leaves sides of bowl and forms a ball. Remove dough from bowl. Shape into 50 balls; chill 15 minutes. Place in ungreased miniature (1¾ inch) muffin pans, shaping dough to make shells. Prick bottom of shells several times with a fork; bake for 8 to 10 minutes or until browned. Remove from pans; cool on wire racks. Just before serving, spoon Crème Fraîche into pastry shells; top with choice of fruit. Yield: 50 tartlets.

Crème Fraîche

1 (3 ounce) package cream cheese, softened	½ cup sour cream
	⅔ cup sifted powdered sugar
1½ cups whipping cream	2 tablespoons amaretto

Beat cream cheese at medium speed with mixer until light and fluffy. Add remaining ingredients; beat until thickened. Cover and chill 8 hours or up to 4 days. (Mixture may thin upon agitation, but will thicken upon standing.) Yield: 2¾ cups.

Pastry shells may be made ahead and frozen in airtight containers up to 1 month. Let thaw at room temperature before filling.

Chocolate Chip Pie

2 eggs	1 cup margarine, melted and cooled
½ cup flour	1 cup chocolate chips
½ cup sugar	1 cup chopped nuts
½ cup brown sugar	

Preheat oven to 325 degrees. Beat eggs until foamy; add flour, sugars, and melted margarine. Stir in chocolate chips and nuts. Pour into pie plate and place pie plate on cookie sheet while baking. Bake 1 hour or until golden brown. Very rich!

Chocolate Pie

3 cups sugar	6 egg yolks
1 cup flour	2 teaspoons vanilla extract
1 teaspoon salt	½ stick margarine
½ cup cocoa	2 (9 inch) baked pie shells
3½ cups milk, divided	

Preheat oven to 350 degrees. Mix sugar, flour, salt and cocoa. Add 3 cups of milk gradually. Mix egg yolks and ½ cup milk; stir into cocoa mixture. Cook until thickened. Add vanilla and margarine; beat 2 minutes with electric mixer. Pour into cooked pie shells, cover with meringue. Bake for 12 to 15 minutes or until brown.

Meringue

½ cup water	3-4 egg whites
½ cup sugar, divided	Dash of salt
1 tablespoon cornstarch	

In a small saucepan cook water, 2 tablespoons sugar and cornstarch until thickened; cool. Beat egg whites with salt until stiff. Add cooked mixture; add remaining sugar, beat until stiff.

Buttermilk Pie

1 stick butter, softened	1 teaspoon lemon extract or
2 cups sugar	1 teaspoon vanilla extract
3 tablespoons regular flour	2 dashes of nutmeg
3 eggs	1 (9 inch) unbaked pie shell
1 cup buttermilk	

Preheat oven to 400 degrees. Cream butter at high speed of an electric mixer; gradually add sugar, beating well. Add flour and beat until smooth. Add eggs; beat until blended. Add buttermilk, lemon extract and nutmeg; beat well. Pour filling into pie crust. Bake at 400 degrees for 5 minutes; reduce heat to 350 degrees and bake an additional 45 minutes or until set. Cool to room temperature; chill.

Double Coconut Cream Pie

⅓ cup sugar
¼ cup cornstarch
¼ teaspoon salt
2 cups milk
8 ounces cream of coconut

3 egg yolks, beaten
2 tablespoons butter
1 cup flaked coconut
2 teaspoons vanilla extract
1 (9 inch) baked pie shell

Meringue:
3 egg whites
½ teaspoon vanilla extract
¼ teaspoon cream of tartar

⅓ cup sugar
2 tablespoons flaked coconut

Preheat oven to 350 degrees. Filling: in a medium saucepan combine the first ⅓ cup sugar, cornstarch, and salt. Stir in milk and cream of coconut. Cook and stir over medium heat until thickened and bubbly. Cook and stir 2 minutes more. Gradually stir about 1 cup of the hot milk mixture into beaten egg yolks, stirring constantly. Return all the mixture to saucepan. Cook and stir until bubbly. Cook and stir 2 minutes more; remove from heat. Stir in butter until melted. Stir in 1 cup of coconut and 2 teaspoons vanilla. Pour filling into baked pastry shell. Meringue: let egg whites stand at room temperature for 30 minutes. In a mixing bowl beat egg whites, ½ teaspoon vanilla, and cream of tartar on medium speed in an electric mixer until soft peaks form. Gradually add ⅓ cup sugar, 1 tablespoon at a time, until stiff peaks form. Evenly spread meringue over hot filling, seal to pastry edge. Sprinkle with 2 tablespoons coconut. Bake for 15 minutes. Cool 1 hour on a wire rack. Cover and chill 3 to 6 hours before serving.

Chocolate Pecan Pie

1 cup sugar
¾ cup light corn syrup
¼ cup melted butter or margarine
3 eggs, beaten
1 teaspoon vanilla extract

½ cup semisweet chocolate morsels
½ cup chopped pecans
1 (9 inch) unbaked pie shell
1 cup pecan halves, optional
Whipped cream, optional

Preheat oven to 350 degrees. Combine first 5 ingredients in a large bowl; stir well. Add chocolate morsels and chopped pecans, stirring well. Pour mixture into pastry shell; if desired, top with pecan halves. Bake for 45 to 50 minutes or until set. Cool completely. Garnish with whipped cream, if desired.

Lemon Chess Pie

5 eggs	¾ stick of butter
2 cups sugar	1 (9 inch) unbaked pie shell
2 lemons	

Preheat oven to 450 degrees. Beat eggs until foamy. Add sugar, juice of 2 lemons and the zest of 1 lemon; add butter and mix well. Pour into unbaked pie shell; bake for 10 minutes. Reduce heat to 350 degrees; continue baking about 30 minutes.

Sarah Bradley's Pecan Pie

Native pecans. Magnificent towering trees. Delicious nuts. The State Tree of Texas.

In the fall, Indians came in great numbers to river valleys and their tributaries to harvest pecans, their major food resource for four months of the year. How appropriate many pecan varieties are named for Indian tribes!

When Sarah Elizabeth Bradley crossed the Red River into Texas and settled on Iron Ore Creek in 1838, she was grateful for nature's bounty. Her pecan pie recipe is 160 years old.

3 eggs, slightly beaten	⅛ teaspoon salt
1 cup dark corn syrup	1 teaspoon vanilla
½ cup sugar	1½ cups pecans
1 tablespoon butter, melted	1 uncooked pie shell

In bowl, stir together first six ingredients. Stir in nuts. Pour in uncooked pie shell. Bake at 350 degrees for 50 to 55 minutes.

Background: Crabtree Farm Pecan Orchard. Tree varieties are largely Cheyenne, Choctaw, Sioux and native early pecans.

Bavarian Strawberry Pie

1	(3 ounce) package sugar-free, strawberry-flavored gelatin	6	ounces frozen whipped dessert topping, thawed
1	cup boiling water	1	cup chopped fresh strawberries
½	cup cold water	1	(9 inch) baked pie shell
1	tablespoon lemon juice		

Dissolve gelatin in boiling water. Add cold water and lemon juice. Chill until slightly thickened. Fold together whipped topping and gelatin, blending well. Fold in strawberries. Pour into pie shell; chill about 3 hours.

Fresh Strawberry Pie

1	quart fresh strawberries	¼	cup cornstarch
3	ounces cream cheese	⅛	teaspoon salt
2	tablespoons milk	¼	teaspoon red food coloring
½	cup water	1	(9 inch) baked pie shell
1	cup sugar	1	cup whipping cream

Wash and stem strawberries. Soften cream cheese with milk; spread in bottom of pie shell. Place one-half of the choicest berries in pie shell. Heat remaining berries in water. When berries are soft, add to mixture of sugar, cornstarch and salt. Return to heat and cook until thickened. Add food coloring. Pour over berries in pie shell; chill. Top with whipped cream before serving. Yield: 6 servings.

Apple Torte

1	cup peeled, cored and chopped cooking apples	½	cup unsifted all-purpose flour
2	rounded teaspoons powdered fruit protector	1	teaspoon baking powder
		1	teaspoon vanilla extract
1	egg	½	cup chopped pecans
¾	cup sugar	1	cup whipping cream
		1	teaspoon sugar

Preheat oven to 325 degrees. Place apples in a small bowl, sprinkle with fruit protector. In another bowl, mix egg and sugar until well blended; stir in flour, baking powder, vanilla and pecans. Fold in apples; stir until well blended. Spread mixture evenly into a greased 8-inch pie pan. Bake for 25 minutes or until puffed and brown. Whip cream to soft peaks; add sugar. Continue whipping until stiff. Cut warm torte into wedges and top with whipped cream. Yield: 6 servings.

Honey Crunch Pecan Pie

4 eggs, lightly beaten	2 tablespoons melted butter or margarine
¼ cup firmly packed brown sugar	1 tablespoon bourbon
¼ cup granulated sugar	1 teaspoon vanilla extract
½ teaspoon salt	1 cup chopped pecans
1 cup light corn syrup	1 (9 inch) unbaked pie shell

Topping

⅓ cup firmly packed brown sugar	3 tablespoons honey
3 tablespoons butter or margarine	1½ cups pecan halves

Preheat oven to 350 degrees. For filling: combine the first 9 ingredients; mix well. Spoon into unbaked pie shell. Bake for 15 minutes. Cover edge of pastry with foil. Bake another 20 minutes. Remove from oven. For topping, combine brown sugar, butter and honey in medium saucepan; cook about 2 minutes or until sugar dissolves. Add nuts; stir until coated. Spoon evenly over pie. Cover edge of pastry with foil. Bake 10 to 20 minutes more or until topping is bubbly and golden brown. Cool to room temperature before serving.

Mom's Pumpkin Chiffon Pie

1 envelope unflavored gelatin	½ teaspoon cinnamon
¼ cup cold water	½ teaspoon nutmeg
3 egg yolks	3 stiffly beaten egg whites
½ cup sugar	½ cup sugar
1¼ cups canned pumpkin	1 (9 inch) baked pie shell
½ cup milk	Sweetened whipped cream or frozen whipped dessert topping, thawed
½ teaspoon salt	
½ teaspoon ginger	

Soften gelatin in ¼ cup cold water; set aside. Beat egg yolks and ½ cup sugar until thick; add pumpkin, milk, salt and spices. Cook in a double boiler until thickened. Add softened gelatin to hot mixture, stirring until dissolved; chill. Beat egg whites with remaining ½ cup sugar until stiff peaks form. Fold into pumpkin mixture. Pour into a cooled, baked pastry shell; chill. Spread sweetened whipped cream over top of pie.

Easy Cobbler

Batter

1	stick margarine	4	teaspoons baking powder
2	cups flour	1	teaspoon cinnamon
1½	cups sugar	1	teaspoon butter flavoring,
1½	cups milk		optional
1	teaspoon vanilla extract		

Fruit Mixture

2   cups or more fruit

¾   cup sugar to sweeten (sour fruit takes more) or you can use canned fruit, thickened with a little corn starch over heat

Melt margarine in a 9 x 13-inch pan in oven. Combine remaining ingredients to make batter. Pour batter into melted margarine and stir slightly. Pour fruit mixture over top of batter. Do NOT stir. Batter will rise over fruit. Bake at 350 degrees for approximately 45 minutes. Should be brown on top. Can broil to brown, but be sure to watch.

Fruit options: berries, peaches, apricots, cherries, or blueberries. With peaches or apricots, brandy or rum extract is good. With cherries, almond extract is good. Can use with vanilla extract or in place of.

Chocolate Truffles

1	(6 ounce) package semisweet chocolate morsels	1	cup finely chopped walnuts, toasted
1	(9 ounce) package chocolate wafers, crushed	½	cup orange juice
2	cups sifted powdered sugar	½	teaspoon rum extract
			Chocolate decorator sprinkles

Place chocolate morsels in top of a double boiler; bring water to a boil. Reduce heat to low; cook until chocolate melts. Remove from heat. Add wafer crumbs and next 4 ingredients; mix well. Cover; chill 30 minutes. Shape mixture into 1 inch balls; roll lightly in chocolate sprinkles. Chill until firm. Store in an airtight container in refrigerator. Yield: about 7 dozen.

☽ Bonbons

3 cups chopped pecans	2 boxes powdered sugar
2 sticks butter or margarine, slightly melted	1 teaspoon vanilla extract
2 cups coconut	1 (12 ounce) package semisweet chocolate chips
1 (14 ounce) can sweetened condensed milk	1 block paraffin

Mix first 6 ingredients together and form into small balls of candy. Refrigerate overnight to set. The next day, melt chocolate chips and paraffin in a double boiler. Dip candy balls into the melted chocolate chips and paraffin. Use round toothpicks to handle balls. Place dipped balls on wax paper. Can be stored in freezer.

🕐 Kelly's Butterscotch Candy

2 (11 ounce) packages butterscotch chips	12 ounces Spanish peanuts
2 tablespoons peanut butter	½ (7 ounce) can shoestring potatoes, do NOT use a full can

Melt butterscotch chips with the peanut butter in a microwave on high for 2 to 2½ minutes. Stir in Spanish peanuts and shoestring potatoes. Drop by spoonful onto foil or cookie sheet.

Date Nut Roll

3 cups sugar	1½ cups chopped nuts
1 cup milk	1 teaspoon vanilla extract
1½ cups chopped dates	Powdered sugar to sprinkle on cloth
1 tablespoon butter or margarine	

Mix sugar and milk. Boil for 15 minutes; use a pancake turner to slowly run across bottom of pan to keep sugar from crystallizing. Add dates; boil for 10 more minutes. Remove from heat; beat until thick as dough. Add butter, nuts, and vanilla. Roll in wet cloth wrung out in cold water and sprinkled with powdered sugar. Let stand until hard. Slice date nut roll in ¾ inch slices.

Perfect Fudge

This recipe for fudge was taped inside a cookbook that was received as a wedding gift in 1947. The following recipe is typed EXACTLY as the original.

2 cups sugar	3 tablespoons white syrup
2 tablespoons cocoa stir well, then	½ cup milk

Stir, mix well; cook until big "blubbers" form about 3 to 5 "minits". Try some in cold water. When soft ball, add large spoon butter and beat.

Orange/Apricot Balls

1 orange	1 cup chopped pecans
1 package dried apricots	Shredded coconut or powdered
1½ cups sugar	sugar

Remove seeds and membrane from orange. Grind orange and apricots in a blender. Add sugar and place in a heavy saucepan. Simmer until clear. Add nuts; cool. Form into small balls and roll into either coconut or powdered sugar.

◷ Hay Stacks

⅔ cup peanut butter	1 (3 ounce) can chow mein noodles
1 (12 ounce) package butterscotch chips	1 cup chopped walnuts

In a double boiler, melt chips and peanut butter. Mix in noodles and nuts until well coated. Drop by teaspoon on wax paper. Put in refrigerator until set.

Mix chips and peanut butter together first in a microwave safe bowl. Microwave for 2 minutes on high, stirring halfway through.

Crack! Crack! Crack! They cracked eggs. And cracked eggs....twenty-four hours a day, seven days a week. The most dexterous could crack four at a time with no shell bits left clinging to the egg.

Women at the Clymers' Denison Poultry and Egg Company were doing their part to provide powdered eggs for the military during World War II. Raw eggs were placed on a conveyor belt traveling into a funnel shaped chamber with hot air blowing up from the smaller bottom end. As the eggs dried, they became lighter and powdery, moving upward to be collected at the top. Invented by M. D. (Bud) Bryant, this process was part of the crucial home front war effort.

Million Dollar Fudge

4½	cups sugar	12	ounces semisweet chocolate bits
	Pinch of salt	12	ounces German chocolate
2	tablespoons butter	1	pint marshmallow creme
1	(12 ounce) can of evaporated milk	2	cups chopped nuts

Boil first 4 ingredients for 6 minutes. Put remaining ingredients in a large bowl; pour boiling syrup over ingredients in the bowl. Beat until chocolate is melted; pour in buttered pan. Let stand a few hours before cutting. Store in tin box.

Never Fail Fudge

1	pound box powdered sugar	1	stick margarine, cut into several
½	cup cocoa		pieces
¼	cup milk	1	teaspoon vanilla extract
		½	cup nuts, optional

Sift sugar and cocoa into medium glass bowl. Add milk and margarine, but do NOT stir. Microwave 2 to 2½ minutes on high. Add vanilla and nuts. Stir to blend well. Put in an 8 or 9-inch buttered pan. Chill 1 hour. Cut into squares. Store in refrigerator.

Allyne's Buttermilk Pralines

2   cups sugar
1   cup buttermilk
1   teaspoon baking soda
1   tablespoon white corn syrup

1½ cups pecans
1   teaspoon vanilla extract
¼   cup margarine

In a heavy saucepan combine sugar, buttermilk, baking soda and syrup. Cook over medium heat to soft ball stage. Remove from heat; add pecans, vanilla and margarine. Stir until margarine has melted. Beat until it begins to thicken; drop from tablespoon onto wax paper.

This was the stark scene on Main Street when the Katy Railroad reached Denison in 1872. Less than three months later, March 7, 1873, Denison officially became a city. It had already mushroomed to over 3,000 inhabitants, albeit with mostly primitive living and eating conditions, and was heralded as the Infant Wonder.

In the same week a **MAJOR NATIONAL HISTORIC MILESTONE** *occurred almost unnoticed. On March 10, 1873, with no golden spikes or big hullabaloo, the Katy Railroad and the Houston & Texas Central Railroad, which had built north from the Gulf Coast, were joined at the Denison Depot. The event connected the North and South just as the East and West had been joined four months earlier.* **FOR THE FIRST TIME, THE ENTIRE UNITED STATES – NORTH, SOUTH, EAST AND WEST – WAS LINKED BY RAIL.**

Spiced Pecans

1	cup sugar	1	teaspoon vanilla extract
⅓	cup evaporated milk	2-3	cups pecan halves
½	teaspoon cinnamon		

Combine first 3 ingredients. Heat to boiling on medium high. Continue to heat, stirring constantly for about 4 minutes until soft ball stage. Add vanilla and pecans; stir to coat well. Pour onto wax paper and break apart when cool.

Stalwart German pioneers played a prominent role in Denison's early days. The Society Vorwaerts, or "Society Forward", from its organization in 1877 was renowned for its "attractive social privileges" e.g. good fellowship and bounteous food and drink. While membership was restricted to those who could speak and write the German language, passive memberships were permitted.

Texas Special

Clearly delighted, Edna Freels (holding gun) poses with two friends about 1913. Was the rifle a new birthday gift? Had she just vanquished a chicken hawk? Her elegant dress and tiny waist contrast with her easy, familiar grasp of the rifle. She evidently was quite a Texas lady!

It's A Texas Thing

TEXAS SPECIAL

December 24, 1944. Christmas Eve. The last winter of World War II. Wartime troop train movements were secret.

But First Presbyterian Church ladies regularly met those trains at Denison's Katy Depot with carts of sandwiches, cookies, coffee and smiles. It seems when the Stationmaster in Muskogee, Oklahoma, called Helen Marie Steele, church secretary, she had about two hours to pass the word before a troop train arrived.

"Miss Betsy" Munson had set up a rotating system so hostesses and food were always ready. Trains were cleaned and serviced in Denison, allowing soldiers about thirty minutes to get out and stretch their legs. Frances Prideaux remembers the boys especially enjoyed talking to the girls who pushed the serving carts.

The Christmas Eve train carried new Colorado-trained ski troopers whose unknown destination would turn out to be the Italian Alps. Along with refreshments, caroling song sheets were handed out. As the singing began, the church choir director was spontaneously lifted onto a baggage cart which was pulled down the length of the train so all could see. The voices of twenty-two carloads of young men swelled in carols until they literally could be heard all over town.

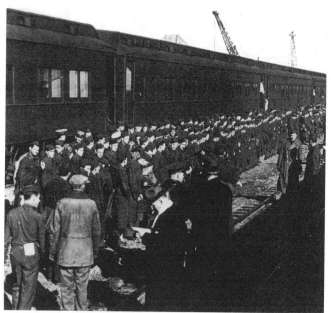

The first contingent of soldiers detraining January 16, 1942, for Perrin Field, then called Grayson County Flying School.

Chicken/Turkey Roll-Ups

16 ounces cream cheese, softened
2 (4¼ ounce) cans black olives,
    drained, chopped
2 (4½ ounce) cans chopped green
    chiles, drained
   Garlic powder to taste

   Salt to taste
   Picante sauce to taste, drained
1 (20 count) package flour tortillas,
    fajita size
20 slices thinly sliced chicken or
    turkey

Combine softened cream cheese, black olives, green chiles, garlic powder, salt and drained picante sauce. Spread mixture on flour tortillas. Place chicken or turkey on top of mixture and roll up. Put the roll-up in plastic wrap and refrigerate until firm. Take out of plastic wrap; slice.

Taco Snack Mix

½ cup margarine, melted
1 package taco seasoning mix
1 tablespoon Worcestershire sauce

½ teaspoon seasoned salt
1 (13½ ounce) box baked cheese
    snack crackers

Preheat oven to 250 degrees. In a small bowl, mix well the first 4 ingredients. Place crackers in a large shallow baking dish; pour butter mixture over crackers and stir well. Bake 1 hour; stir every 15 minutes. Put onto waxed paper and cool. Store in airtight container. Yield: about 6 cups.

Easy Texas Caviar

2 large tomatoes, chopped
4 green onions, chopped
1 (4¼ ounce) can chopped ripe
    olives
1 (4½ ounce) can chopped green
    chiles

1-2 tablespoons salad oil
1   teaspoon garlic salt
1   tablespoon vinegar
    Black pepper

Mix all the above ingredients; pour into a covered dish. Sprinkle with pepper. Cover; marinate overnight. Serve with chips.

Texas Black Bean Caviar

1 (16 ounce) can black beans, drained	1 cup chopped tomatoes
1 (8 ounce) can small white corn, drained	½ bunch chopped cilantro
1 (16 ounce) can tomatoes with diced jalapeños	⅛ cup red wine vinegar
	Juice of one lemon
½ cup diced green onions	1 garlic clove, minced
½ cup diced yellow peppers	Cayenne pepper to taste
½ cup diced green peppers	Chili powder to taste
	Garlic salt to taste
	Dash of cumin

Combine ingredients in a large bowl. Season to taste. Chill; serve with tortilla chips.

Creamy Olive and Tomato Dip

16 ounces cream cheese, softened	Dash Worcestershire sauce
½ cup green olives with pimentos, chopped	½ teaspoon lemon juice
1 (10 ounce) can diced tomatoes and green chiles	Seasoned Salt to taste
	Black pepper to taste

Mix all ingredients thoroughly; chill. Serve with crackers or raw vegetables. Yield: 8 to 10 servings.

Green Chili and Bacon Dip

16 ounces cream cheese, softened	½ large bell pepper, finely minced
½ cup mayonnaise	8 strips bacon, fried crisp and crumbled
1 tablespoon lemon juice	
1 small clove garlic, crushed	1 (4½ ounce) can chopped green chiles
½ large onion, finely minced	

Mix first 3 ingredients in a food processor until smooth. Put in a mixing bowl; add remaining ingredients. Chill 3 to 4 hours before serving. Serve with melba toast or corn chips. Yield: 3 cups.

Picante Sauce

2   large cans whole tomatoes,
    drained
1   medium onion
1   large jalapeño, or to taste

5-6 fresh leaves of cilantro
    Garlic salt to taste
    Salt to taste

Drain tomatoes. Put 2 or 3 tomatoes in a blender; add onion and jalapeño (cut in fourths). Chop until fine. Add cilantro and remaining tomatoes; touch the "CHOP" button a few times until tomatoes are chopped, but not blended. Add seasoning to taste, stirring by hand. Serve immediately, or may be refrigerated for later use. Yield: approximately 4 cups.

☾ Piña Colada Dip

1   (8 ounce) can crushed pineapple
    in its own juice, undrained
1   (3.4 ounce) package instant
    coconut pudding and pie filling
    mix

¾   cup milk
½   cup sour cream

In a food processor bowl with metal blade or a blender, combine all ingredients. Cover and blend 30 seconds. Refrigerate several hours or overnight to blend flavors. If using a blender, stir after 15 seconds. Good dip for fruit.

May use pistachio pudding instead of coconut pudding.

Salsa Fresca

1   cup chopped tomatoes
⅓   cup finely chopped white onions
2   serrano chile peppers, seeded and
    finely chopped

1   tablespoon freshly squeezed lime
    juice
2   teaspoons finely chopped fresh
    cilantro
    Salt to taste

In a medium bowl place all ingredients; mix together. Cover bowl with plastic wrap; refrigerate for 30 minutes. Yield: approximately 1½ cups.

Texas Fudge

3	(4½ ounce) cans chopped green chiles	1	pound grated Cheddar cheese
1	(5½ ounce) can evaporated milk	1	pound grated Monterey Jack cheese
6	eggs		

Spread green chiles on bottom of a lightly sprayed 8 x 12-inch baking dish. Mix other ingredients together; spread over chiles. Bake at 350 degrees for 30 minutes until center is firm and top is golden brown. Cut into small squares and serve with wheat thins.

Sherry's Southwestern Dip

1	(10¾ ounce) can cream of mushroom soup	1	cup crushed corn chips
1	(4½ ounce) can green chiles	1	inch slice from a 2 pound loaf of processed cheese, cubed
1	(5 ounce) can chicken, drained		

Mix all ingredients; microwave 4 to 5 minutes. Serve with chips while warm.

History in the making. All it took was a refrigerated railroad car. Early Denison pioneer R. L. Rankin built one, accumulating over two dozen patents along the way.

With whirlwind speed, Rankin founded the Denison Artic Ice Co., found capital to finance his vision of rail shipment of fresh meat to the East, was voted bond funds by Denison to build slaughter pens and packing sheds, and persuaded his friend Joseph McCoy to move to Denison to provide cattle shipping experience.

The Quick Meat Transit Co. on November 24, 1873, shipped 130 head of dressed prime beef in refrigerated cars on the Katy railroad. Denison was not yet one year old. Incredible!

Tortilla Roll-Ups

16 ounces sour cream
8   ounces cream cheese, softened
1½ cups grated Cheddar cheese
2   tablespoons dried onions

1   (4½ ounce) can chopped chiles, drained
1   (4¼ ounce) can chopped black olives, drained
1   package flour tortillas

Mix first 6 ingredients well. Spread on tortillas; roll up and slice. Serve!

A Dining Car Menu for

Fiesta Time

Picante Sauce
Taco Soup
No-Fuss Chicken Fajitas
Sour Cream Enchiladas
Allyne's Buttermilk Pralines
Texas Fudge
Mango Melon Colada

Sopaipillas

4   cups flour
1   teaspoon salt
2   tablespoons baking powder
4   tablespoons shortening

¾   cup warm water
Vegetable oil for frying
Honey or cinnamon and sugar for dipping

Combine dry ingredients and cut in shortening until mix resembles cornmeal. Add water and mix until dough is nice and smooth. Knead a couple of minutes on a floured board. Cover dough and let rise ½ hour in a warm, draft free area.

Roll dough into a rectangle, about a ⅓ inch thickness and cut into about 3 inch squares. Heat oil in a deep fryer to 375 degrees. Drop squares into oil, turning at once so they will puff evenly. Brown on both sides; drain on paper towels.

Traditionally, sopaipillas are served warm with honey, or you can roll them (while hot) in a mixture of ½ cup sugar mixed with 1 teaspoon cinnamon.

Mango Melon Colada

⅓ cantaloupe, chunked (about 2 cups)	2 tablespoon fresh lime juice
1 mango, chunked (about 1½ cups)	2 tablespoons superfine sugar
3 tablespoons cream of coconut	4 ounces light rum
	2 cups crushed ice

Process all ingredients and 2 cups crushed ice in blender until smooth (about 20 seconds). Pour into glasses and serve immediately. Yield: 4 drinks.

Margarita Smoothie

1 (6 ounce) can frozen limeade concentrate	1 lime, peeled
½-1 can Tequila	Ice
	½ cup whipped dessert topping

Place first 3 ingredients in a blender. Add enough ice to fill blender about ⅔ full. Add whipped dessert topping. Blend until smooth. Serve!

Texas Twister

1½ ounces citrus flavored vodka	1 tablespoon lemon juice
½ ounce triple sec	Sweet and Sour mix

Fill a tall glass ¾ full with crushed ice; pour vodka, triple sec and lemon juice over ice. Fill glass with Sweet and Sour mix. Stir and Serve!

Chili Relleno Bake

½ pound ground beef	2 cups sharp shredded cheese, divided
½ pound pork sausage	
1 cup chopped onion	4 eggs
2 cloves garlic, minced	¼ cup flour
2 (4½ ounce) cans whole green chiles, drained and seeded, divided	1½ cups milk
	Salt to taste

Brown meats; add onion and garlic and cook until onion is soft. Drain off fat. Lightly spray a 9-inch square baking dish and line with half of the chiles; top with 1½ cups cheese. Add meat mixture and top with remaining chiles. Beat eggs and flour until smooth. Add milk, season to taste and blend well. Pour over casserole. Bake at 350 degrees for about 40 minutes or until knife inserted comes out clean. Top with remaining cheese. Let stand 5 minutes before serving.

Huevos Revueltos A La Mexicana

This is a classic Mexican breakfast which includes salsa ingredients mixed in with scrambled eggs.

2 tablespoons vegetable oil	10 eggs, beaten with 2 tablespoons
½ cup chopped tomatoes	water
¼ cup chopped white onions	¼ teaspoon salt
1-2 serrano chile peppers, seeded, and chopped small	

In a medium skillet place the oil and heat on medium until hot. Add tomatoes, onions and serrano chile peppers. Sauté for 2 minutes, or until onions are translucent. Add eggs and salt stirring occasionally for 5 minutes, or until firm. Yield: 4 servings.

Serve eggs with refried beans, cheese and warm tortillas. A lot of people like to put everything in a tortilla, roll it up and then eat it.

Corn and Cheese Bake

2 eggs, beaten	2-3 teaspoons sugar
1 cup creamed cottage cheese	1 teaspoon onion salt
½ cup sour cream	¼-½ teaspoon pepper
⅓ cup chopped green chiles, drained	1 (15 ounce) can whole kernel golden sweet corn
3 tablespoons flour	3 tablespoons chopped ripe olives
3 tablespoons milk	¼ cup shredded Cheddar cheese

Heat oven to 350 degrees. In a large bowl combine eggs and cottage cheese; blend well. Add sour cream and chiles; mix well. In a small bowl combine flour and milk; beat until smooth. Add to cottage cheese mixture. Stir in sugar, onion salt, pepper and corn; blend well. Pour into ungreased 2-quart baking dish. Bake for 30 to 40 minutes or until knife inserted in center comes out clean. Sprinkle top with olives and Cheddar cheese. Bake an additional 1 to 2 minutes or until cheese is melted. Yield: 6 to 8 servings.

Hot Rice

1	stick margarine, melted	1	chopped jalapeño pepper or
1	cup chopped onion		1 (4½ ounce) can chopped green
1	cup regular long grain rice		chiles
1	(10¾ ounce) can chicken broth	4	ounces processed cheese loaf,
1	cup water		cubed
			Garlic powder

Mix all ingredients in a saucepan and bring to a boil. Simmer for about 20 minutes until all liquid is absorbed.

Dirty Rice

1½	pounds ground beef	2	tablespoons picante sauce, or to
1	medium onion, chopped		taste
1	bell pepper, chopped	½-¾	pound processed cheese loaf,
1	cup celery, chopped		chopped into pieces
1	(10¾ ounce) can chicken and rice soup		Salt and pepper to taste
1	(10¾ ounce) can cream of mushroom soup	1	cup white rice, cooked

Cook and drain meat and vegetables. Add other ingredients until cheese melts. Stir in cooked rice and serve. Yield: 6 to 8 servings.

Texas Sour Dough Biscuits

2	packages active dry yeast	1	teaspoon salt
1	cup warm water	2½	tablespoons sugar
5	cups self-rising flour	⅔	cup olive oil
1	teaspoon baking soda	2	cups buttermilk

Dissolve yeast in water; set aside. Mix all dry ingredients. Then add yeast, oil and buttermilk; mix well. Form mixture into a ball and store in an airtight container in refrigerator. Dough keeps in refrigerator for 6 weeks. Cut off amounts as needed and make rolls any shape desired. Bake on a lightly greased pan at 350 degrees for 20 to 25 minutes or until golden brown.

If dough is sticky, lightly flour hands for shaping into a ball.

Val's Texas Cornbread

5	tablespoons shortening	1	tablespoon sugar, optional
1	cup yellow cornmeal	3	teaspoons baking powder
2	cups milk	2	eggs
1	teaspoon salt		

Preheat oven to 350 degrees. Put shortening in a 9-inch square or similar size pan and put in oven to melt. Add cornmeal to mixing bowl. From pan pour into cornmeal 3 tablespoons melted shortening, leaving approximately 2 tablespoons in pan. Return pan to oven and heat shortening to very hot. Mix shortening into cornmeal. In saucepan, bring milk to boil. Watch milk as it begins to boil and let it climb the sides of the pan before pouring into cornmeal. Stir well. Add salt, sugar and baking powder to cornmeal mixture. Add eggs and mix well. Pour mixture into pan and cook about 30 minutes or until nicely browned.

Dairy farms dotted the Denison countryside. One of Bill Sharp's earliest memories is hearing his father calling before sunrise for him and his brother, Joe, to hit the floor and get the milking done. Less than ten years old and still half asleep, the boys rested their foreheads on the cows' warm flanks, only raising them to respond to the barn cats with well aimed streams of warm milk in their mouths.

Bill Ashburn recalls as a child, his grandfather contracted with cow-owning city folk to graze their stock in his ample pastures in the summer so they didn't have to buy hay. In the morning, Bill and his brothers herded the bossies to pasture, then walked them home each evening. Going home, the cows would peel off and go to their own barn without any help from the boys.

Ashburn's Dairy door-to-door delivery routes, first by wagon then by truck, served home customers. After 1907 the milk was pasteurized for both home and wholesale customers.

Mexican Cornbread

1 cup cornmeal	1 small onion, chopped
1 cup milk	Garlic salt or garlic powder to
2 eggs	taste
½ cup bacon drippings	4-5 jalapeño peppers, seeded and
1 cup cream style corn	chopped
½ teaspoon baking soda	½ pound sharp Cheddar cheese,
¾ teaspoon salt	finely grated

Preheat oven to 425 degrees. Mix all ingredients together. This makes a thin batter. Bake for 25 minutes.

Migas

2 corn tortillas	2 tablespoons minced pepper, hot
Oil for cooking	or sweet
¼ cup chopped onion	4 eggs, beaten
¼ cup chopped tomato	Salt and pepper to taste

Cut tortillas into 1 inch square pieces. Cook in a skillet with oil until crisp. Cook onion, tomato, and pepper in oil until tender; remove. Cook 4 eggs, salt and pepper until half done; add tortillas and veggies. Cook until eggs are still moist. Yield: 2 servings.

Mexican Quiche

15 eggs, beaten	½ pound Monterey Jack cheese, grated
½ cup flour	1 (7 ounce) can chopped green
1 pint cottage cheese	chile peppers
½ pound Cheddar cheese, grated	1 teaspoon baking powder

Toppings: sour cream, scallions and red salsa on the side

Preheat oven to 350 degrees. Place all ingredients in a large bowl; beat together well. Place mixture in a greased medium baking pan. Bake for 30 minutes, or until a knife inserted in the center comes out clean. Yield: 10 to 12 servings.

Easy Chili Relleno

2 (4½ ounce) cans chopped green chiles	4 eggs, slightly beaten
1 pound Monterey Jack cheese, cut in small cubes	½ cup milk
	½ teaspoon dry mustard
½ cup chopped ripe olives	Salt to taste

Preheat oven to 325 degrees. In a greased baking dish; layer chiles, cheese and olives. Repeat twice more. Mix beaten eggs, milk, mustard and salt; pour over chile mixture. Put baking dish in a pan of hot water. Bake for 35 minutes or until eggs are firm.

☽ Salpiçon (Mexican Roast)

8 pound top sirloin roast	½ cup chopped fresh cilantro
2 cloves garlic, minced	Salt and pepper to taste
2 bay leaves	1½ cups chopped green chiles
1 tablespoon peppercorns	½ pound Monterey Jack cheese cut into ½ inch chunks
5-6 dried red chiles OR 2 tablespoons crushed dried red chiles	¼ cup chopped fresh parsley
1 (16 ounce) can tomatoes, diced	

Suggested toppings: guacamole, flour tortillas, picante sauce

Marinade

6 ounces oil	½ teaspoon dried oregano
2 ounces red wine vinegar	½ teaspoon dried basil
Salt and pepper	

First Day: Place beef in a large pot. Cover with water and add garlic, bay leaves, peppercorns, red chiles, tomatoes, ¼ cup cilantro and about a tablespoon of salt. Bring to a boil; simmer 5 hours. Remove meat and cool. Cut into pieces, about 2 inches square, then shred. Place in 8 x 11-inch baking dish and cover with marinade. Marinate overnight.

Second Day: Top beef with chopped green chiles and cheese squares; sprinkle with remaining cilantro and chopped parsley. Bake at 325 degrees for 20 to 30 minutes until meat is heated through. Yield: 16 servings.

☽ Barbecue Brisket

5-6 pound trimmed boneless beef brisket Celery salt Onion salt Garlic salt	3 ounces liquid smoke Salt and pepper to taste Worcestershire sauce 6 ounces barbecue sauce Flour or corn starch

Place trimmed boneless beef in a large freezer bag. Sprinkle generously with celery salt, onion salt and garlic salt. Add 3 ounces liquid smoke. Turn occasionally to coat meat with liquid smoke. Refrigerate overnight.

Sprinkle both sides of meat with salt, pepper and Worcestershire sauce. Place in a tightly covered roaster and cook at 275 degrees for 5 hours. Uncover meat and pour 6 ounces of commercial barbecue sauce over meat and cook 1 more hour, uncovered. Remove meat; skim fat from sauce. Thicken sauce with flour or corn starch. Let meat cool for easier carving. Heat the sauce and serve hot. Yield: 10 generous servings. Freezes well.

Beef Enchiladas

2 tablespoons butter
¼ cup diced onion
2-3 chopped jalapeño peppers
2 tablespoons flour
2 cups milk
¾ pound processed cheese loaf,
    grated
	1 pound ground beef, can use
	    up to ½ pound more
	½ onion, chopped
	1½ teaspoons salt
	1½ teaspoons black pepper
	1½ teaspoons chili powder
	Flour tortillas
	Cooking oil

Melt butter; brown onion and peppers. Add flour and milk. Bring to a simmer; remove from stove. Add cheese; set aside to cool. While meat is browning, add chopped onion and seasonings. When browned, remove from heat and drain in a colander. Heat tortillas in just enough cooking oil to coat; drain. On tortilla, put 2 tablespoons of meat mixture and roll. Place in a casserole and pour cheese sauce over them. Make sure all are covered. Bake at 350 degrees for 15 to 20 minutes.

A Dining Car Menu for a *Fireside Dinner for Eight*
Blackened Ribeye with Roasted Vegetable Salsa
Spinach and Garlic Sauté
The Adolphus Hotel Scalloped Potatoes
Mattie Howard's Hot Rolls
Creamy Mocha Frozen Dessert

Blackened Rib-Eye
with Roasted Vegetable Salsa

1	tablespoon ground cumin	2	tablespoons kosher salt
1	tablespoon ground dried oregano	8	rib-eye steaks
1	tablespoon ground coriander	2	tablespoons canola oil, or as needed
1	tablespoon red chili pepper		Roasted Vegetable Salsa, recipe follows
1	teaspoon cayenne pepper		
½	tablespoon black pepper		

In a low-sided dish, place all spices and seasonings; mix well. Dredge each steak in mixture so that it is well coated on both sides. In a large heavy skillet, place oil and heat on medium until hot. Sear steaks on both sides until the desired doneness is achieved. Serve steaks with Roasted Vegetable Salsa on top, recipe follows. Yield: 8 servings.

Roasted Vegetable Salsa

4	ears fresh corn, husked, grilled and kernels removed	1	large red onion, peeled, roasted and thinly sliced
1	green bell pepper, roasted, peeled, seeded and chopped	½	cup fresh cilantro, chopped
1	red bell pepper, roasted, peeled, seeded and chopped	2	tablespoons freshly squeezed lime juice
1	poblano chili pepper, roasted, peeled, seeded and chopped	1	teaspoon red chili powder
			Salt and pepper to taste

In a medium bowl, combine all ingredients and toss well. Yield: approximately 3 cups.

To roast peppers, place on cookie sheet and broil until skin turns black. Turn peppers so they blacken on all sides. Remove from oven; place in bag and cool. Core and remove skin.

Mexican Beef Casserole

1½ pounds ground beef	1 (10¾ ounce) can cream of
1 medium onion, chopped	chicken soup
1 (4½ ounce) can chopped green	1 (16 ounce) can enchilada sauce
chiles	(mild or medium, your choice)
1 (10¾ ounce) can cream of	12 corn tortillas
mushroom soup	8 ounces grated Cheddar cheese
	Salt and pepper if desired

Brown meat and onion; drain. Add next 4 ingredients and cook until well blended. In a 9 x 13-inch baking dish place a layer of tortillas, cover with a layer of meat sauce; repeat layers. Cover with grated cheese. Bake at 350 degrees for 20 minutes or until cheese melts. Can be made in advance.

⊘ Tortilla Soup

2 (10¾ ounce) cans chicken with	1 can Mexican vegetables, drained
rice soup	⅓ cup sherry, optional
4 soup cans of water	Basil, chives, parsley to taste
1 (10 ounce) can diced tomatoes	(your choice)
with green chiles	1 teaspoon chili powder
1-2 (6 ounce) cans premium chunks	1 teaspoon cumin
chicken or turkey white meat	Garlic powder to taste

Toppings: grated Cheddar cheese and chopped green onion

Combine all ingredients. Bring to a boil; simmer for 10 minutes. Serve with suggested toppings.

Quick Mexican Pizza

½ pound ground beef	2 cups shredded Colby/Monterey
1½ teaspoons chili powder	Jack cheese
½ teaspoon cumin	Green/red peppers, onions,
1 cup salsa	mushrooms, etc., as desired
4 (10 inch) flour tortillas	

Preheat oven to 400 degrees. Cook meat; drain. Stir in seasonings. Spread ¼ cup of salsa and ½ cup of meat mixture on each tortilla. Top each with ½ cup of cheese and desired toppings. Bake 8 to 10 minutes or until crisp and lightly browned. Yield: 4 servings.

Mexican Salad

1½ heads of lettuce, chopped
1½ pounds yellow cheese, shredded
22 ounces of Ranch Style beans,
     rinsed, drained and chilled
2½ tomatoes, chopped
1½ onions, chopped

1½ pounds ground beef, cooked,
     drained and chilled
12 ounces Catalina dressing, chilled
2½ avocados, chopped
1   (2 ounce) jar chopped pimentos,
     optional
1   large bag corn chips, crushed fine

Place first 6 ingredients in a large bowl; refrigerate 4 hours. Before serving mix in dressing. Arrange on a long platter or tray; garnish with avocados, pimentos and crushed corn chips.

Can substitute Catalina dressing with picante sauce.

Tortilla Casserole

1½ pounds ground beef
1   medium onion, diced
     Salt, chili powder, and garlic salt
     to taste
12 corn tortillas
1   (15 ounce) can Ranch Style beans
1   pound sharp Cheddar cheese,
     grated

1   (10¾ ounce) can cream of
     mushroom soup
1   (10 ounce) can diced tomatoes
     and green chiles
1   (4½ ounce) can chopped green
     chiles

Cook ground beef in skillet with onion until brown. Season with salt, chili powder and garlic salt. Line a large, deep, greased casserole with half the tortillas. Place a layer of meat and onion over the tortillas; spread beans and a layer of cheese over the meat mixture. Top with remaining half of tortillas. Mix soup and tomatoes together and spread over all. Sprinkle chopped green chiles. Cover with foil and bake at 350 degrees for 1 hour.

Can cook beef with 1 package taco seasoning if desired.

Spanish Green Beans

3-4 slices bacon, chopped
½ cup chopped onion
4 tablespoons chopped green peppers
1-2 tablespoons flour

2 (14½ ounce) cans tomatoes
2 (14½ ounce) cans green beans, drained
Salt and pepper to taste
Picante sauce to taste

Cook bacon, onion, and green pepper until crisp. Stir in flour. Add tomatoes and green beans. Season to taste. Add picante to taste. Bake at 350 degrees for 30 minutes.

◷ Fancy Ranch Style Beans

This recipe from Susie Luchsinger is ample to serve her large family or please a crowd. Her name may be Susie McEntire Luchsinger, but she's much more than Reba's little sister. She has won a string of awards and honors with several Number One hits on the Christian Country charts. One of the reasons Susie is so popular is that her songs are about maintaining hope through struggles and hardships of everyday life. Susie, Paul and their family travel across the U.S. and as far away as Australia performing at concerts, churches, rodeos, conventions and special events.

1 pound ground beef
1 onion, chopped
1 gallon Ranch Style Beans

1 (28 ounce) can chopped stewed tomatoes
½ cup chopped celery

Brown meat in skillet with onion; drain. Add remaining ingredients. Simmer for 15 minutes. Serve with cornbread or crackers.

◷ Hot Beef Dish

1 pound ground beef
1 small onion, chopped
1 (10 ounce) can diced tomatoes and green chiles

1 (15 ounce) can chili beans
1 package taco seasoning mix
Tortilla chips, crushed
Grated cheese

Brown meat and onion in a skillet; drain meat. Stir in tomatoes and green chiles, chili beans and taco seasoning mix. Continue to simmer for about 10 minutes. Pour into a baking dish lightly sprayed with a nonstick cooking spray. Sprinkle crushed tortilla chips over mixture. Sprinkle grated cheese over top. Heat at 350 degrees until cheese is melted into mixture.

Sour Cream Enchiladas

12	corn tortillas	¼	cup flour
	Cooking oil for tortillas	1	(10½ ounce) can chicken broth
3-4	cups Monterey Jack cheese, grated		Chopped jalapeño peppers, to taste
1	large onion, chopped	8	ounces sour cream
¼	cup cooking oil		

Cook tortillas in hot oil until soft. Drain on paper towels. Put grated cheese and chopped onion on each tortilla and roll up; place in baking dish. In a saucepan put approximately ¼ cup cooking oil. Add an equal amount of flour and stir until smooth. Gradually add chicken broth and chopped peppers; heat to boiling. This should be slightly thick. Add sour cream; heat and stir, but do not let boil. Pour over enchiladas and bake at 350 degrees for about 45 minutes until onions are done.

To keep enchiladas from getting hard on the bottom, move them slightly with a fork so sauce can get under them.

❄ Mexican Chicken Casserole

1½	pounds boneless chicken breasts, cooked and cubed	1	(2 ounce) jar chopped pimento, drained
1	large onion, chopped	1-2	(4½ ounce) cans green chiles, mashed
1	stick butter	3	(10¾ ounce) cans cream of chicken soup
1	medium can sliced mushrooms		
1-2	(8 ounce) cans sliced water chestnuts, drained	18	corn tortillas, cut in pieces
		1	pound grated Cheddar cheese, sharp or mild, to taste

Prepare chicken; set aside. Sauté onion in butter; add mushrooms, water chestnuts, pimento, chiles, soup and tortilla pieces. Alternate layers of tortilla mixture with layers of chicken pieces in a 3-quart casserole. Top with cheese; bake at 350 degrees for 30 minutes. Yield: 8 to 10 servings.

No Fuss Chicken Fajitas

2	tablespoons lemon juice	6	flour tortillas
½	teaspoon salt	2	tablespoons vegetable oil
¼	teaspoon black pepper	1	medium onion, sliced and
¼	teaspoon garlic powder		separated into rings
½	teaspoon liquid smoke	1	green pepper, cut into thin strips
3	boneless, skinless, chicken breast halves, cut into small strips		

Toppings: chopped onion, lettuce, shredded cheese and picante sauce

Combine lemon juice, salt, pepper, garlic powder and liquid smoke in a small bowl. Add chicken; stir to coat. Cover; chill at least 30 minutes. Drain chicken, reserving marinade. Wrap tortillas in aluminum foil; bake at 350 degrees for 15 minutes. Heat oil in a heavy skillet. Add chicken; cook until no longer pink, stirring constantly. Add marinade, pepper and onion; sauté until vegetables are crisp-tender. Remove from heat. Divide mixture evenly; spoon a portion on to each tortilla. Top with desired toppings; roll tortilla.

Chicken Enchilada Casserole

1	large onion, chopped	1	(10¾ ounce) can cream of mushroom soup
2	tablespoons butter		
1-2	(4½ ounce) cans of chopped mild green chiles	1	(10½ ounce) can chicken broth
1	(10¾ ounce) can cream of chicken soup	2	large cans of white chicken OR 4 to 5 cooked chicken breasts
		1	bag tortilla chips
		2	cups grated Cheddar cheese

Serve with ranch dressing, sour cream and/or hot sauce

Sauté onion in butter until tender; add green chiles, soups and cubed chicken. Pour tortilla chips in a lightly sprayed 9 x 13-inch baking dish. Add mixture; cover with cheese and bake at 350 degrees for 30 minutes or until cheese melts. Serve hot with suggested toppings.

Salsa Topped Chicken Breasts

1 (15 ounce) can black beans, rinsed and drained	1½ tablespoons Dijon mustard
1¼ cups frozen whole kernel corn, thawed	¼ teaspoon salt
	⅛ teaspoon black pepper
¾ cup finely chopped red onion	1 tablespoon chili powder
¾ cup finely chopped sweet red pepper	1 teaspoon ground cumin
	¼ teaspoon salt
2 jalapeño peppers, seeded and finely chopped	⅛ teaspoon pepper
	4 boneless, skinless chicken breast halves
½ cup balsamic vinegar	2 tablespoons butter
¼ cup olive oil	¼ cup chopped fresh cilantro

Combine first 10 ingredients; cover and chill at least 2 hours. Combine chili powder and next 3 ingredients; sprinkle over chicken. Melt butter in a nonstick skillet; add chicken and cook 5 to 7 minutes on each side or until done. Stir cilantro into black bean mixture. Serve over chicken. Yield: 4 servings.

Turkey Casserole

1 pound ground turkey	1 (15 ounce) can black beans, drained
⅓ cup chopped onion	
1 clove garlic, minced	¼ cup water
1 tablespoon vinegar	1 (16 ounce) jar mild or medium salsa
2 teaspoons chili powder	
1½ teaspoons dried oregano, crushed	6 (6 inch) corn tortillas, cut into 1 inch strips
½ teaspoon ground cumin	
Dash ground red pepper, optional	¾ cup shredded reduced fat Cheddar cheese

Cook turkey, onion and garlic in a large skillet until turkey is no longer pink; drain fat. Add vinegar, chili powder, oregano, cumin and red pepper, if desired. Cook and stir for 1 minute more. Stir in beans and water; remove from heat. Place about 2 tablespoons of salsa on the bottom of a 2-quart baking dish. Place half of the tortilla strips in the dish. Top with half of the turkey mixture and half of the remaining salsa; repeat layers. Cover and bake at 325 degrees for 30 minutes. Uncover; sprinkle with cheese. Bake 5 to 10 minutes more or until cheese is melted and mixture is heated through. Yield: 6 servings.

Guadalajara Chicken

½ cup flour seasoned with salt and pepper
4-6 boneless, skinless chicken breasts, cut into strips
4-5 tablespoons margarine, divided
1 small onion, sliced

1 (4½ ounce) can whole green chiles, sliced lengthwise
½ pint whipping cream
1 cup grated Monterey Jack cheese, garnish
Cooked white rice, if desired

Flour chicken and sauté in margarine until cooked. (Do NOT overcook) Remove chicken from skillet. Sauté onion in remaining margarine; add green chiles and cook briefly. Add whipping cream, mix well; add chicken strips. Cook until chicken is reheated. Turn off heat; sprinkle with one cup Monterey Jack cheese. Serve over white rice.

Vegetable Chili with Cornmeal Biscuits

1 (15 ounce) can chili without beans
1 (14½ ounce) can Mexican-style stewed tomatoes, chopped
1 cup cooked black-eyed peas
1 cup cooked corn

1 cup diced green bell pepper
1 cup diced zucchini
1 cup diced yellow squash
½ cup minced fresh cilantro
Cornmeal biscuits, recipe follows

Toppings: shredded cheese, minced green onion, sour cream

Combine first 8 ingredients in a 3-quart pan; bring to a boil. Cover, reduce heat and simmer 15 minutes or until vegetables are tender. Prepare biscuits. Ladle chili into bowls; add toppings as desired and serve with biscuits.

Cornmeal Biscuits

1½ cups biscuit baking mix
½ cup self-rising cornmeal
½ teaspoon ground red pepper

3 tablespoons firm margarine or butter
⅔ cup milk
Butter, melted

Heat oven to 450 degrees. Combine baking mix, cornmeal and pepper. Cut butter into ¼ inch pieces; add to baking mix. Toss with fork until coated. Stir in milk until just moistened. Turn dough onto surface coated with baking mix and knead 10 times. Roll dough into 8 inch squares and cut into 8 triangles. Place on ungreased cookie sheet. Brush lightly with melted butter. Bake 8 to 10 minutes or until golden.

King Ranch Chicken

¼ cup margarine
1 medium green bell pepper,
 chopped
1 medium onion, chopped
1 (10¾ ounce) can cream of
 mushroom soup
1 (10¾ ounce) can cream of
 chicken soup

1 (10 ounce) can of diced tomatoes
 and green chiles
2 cups cooked cubed chicken
12 corn tortillas, torn into bite-size
 pieces
2 cups (8 ounces) shredded
 Cheddar cheese

Preheat oven to 325 degrees. In a large saucepan, cook pepper and onion in margarine until tender, about 5 minutes. Add soups, tomatoes and chiles, and chicken, stirring until well blended. In a lightly sprayed 9 x 13-inch baking dish, alternately layer tortillas, soup mixture and cheese; repeat layer. Bake 40 minutes or until hot and bubbling. Yield: 8 servings.

Gourmet Chili Con Carne

 Cooking oil
2 medium onions, finely chopped
1 cup finely chopped green and red
 peppers
6 cloves garlic, pressed
4 tablespoons chili powder
2 teaspoons ground cumin
3 teaspoons oregano

2 pounds ground beef
1 tablespoon salt
½ teaspoon black pepper
3½-4 cups fresh tomatoes or
 1 (32 ounce) can tomatoes,
 undrained
2 (16 ounce) cans red kidney
 beans, undrained

Heat oil in a 4 or 5-quart pot. Sauté onions until clear. Add peppers and garlic; sauté until soft. Add chili powder, cumin, oregano, ground beef, salt and pepper. Cook slowly, stirring often until meat is brown and broken apart. Add tomatoes and kidney beans, including liquid. Stir well to combine ingredients. Cover; simmer slowly at least 1 hour, preferably 2 to 3 hours. Taste and adjust seasonings, if necessary. Stir often to avoid burning. Yield: 6 to 8 servings.

San Antonio Chili

3	pounds coarsely ground beef	¼	tablespoon cayenne pepper, optional
6	tablespoons chili powder		
1	tablespoon oregano	2	large cloves garlic, minced
1	tablespoon cumin	1	teaspoon hot pepper sauce
1	tablespoon salt	1½	quarts water
		¼	cup white cornmeal

In a Dutch oven, brown ground beef; drain. Add seasonings and water; heat to boil. Reduce heat; cover and simmer for 1 hour and 30 minutes. Skim off fat. Stir in cornmeal and simmer uncovered for 30 minutes; stir occasionally. Yield: 8 servings.

Can use part ground beef, pork and venison. Use cayenne pepper for "hot" chili.

Chili Blanco Soup

½	pound turkey or chicken breast, diced	1	cup diced fresh tomatoes
		1	cup diced squash
1	tablespoon vegetable oil	1	cup whole kernel corn
½	cup diced celery	½	teaspoon salt
½	cup chopped onion	½	teaspoon ground cumin
½	cup chopped green chiles	⅛	teaspoon black pepper
2	cups water or chicken broth	⅛	teaspoon cayenne pepper
1	(16 ounce) can white navy beans		

Toppings: grated Cheddar cheese, chopped green onion and chopped cilantro

Brown turkey breast in oil in a stew pot. Add next 3 ingredients; cook until tender. Add remaining ingredients; mix well. Bring to a boil; reduce heat and simmer 30 minutes. Serve with suggested toppings. Yield: 6 to 8 servings.

Drain juice after simmering. Pour into a large casserole dish; cover with a batch of cornbread mix. Bake at 350 degrees for 30 to 45 minutes.

Taco Soup

1 pound lean ground beef	1 (15 ounce) can tomato sauce
1 large onion, chopped	1½ cups water
3 (16 ounce) cans Mexican-style chili beans, undrained	1 (4½ ounce) can chopped green chiles
1 (16 ounce) can whole kernel corn, undrained OR yellow hominy	1 (1¼ ounce) package taco seasoning mix
1 (16 ounce) can chopped tomatoes, undrained	1 (1 ounce) envelope ranch salad dressing mix

Toppings: tortilla chips, shredded lettuce, chopped tomato, sour cream, chopped avocado

Cook ground beef and onion in a large Dutch oven over medium-high heat until meat is browned, stirring until it crumbles; drain. Stir in beans and next 7 ingredients. Bring to a boil; reduce heat and simmer uncovered 15 minutes. Serve with desired toppings. Yield: 3½ quarts.

Cowboy Steak and Veggie Soup

1 pound boneless beef sirloin	1 pound package frozen mixture green beans, potato, onions and red peppers
1 teaspoon dried basil leaves	
2 garlic cloves, crushed	
Salt and pepper to taste	1 (15½ ounce) can great northern beans, drained, rinsed
1 tablespoon oil	
2 (14½ ounce) cans beef broth	1 cup torn fresh spinach
8 ounces thick salsa	Fresh basil, garnish

Cut beef into 1 inch chunks. Cook beef, basil, garlic, salt and pepper in oil 4 to 5 minutes or until brown. Stir in broth, salsa and vegetables. Bring to a boil over medium-high heat. Reduce heat to low; simmer 10 minutes. Stir in beans; cook 5 minutes. Stir in spinach. Garnish with fresh basil. Yield: 6 (1½ cups) servings.

Cowboy Stew

1	pound ground beef	1	(15 ounce) can Ranch Style beans
1	medium onion, chopped	1	(10¾ ounce) can cream of tomato
1	(4½ ounce) can chopped chiles		soup
3-4	new potatoes, cubed	2	soup cans of water
3	carrots, sliced	1	teaspoon chili powder or to taste
2	stalks celery, diced		Salt and pepper to taste

Sauté meat and onions; drain. Add small can of chopped chiles, new potatoes, carrots and celery (more if you like). Add beans, tomato soup, water, and seasonings. Simmer until done, about 30 minutes. Do NOT overcook vegetables.

Ike's Hot Tamales

When Dwight Eisenhower was almost two years old, the family moved to Abilene, Kansas. But while they still lived in Denison, Ike's mother learned to make Mexican hot tamales. Growing up, Ike needed to earn spending money, so he, too, mastered the recipe. He sold his tamales all around town, three for a nickel. Ike came to be an enthusiastic and lifelong cook. Cornmeal flapjacks for breakfast were a specialty.

2	dozen dried cornhusks	1½ teaspoons salt
⅓	cup lard	1½ teaspoons baking powder
2	cups finely ground yellow cornmeal, preferably masa harina	1¼ cups warm beef broth
		1½ cups filling (see note below)

Soak cornhusks in hot water until pliable, about one hour. Cream lard until it is very light and fluffy. Mix the cornmeal with the salt and baking powder and beat into the lard, a little at a time. Slowly beat in enough broth to make a rather mushy dough. Shake excess water from the softened cornhusks. Spread one tablespoon of the dough on the center part of each husk, allowing room to fold over the ends at top and bottom. Place a tablespoon of filling in the center of the dough, and fold like a jelly roll, so that the filling is completely covered by the dough. Fold the ends of the husk over the top and bottom. Put tamales in a steamer, with the bottom ends of the cornhusks down. Steam for about an hour, or until the dough comes away from the husks.

Note: Any leftover meat or poultry can be shredded or ground and used as filling. Season with hot sauce, chile peppers or chili powder to taste.

Tortilla Soup with Cheese

6   corn tortillas, cut into ½ inch
    strips
2   tablespoons vegetable oil
1   bunch green onions, chopped
1   clove garlic, minced
1   (4½ ounce) can chopped green
    chiles
1   (10½ ounce) can beef broth
1   (10½ ounce) can chicken broth
1   (10¾ ounce) can cream of
    chicken soup

2   (6 ounce) cans chicken OR
    4 boneless chicken breasts,
    cooked and cubed
1   cup water
2   teaspoons Worcestershire sauce
1   teaspoon ground cumin
1   teaspoon chili powder
    Pepper to taste
12 ounces processed cheese loaf,
    cubed
    Paprika

Lightly brown tortilla strips in hot oil. Drain and pat off oil with paper towel; set aside.
Add all ingredients together except tortillas, cheese and paprika; simmer for 1 hour.
Add cheese and tortilla strips; warm until cheese melts. Sprinkle with paprika. Yield:
8 cups.

Cheddar-Topped Chicken Chili Stew

1   medium onion, chopped
1   medium green pepper, diced
2   cloves garlic, minced
2   teaspoons vegetable oil
1½ pounds boneless chicken breasts,
     cut into ½ inch cubes
1   (14½ ounce) can diced tomatoes
1   (15 ounce) can pinto beans,
     drained

1   (15 ounce) can Ranch Style
     beans, drained
1   cup chunky salsa
1½ teaspoons chili powder
½   teaspoon ground cumin
2   cups (8 ounces) grated Cheddar
     cheese
4   green onions, sliced

Cook first 3 ingredients in oil 3 to 4 minutes. Place in a lightly greased 9 x 13-inch
baking dish. Add chicken to skillet and cook over medium-high heat, stirring frequently, until chicken is browned. Drain, arrange over vegetables in baking dish. Add
tomatoes and next 5 ingredients; stir to combine. Bake at 375 degrees for 30 to 35
minutes. Sprinkle evenly the cheese and onion. Bake an additional 3 to 5 minutes.
Serve with cornbread or chips.

Southwest Stew

1 pound ground beef	1 (15 ounce) can Ranch Style beans
1 medium onion, diced	1 (10½ ounce) can beef broth
1 teaspoon minced garlic	1 teaspoon cumin
2 (10¾ ounce) cans minestrone soup	1 teaspoon dry cilantro, more if desired
1 (10 ounce) can diced tomatoes and green chiles	Tortilla chips Grated Cheddar cheese

Brown meat, onion, and garlic; drain. Add all ingredients together except chips and cheese; simmer 1½ hours on top of stove or cook slowly in oven for 3 hours. Top with crushed tortilla chips and grated cheese.

Green Chile Rice

1 cup raw white rice, cooked	1 cup Monterey Jack cheese, grated
1 cup green chile peppers, roasted, peeled and chopped	1 cup mozzarella cheese, grated Salt to taste
8 ounces sour cream	

Preheat oven to 350 degrees. In a large bowl, place all ingredients and mix well. Place mixture in a greased baking dish. Bake for 35 minutes, or until cheese is bubbly and everything is hot. Yield: 4 servings.

Green Chili Sauce

4 sweet green chiles	½ of one jalapeño, finely chopped
1 large tomato, chopped	Salt and pepper to taste
6 sprigs of parsley (or dried flakes)	Pinch of sugar
1 small onion, chopped	3 tablespoons salad oil
1 clove garlic, minced	

Combine ingredients except oil and serve fresh, or heat oil in skillet and cook mixture stirring constantly for 2 to 3 minutes. Yield: about 1½ cups.

Green Beans De San Antonio

8	slices bacon	¼	teaspoon pepper
1	cup chopped onion	4	ounces mild jalapeños, chopped
1	teaspoon minced garlic	2	pounds fresh green beans,
1	(28 ounce) can tomatoes, drained		trimmed & steamed until crisp
	and chopped		tender
1	teaspoon salt		

Fry bacon in a large heavy skillet until crisp. Remove to paper towels; drain. Pour off all but 4 tablespoons of drippings. Process next 5 ingredients in blender until smooth. Heat drippings over medium heat until very hot. Add tomato mixture all at once. Cook 1 minute. Stir in chopped jalapeños and cook 5 to 10 minutes until sauce is slightly reduced. Add green beans; stir to coat with sauce. Cook 5 minutes or until green beans are tender. Crumble bacon over the top. Yield: 10 servings.

Come butter, come.

Come butter, come.

Old man at the gate

Is waiting for some.

The six year old chanted this verse as she worked the plunger up and down in the churn. Her handmade ladder-back chair with a cowhide seat was near the cistern on the wide screened-in back porch. She frequently peeked under the churn lid wishing the butter would hurry.

The impatient helper could hardly believe her grandmother actually liked to churn. It was many years before she realized that with thirteen children, Mama Cora welcomed the opportunity to sit down and read her Bible. The churning part was automatic and the butter seemed to come too soon.

A churn in the Judge James G. Thompson home, built in the early 1840's, at Denison's Frontier Village.

HOT TAMALE JOE. His name was Jose Ignacio Espinosa. Everyone knew him for he was an ever present figure in downtown Denison. Hot Tamale Joe had a two wheeled cart filled to the brim with the most wonderful tamales in the world. What a satisfying treat, especially during the chill of winter, to stop by Joe's cart to buy tamales wrapped in real corn shucks, and take them home for dinner always piping hot.

His daughter, Margarite Espinosa Escalera, still lives at the old home place and recalls the family assembly line. Her mother did the cooking while the children did the filling and wrapping in corn shucks, all with Dad's help. He knew exactly how to line the cart with newspapers for insulation to keep his tamales hot from daylight to dark.

The old tamale cart still stands outside Margarite's home as a gentle reminder of the days gone by.

Home Cured Jerky

1½-2 pounds lean, boneless meat
¼ cup soy sauce
1 tablespoon Worcestershire sauce
¼ teaspoon pepper
¼ teaspoon garlic powder

½ teaspoon onion powder
1 teaspoon hickory smoke flavored salt
Hot pepper sauce, optional
Coarse ground black pepper

Trim and discard all fat from meat. Cut meat into ⅛ to ¼ inch thick slices. In a bowl, combine remaining ingredients except for coarse ground black pepper. Stir until seasonings are dissolved. Add all meat strips and work them thoroughly into the mix until all surfaces are well coated. The meat will absorb most, if not all, of the liquid. Cover tightly and let stand overnight in the refrigerator. Shake off any excess liquid; sprinkle coarse ground black pepper on both sides. Arrange strips of meat close together, but not overlapping, directly on oven racks or cake racks set in shallow rimmed pans. Dry meat in oven at the lowest possible oven setting, 150 degrees or 200 degrees, until it turns brown, feels hard and is dry to the touch. This will take 5 hours for chicken and turkey, 4 to 7 hours for beef and venison. Pat off any beads of oil. Cool and store in airtight plastic bags or in jars with tight fitting lids. Keeps in refrigerator or at room temperature indefinitely. Men love to make this! This particular jerky can be made from beef flank, brisket or top round steak, venison or the white meat from chicken or turkey. Partially freezing meat makes it easier to slice evenly. Cut with the grain for chewy jerky, across the grain for more tender, brittle jerky.

Half Fare

Groce's Grocery, Market and Confectionery
GASOLINE AND OIL
Open Daily and Sunday for Your Convenience
From 6 A.M. to 10 P.M.
Phone 3602   720 N. Mirick Ave., DENISON, TEXAS

This charming picture is an advertising calendar promoting Groce's Grocery. One of the many establishments owned and operated by successful black entrepreneurs, Groce's served neighborhood families in the 60's and 70's.

Fun For Kids

Ants on a Log

1 bunch of celery	½ cup of raisins
Peanut butter	

Clean celery; remove leafy top and cut off bottom section. Fill each celery stalk with peanut butter and spread it over the length of the stalk. Place 5 to 10 raisins on top of the peanut butter in each celery stalk. May also be made with half a banana sliced lengthwise.

Song: Ants Go Marching

Apple Leather

3 cups applesauce	¼ teaspoon nutmeg
½ cup sugar	Powdered sugar

Mix applesauce, sugar and nutmeg. Spread ½ inch thick in a shallow pan; bake at 250 degrees for 3 hours. Remove when nearly dry; roll in powdered sugar like a jelly roll. Slice thin; serve.

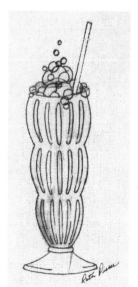

ICE CREAM SODA: Into a tall glass dip some ice cream, add flavored syrup, then spritz with a strong stream of carbonated water until big bubbles fizz over the glass edge. Serve with a straw and an ice tea spoon.

The ice cream soda was invented in Denison by Joseph A. Euper in the early 1870's. He operated the town's first confectionery when Denison was a rough frontier town more inclined to saloon traffic.

While he is remembered for his delicious concoction, Euper helped in establishing Denison, served as a city councilman, joined in building the first street railway system and was identified with industrial developments.

A Dining Car Menu for

Children's Summertime Fun
Peanut Butter Sandwiches
Ants on a Log
Kid's Snacks
Kid's Koolaid Punch

Apple Rounds

1 apple	2 tablespoons peanut butter

Wash and core the apple. Fill cavity with peanut butter. Turn the apple onto its side and slice. Each slice should have a peanut butter center.

Cream cheese and pimento cheese also work well in Apple Rounds.

Successfully fetching a cup of water took a certain amount of skill. This little lady had opened a folded paper cup, held a button down to fill it with water from the wall dispenser at the end of the car, then managed to make it back to the smiling grandmother. That meant the water wasn't mashed out from holding the cup too tightly or sloshed out from the rocking of the train. Good for her!

Applesauce

4	apples	3	tablespoons honey
½	cup water		Cinnamon

Chop apples and boil in water. Add honey; continue to cook until apples are very soft. Sprinkle with cinnamon.

Nursery Rhyme: Criss-Cross Applesauce

Ice Cream in a Can

¼	cup whipping cream
⅛	teaspoon vanilla extract
½	teaspoon maple syrup

Salt
Crushed ice

Mix whipping cream and vanilla in a small metal can. Add syrup and a pinch of salt. Stir until well blended. Place can in a larger container and surround with ice that has been sprinkled with salt. Stir ice cream every 5 minutes and refill ice as needed. Ice cream should be ready in about 30 minutes.

Rhyme: I scream, you scream, we all scream for ice cream.

Mud

1 package chocolate sandwich cookies, finely ground in a blender

1 large package instant vanilla pudding, prepared with 2¾ cups milk
8 ounces cream cheese
1½ cups powdered sugar

Blend pudding, cream cheese, and powdered sugar. Layer mixture with ground cookies in a cute flower pot or sand bucket.

You can make SAND by using lemon-filled cookies and lemon jello. Add gummy worms to MUD for WORMS IN DIRT. ENJOY!

Peanut Butter

1	cup roasted, unsalted peanuts	½	teaspoon salt
1	tablespoon peanut oil	1	teaspoon sugar or honey; optional

Pour all ingredients into a blender or food processor, adding sugar or honey depending on desired sweetness. Blend for several minutes until smooth. Serve!

It may be necessary to add more peanut oil. Store in airtight container. Homemade peanut butter will separate while standing. Stir before using.
Song:
A peanut sat on a railroad track
It's heart was all a flutter
Around the ben' came the number ten
And, SMASH, peanut butter!

A Taste for Politics: W. Lee O'Daniel
Governor of Texas 1939-1941

PASS THE BISCUITS, PAPPY! The flamboyant W. Lee "Pappy" O'Daniel ran for governor of Texas on that campaign slogan. It still rings the memory bell for Denisonians. Betty Turner recalls the Saturday afternoon her mother's family took her to town to hear the candidate. Pappy traveled with a band, The Lightcrust Doughboys, who were regulars on his popular Dallas radio show sponsored by Lightcrust Flour producers Burrus Mills. It was quite an exciting event for the little girl. To top it all off, biscuits were served to everyone in the crowd and song sheets were passed out for "Beautiful Texas", which had been composed by the candidate. The chorus is:

(Oh) Beautiful, beautiful Texas,
Where the beautiful bluebonnets grow,
We're proud of our forefathers
Who fought at the Alamo.
You can live on the plains or the mountain
Or down where the sea breezes blow,
And you're still in beautiful Texas,
The most beautiful State that we know.

Peanut Butter Balls

½   cup peanut butter
2½ tablespoons nonfat dry milk
2   tablespoons raisins

2   tablespoons honey
¼   cup coconut
     Sesame seeds

Mix all ingredients except sesame seeds; form into balls. Roll balls in sesame seeds. Eat!

Purple Cows

1   scoop vanilla ice cream
2   tablespoons grape juice
       concentrate

2   tablespoons milk

Place all ingredients in a small jar (baby food jars work well). Shake! When mixed well, serve. Makes 1 child size serving.

Nursery rhyme:
"I never saw a purple cow,
I never hope to see one.
But I can tell you anyhow
I'd rather see than be one."
Gelett Burgess 1895

Toasted Pumpkin Seeds

Seeds from a pumpkin
Butter/corn oil

Salt

Wash seeds and remove stringy pulp. Coat seeds with melted butter or oil. Season with salt. Place on cookie sheet; bake at 350 degrees until toasted.

Nursery Rhyme: Peter, Peter, Pumpkin Eater

Reindeer Sandwich

1	slice bread	2	pieces coated chocolate candies
	Peanut butter	1	cherry
2	pretzels		

Spread peanut butter on bread; cut in half diagonally. Add candy for eyes, cherry for nose and pretzels for antlers.

Song: Rudolph the Red Nosed Reindeer

Colored Sugar

1	cup sugar

Food coloring

Add a few drops of food coloring to sugar in a jar. Shake until color is evenly distributed. Use to sprinkle on sugar cookies, cakes or cupcakes, and to sweeten lemonade.

Shocking peanuts is kid's work. Farmer Henry Shearer's children knew when peanuts ripened it was their job to pull up the big clumps, shake out the sand and stack them around a pole stuck in the ground, or a shock, until Sug Moser's thrashing crew showed up to finish the job.

Peanuts were big business in Denison. After almost fifty years of operation, the Denison Peanut Company in 1964 added a mammoth automated warehouse

and drying system, capable of holding 7,500 tons of peanuts.

Today it is Southern Style Nuts. Think unique party mixes like Texas Trash or Redneck Caviar plus peanuts seasoned, glazed, and packaged in every way imaginable being shipped from a meticulously restored 1896 brick building.

Good for Kids Fruit Punch

1 (12 ounce) can frozen, orange juice concentrate, thawed

1½ cups unsweetened pineapple juice, chilled
4 cups apple juice, chilled

Mix orange juice according to directions. Add to chilled pineapple and apple juices. Serve.

Kids Koolaid Punch

3 packages koolaid, any flavor
3 quarts water
3 cups sugar

1 (46 ounce) can pineapple juice
1 quart ginger ale

Combine all ingredients. Yield: 36 servings. Good and inexpensive.

Kid's Snacks

2 cups animal crackers
2 cups chocolate covered raisins

1 cup jelly beans
1 cup unsalted peanuts

Combine all ingredients and store in an airtight container. Yield: 6 cups.

Variation:
2 cups candy corn
2 cups candy coated chocolates
2 cups unsalted peanuts

Sundae Waffles

1   (11 ounce) package frozen waffles
1   quart vanilla ice cream

Warm maple syrup or chocolate
syrup
Chopped nuts

Toast waffles as directed on package. Top each waffle with a scoop of ice cream. Pour syrup or sauce over ice cream and waffle. Sprinkle with nuts.

Quick and Easy
Peanut Butter (PB) Sandwiches

The Big Apple - PB and apple butter on white toast.

The Jelly Roll - PB and jelly on a hard roll.

The Stripper - PB and bacon strips on rye bread.

The Pickle Dilly - PB with sliced pickle on toast.

The Breath Tester - PB and sliced onions on white bread.

The Purist - PB and lettuce or cole slaw on toast.

The Garden Of Eden - PB and chopped apple salad with lettuce on a bun.

The Cheese-It - PB with a slice of American cheese under the broiler.

The P-B-L-T - PB, chopped bacon, lettuce, and tomato on toast.

The French Grill - PB on white bread, covered with a second slice of bread and dipped in French toast egg batter, then fried on both sides and served with powdered sugar.

Bunny Trail Mix

1 (6 ounce) package butterscotch
    flavored morsels
½ cup chunky peanut butter

4 cups granola cereal
1 cup jelly beans (about 8 ounces)

Line the bottom of a 9 x 13-inch pan with wax paper; set aside. Combine butterscotch morsels and peanut butter in a large heavy saucepan; cook over low heat, stirring constantly, until melted. Add cereal, stirring well; press mixture into prepared pan. Cover; chill until firm. Break into pieces, stir in jelly beans. Store in an airtight container at room temperature. Yield: 8 cups.

The 1926 Denison High School Senior Domestic Science Class From The Yellow Jacket Yearbook.

Ice Cream

1	cup milk	3	trays of ice cubes
4	teaspoons sugar		Rock salt
½	teaspoon vanilla extract		

Take a sandwich zip-top plastic bag and pour in first 3 ingredients; seal. Take a large zip-top plastic bag, put in 3 trays of ice and pour in some rock salt; put small bag in and shake. You will have ice cream in about 10 minutes.

Not to forget our furry and feathered friends...

Doggie Cookies

1½ cups flour (hold back ½ cup)
1   teaspoon baking powder
¾   cup quick oats
¼   cup Honey Crunch wheat Germ
¼   cup peanut butter

¼   cup oil
¼   cup honey
½   cup water
    Dog bone cutter or cookie cutter
    of your choice

Mix 1 cup flour with remaining ingredients plus ½ cup water until blended. Put remaining ½ cup flour on flat surface and knead dough until it holds together. Roll out dough; cut in bone shapes. Re-roll; cut again. Bake on ungreased cookie sheet at 350 degrees for 20 minutes. Turn oven off and leave cookies in oven for 1 hour. Cool on rack. Store in airtight container.

Kitty Cookies

1   cup whole wheat flour
2   tablespoons wheat germ
⅓   cup soy flour
⅓   cup powdered milk
1   tablespoon kelp
½   teaspoon bone meal

1   teaspoon crushed dried catnip
    leaves
1   tablespoon unsulfured molasses
1   egg
2   tablespoons oil, butter or fat
⅓   cup milk or water

Mix all dry ingredients together. Add remaining 4 ingredients. Roll out flat on a greased cookie sheet; cut into narrow strips. Bake at 350 degrees for 20 minutes or until lightly toasted. Break into small pea-size pieces suitable for cats. Good only as a treat.

For The Hummingbirds

Bring 4 parts water to a boil. Add 1 part white granulated sugar. Stir until sugar is dissolved; cool. Pour into a red feeder. Do NOT Use Red Food Coloring as it could harm their kidneys.

A Year Round Treat for The Birds

Keep your grapefruit or orange rinds and combine with cut up apples, apricots, bananas, blueberries, cherries, cranberries, dates, grapes, peaches, pears, raisins, and/or watermelon. Place on a platform feeder or secure to a tree.

Denison Crystal Ice & Storage Co. from the late 1870's operated horse-drawn delivery wagons on routes throughout town and supplied the Katy Railroad. Motor trucks began showing up in the 1930's as seen in the photo.

Icemen on their routes looked at their customers' windows where cardboard signs with numbered corners — 25, 50, 75, 100 — indicated how many pounds of ice was needed. The number showing at the top of the card was the size block the iceman would sling over his padded shoulder and carry in to place in the icebox.

Contributors

Candy Allen	Ada Everett	Sharon Luker
Dawn Archer	Bonnie Francis	Tracy Madden
Charla Atwell	Sarah Frietsch	Joyce Mahaffey
Linda Avila	Delores Gaines	Mary Markham
Candace Baugh	Ruth Gear	Patricia Mason
Linda Beckelman	Gloria Gordon	Gayle McKinley
Virginia Blankenship	Joan Gordon	Margaret Melvin
Julie Blount	Jane Green	Lisa Morgan
Martha Bostwick	Helen Griffin	Delonia Mullins
Carolyn Brady	Rita Gundlach	Jane Ellen Myers
Andrea Bratcher	Joan Harner	Candy Neaves
Emma Lee Brown	Judy Harris	Vivian Nelson
Nondas Bullard	Dorothy Harrison	Kelly Nicholson
Tracey Bullard	Pat Hartsell	Annette Oro
Betty Cabaniss	Karen Hubbard	Patsey Palmer
Shelle Cassell	Barbara Hutchison	Sandra Phillips
Frances Cherry	Jo Hutchman	Nancy Pike
Mary Louise Chesnutt	Charlotte Hyman	Cathy Pilkilton
Janet Ciaccio	Laura Jacobs	Sheryl Pool
Elise Cole	Mary James	Skeet Pool
Rita Cole	Ruenell Jarriel	Mitzi Power
Patricia Corcoran	Carol Jennings	Sherry Pruiett
Mary Crawford	Martha Jordan	Ava Ray
Roberta Daniels	Beth Keese	May Richards
Willa Mae Davis	Jana Keese	Carolyn Riggins
Maxine Delaney	Mason Keller	Norma Roush
Pat Deligans	Betsy Keown	Anna Rowland
Pat Dieterichs	Edith Ketcham	Sherry Rumsey
Lucy Dossey	Martha Landrum	Ruth Sanderlin
Katie Eaton	Kathryn Laughlin	Evelyn Scoggins
Cathy Eubank	Carole Linsteadt	June Scott

CONTRIBUTORS

Mary Sherrard
Sherry Simmons
Kay Skelton
Christine Smart
Lois Smith
Carolyn Spencer
Sara Jane Stagner
Pate Stanphill
Harriet Steward
Charla Stubbs
Willene Sweeney

Betty Taylor
Denise Tucker
Betty Turner
Sandy Underwood
Carolyn Walton
Carol Washburn
Vicki Washburn
Pat Watson
Linda West
Gayle Williams
Madell Wilson

Beverly Young
Vicki Zakin
Julie Nixon Eisenhower
Ivy Blue Bed and Breakfast
Molly Cherry Bed and Breakfast
The Inn of Many Faces Bed and Breakfast
Susie Luchsinger

To have *The Dining Car* perfect would be wonderful, but glitches are inevitable. We apologize sincerely for any mistakes, either done or undone, which may slip by even our best efforts.

Acknowledgments

Bill Ashburn
Blue Moon Antique Mall
Joy Bryant
Mavis Anne Bryant
Verna Blood
Evelyn Carlat
Nick Ciaccio
Ralph Douglas
Denison Chamber of Commerce
Denison Public Library
Sarah Dye

Eisenhower Birthplace State Historical Park
Dixie Foster
Valerie Freels
Jon Geer
Grady's Charters
Grayson County Frontier Village
Vickie Hempkins
Hickory House
Ann Grant Holmes
Lake Texoma Association

Donna Hunt
Jack Maguire
Dorothy Mills
Ruth Pierce
Doug Pilcher
Red River Railroad Museum
Butch Roberson
Rock Computers
Delbert Taylor
Marla Tortorici
Pat Welsh

Cookbook Committee

1996-1997

Barbara Hutchison, Chairman
Margaret Melvin, Historian
Tracey Bullard
Ruth Gear
Charlotte Hyman
Beth Keese
Jana Keese
Betsy Keown
Martha Landrum
Kay Skelton

1997-1998

Barbara Hutchison, Chairman
Margaret Melvin, Historian
Martha Bostwick
Tracey Bullard
Janet Ciaccio
Ruth Gear
Charlotte Hyman
Beth Keese
Jana Keese
Betsy Keown
Candy Neaves
Pate Stanphill

1998-1999

Barbara Hutchison, Chairman
Margaret Melvin, Historian
Tracey Bullard, Recipe
Testing Coordinator
Charlotte Hyman
Ruenell Jarriel
Betsy Keown
Candy Neaves
Betty Turner

Proofers

Martha Bostwick
Betty Cabaniss
Ruth Gear
Cathy Pilkilton
Sherry Simmons
Carolyn Spencer
Betty Turner
Sandy Underwood
Carolyn Walton
Vicki Zakin

Bibliography

Dye, Sarah Elizabeth, *The Cabin By The Spring,* 1995.

Grayson County Frontier Village, *The History of Grayson County Texas,* Volume 1, Hunter Publishing Company, Winston-Salem, North Carolina, 1979.

Grayson County Frontier Village, *The History of Grayson County Texas,* Volume II, Heritage Publishing Company, Tulsa, Oklahoma, 1981.

Maguire, Jack, *A President's Country,* Shoal Creek Publishers, Inc., Austin, Texas, 1964

Maguire, Jack, *Katy's Baby: The Story of Denison, Texas,* Nortex Press, Austin, Texas. 1991.

Munson, T. V., D. Sc., *Foundations of American Grape Culture,* T. V. Munson & Son, Denison, Texas, 1909.

Pool, William C., *A Historical Atlas of Texas,* The Encino Press, Austin, Texas, 1975.

The Denison Herald, clippings.

The Denison Press, discarded old newspapers.

The Sherman Democrat, clipping.

The Opening of the Great Southwest, A Brief History of the Origin and Development of the Missouri-Kansas-Texas Railroad Better Known As The Katy, M-K-T R. R. Co., May 1970.

A

B

INDEX

C

INDEX

INDEX

E

F

G

INDEX

INDEX

INDEX

INDEX

Please send *The Dining Car* to:

Name _____

Address _____

City _____ State _____ Zip _____

Telephone _____

Price per book	Quantity	Total
$19.95	_____	_____

Shipping and Handling $4.00 per book   _____

Texas residents include $1.65 sales tax   _____

Total amount enclosed   _____

Please enclose a check payable to The Denison Service League, Inc. Please do not send cash.
The Dining Car
The Denison Service League, Inc,.
P.O. Box 4
Denison TX 75021-0004

Please send *The Dining Car* to:

Name _____

Address _____

City _____ State _____ Zip _____

Telephone _____

Price per book	Quantity	Total
$19.95	_____	_____

Shipping and Handling $4.00 per book   _____

Texas residents include $1.65 sales tax   _____

Total amount enclosed   _____

Please enclose a check payable to The Denison Service League, Inc. Please do not send cash.
The Dining Car
The Denison Service League, Inc,.
P.O. Box 4
Denison TX 75021-0004

Please send *The Dining Car* to:

Name _____

Address _____

City _____ State _____ Zip _____

Telephone _____

Price per book	Quantity	Total
$19.95	_____	_____

Shipping and Handling $4.00 per book   _____

Texas residents include $1.65 sales tax   _____

Total amount enclosed   _____

Please enclose a check payable to The Denison Service League, Inc. Please do not send cash.
The Dining Car
The Denison Service League, Inc,.
P.O. Box 4
Denison TX 75021-0004